D0197759

the series on school reform

Patricia A. Wasley	Ann Lieberman	Joseph P. McDonald
Bank Street College of Education	NCREST	New York University

SERIES EDITORS

(Continued)

the series on school reform, *continued*

What's Happening in Math Class?: Envisioning New Practices Through Teacher Narratives (Volume 1)
    DEBORAH SCHIFTER, Editor

What's Happening in Math Class?: Reconstructing Professional Identities (Volume 2)
    DEBORAH SCHIFTER, Editor

Reaching for a Better Standard: English School Inspection and the Dilemma of Accountability for American Public Schools
    THOMAS A. WILSON

Restructuring Urban Schools: A Chicago Perspective
    G. ALFRED HESS, JR.

The Subjects in Question: Departmental Organization and the High School
    LESLIE SANTEE SISKIN AND JUDITH WARREN LITTLE, EDITORS

Authentic Assessment in Action: Studies of Schools and Students at Work
    LINDA DARLING-HAMMOND, JACQUELINE ANCESS, AND BEVERLY FALK

School Work: Gender and the Cultural Construction of Teaching
    SARI KNOPP BIKLEN

School Change: The Personal Development of a Point of View
    SEYMOUR B. SARASON

The Work of Restructuring Schools: Building from the Ground Up
    ANN LIEBERMAN, Editor

Stirring the Chalkdust: Tales of Teachers Changing Classroom Practice
    PATRICIA A. WASLEY

This series also incorporates earlier titles in the Professional Development and Practice Series

TEACHERS CAUGHT IN THE ACTION

Professional Development That Matters

ANN LIEBERMAN
LYNNE MILLER
Editors

TEACHERS COLLEGE PRESS

Teachers College, Columbia University
New York and London

Published by Teachers College Press, 1234 Amsterdam Avenue, New York, NY 10027

Library of Congress Cataloging-in-Publication Data

Teachers caught in the action: professional development that matters / Ann Lieberman, Lynne Miller, editors.
    p. cm.— (The series on school reform)
    Includes bibliographical references and index.
    ISBN 0-8077-4100-0 (cloth alk. : paper) — ISBN 0-8077-4099-3 (pbk. : alk. paper)
    1. Teachers—In-service training—United States. 2. Educational change—United States. I. Lieberman, Ann. II. Miller, Lynne, 1945– III. Series.
    LB1731 .T4198 2001
    370'.71'55—dc21   00-054501

ISBN 0-8077-4099-3 (paper)
ISBN 0-8077-4100-0 (cloth)

Printed on acid-free paper
Manufactured in the United States of America

08 07 06 05 04 03 02 01   8 7 6 5 4 3 2 1

Contents

Introduction

ANN LIEBERMAN
LYNNE MILLER

We have been "caught in the action" of professional development for over 20 years. During that time, we have joined with school and university colleagues to develop theory, describe practice, and identify principles that describe and inform what happens when teachers work together over time to deepen their knowledge, improve their craft, and transform schooling for their students and for themselves. This volume represents our third effort to gather the best of what is known and practiced about professional development in schools.

Our first collection (Lieberman & Miller, 1979) was published when the effective schools movement and mastery learning were commanding the limelight. We had the uneasy feeling then that most of the prescriptions for change that abounded were neglecting a critical element—the teacher. We built our first volume on the premise that teachers were at the center of instructional improvement and that staff development was the linchpin of school reform. In compiling the collection, we sought authors who could offer alternatives to the isolated workshops and traditional in-service that dotted the educational landscape.

Our second collection (Lieberman & Miller, 1992) responded to the developments of the next decade. The publication of *A Nation at Risk* (National Commission on Excellence in Education, 1983) and *A Nation Prepared* (Carnegie Corporation, 1986), coupled with the dissemination of comparisons between the United States and other industrialized nations in math and science achievement, had set the stage for an intense national discussion about America's schools and their capacity for success. We approached scholars and practitioners who could help unravel new complexities and extend the literature on professional development to consider issues of local and national context, personal and social learning, the professionalization of teaching and the development of craft knowledge, and expanded roles for teachers as leaders in curriculum, instruction, and school redesign.

This brings us to the current volume, published at a time when standards-based reforms and high-stakes assessments dominate as the new fixes for public education, when technology offers an antidote to limited resources, when charter schools and voucher plans promise to revitalize schools, and when a major teacher shortage looms large. Amid much talk of "teacher quality" (National Commission on Teaching and America's Future, 1996), there are renewed efforts to deprofessionalize teaching, to fast-track teacher preparation and licensure procedures, to disband tenure, and to devalue teacher experience, discretion, and knowledge in everyday classroom decisions. We think it is time to reiterate the message of our first book, that teachers are at the center of all efforts to reform and improve schools, and to support this proposition with solid evidence from research and powerful exemplars from practice. It is with this intention that we identified our current authors, each of whom has made major contributions to the field through research and practical experience, and each of whom has been "caught in the action" of enhancing the capacity of teachers to lead their classrooms and schools toward authentic standards of excellence.

This book begins with a discussion of purpose, a topic that has long been neglected in the professional development literature. When we began thinking about this book, we decided that one big problem in professional development was that it was rarely tied to larger purposes. Districts adopt cooperative learning without considering the larger idea that we are seeking to create more democratic schools. Or curriculum is rewritten or new books adopted with little or no time for building in, as part of the deliberation, inquiry on how teachers use the new ideas and come to make them part of their practice. Professional developers need to understand the dynamics of the change process when they work to improve practice. To deal with this void, we invited a distinguished group of public intellectuals (Maxine Greene, Carl Glickman and Derrick Aldridge, Judith Warren Little, and Marilyn Cochran-Smith and Susan Lytle) to answer the question: What is staff development for? What ends does it seek? In so doing, they set the stage for the chapters that follow and remind us that it is essential to tie what we do in staff development to larger goals.

What we do in staff development can best be understood in terms of contexts, strategies, and structures. In the nine chapters that comprise the second part of the book, people step back to describe their practical work and identify key elements of its effectiveness, all the while grounding what they do in scholarship and connecting it to purpose.

Each author writes from a unique experiential and theoretical stance. In Chapter 5, Jacqueline Ancess describes how teachers in three high-performing secondary schools in New York City increase their own learning when they engage in activities aimed at school development and improving student outcomes. In Chapter 6, Milbrey McLaughlin and Joel Zarrow demonstrate how teachers learn to use data to improve their practice and to meet the educational standards they have set for their students. Lynne Miller, in Chapter 7, presents a case study of a long-lived school–university partnership and depicts how its members make use of the collaboration to improve both school and university policies and practices. In Chapter 8, Beverly Falk recounts stories of how teachers who work together to develop and implement performance assessments expand their knowledge base, understand their students' learning, rethink their curricular and instructional strategies, and develop the capacity for reflection and collaboration. Laura Stokes, in Chapter 9, meticulously analyzes a school that uses inquiry groups to better understand the problems and practices of the school. Turning to novice teachers, Anna Richert Ershler, in Chapter 10, describes the use of narrative to help new teachers make sense of the complexity of their classrooms. In Chapter 11, Ann Lieberman and Diane Wood, in reporting on their study of the National Writing Project, develop a set of principles for effective staff development efforts. Sarah Freedman in Chapter 12 describes the ways in which teachers use their own research to reveal teaching problems and try to resolve them. Finally, in Chapter 13, Joe McDonald discusses the historical and contemporary uses of focusing on student work as the primary object for teacher learning.

Though each of the nine chapters in this section stands on its own merit, when taken together, they provide a broad overview of what matters and what works in professional development. Some common themes emerge, including the importance of

- Explicitly connecting teacher and student learning
- Supporting professional collaboration and collegial accountability
- Creating and sustaining communities of practice where there is time and space for conversation, joint action, and critique
- Coupling teaching and assessment practices
- Encouraging the development of a common language through oral and written communication
- Developing and using structured tools and protocols to guide discussion
- Using the real-life events of teaching as the source of professional development

We invite you to join our authors in this lively discussion of professional development. Our hope is that you will come away with fresh ideas, deeper understanding, and persuasive evidence to support your own work in helping teachers deepen their practice and enhance their professional learning.

REFERENCES

Carnegie Corporation of New York. (1986). *A nation prepared: Teachers for the twenty-first century*. New York: Author.

Lieberman, A., & Miller, L. (1979). *Staff development: New demands, new realities, new perspectives*. New York: Teachers College Press.

Lieberman, A., & Miller, L. (1992). *Staff development for education in the nineties: New demands, new realities, new perspectives*. New York: Teachers College Press.

National Commission on Teaching and America's Future. (1996). *What matters most: Teaching for America's future*. New York: Author.

National Commission on Excellence in Education. (1983). *A nation at risk: The imperative of educational reform*. Washington, DC: U.S. Department of Education.

PART I

The Purposes of
Professional Development

CHAPTER 1

Educational Purposes and Teacher Development

MAXINE GREENE

How are we to understand the purposes of American education? Who defines them, and how are they defined? In what ways do statements of purpose affect teaching and learning within particular schools? Does the social class or ethnic identity of the students influence concepts of what public schools are for? How do the presumed purposes of private and parochial schools differ from those governing public schools? And how do the various articulations of purpose affect teachers' growth and development?

Teaching basic literacy and a "voluntary compliance" with the moral law were the dominant concerns of the first common schools. Granted, there was talk of a "social balance wheel" and equality of opportunity, but, at least in the city schools, there was a tacit commitment to training the young to work in the fast-growing factories. Occasionally there was talk of enabling students to understand the democratic *ethos* and some of the meanings of freedom in the 19th century (when, it should be recalled, neither African Americans nor women, by and large, were granted human rights on an equal basis, and were denied the range of freedoms enjoyed by most white men).

In private schools and public schools in well-to-do districts, purposes were identified with some notion of cultivation in mind. They might refer to the humanizing consequences of courses in the arts and humanities, or to the contributions to progress to be made by well-equipped students of the sciences, or to the need to keep alive old traditions of learning. Little specific attention was paid to the distinctive obligations of schoolteachers, who were expected to serve as transmission belts for the male university scholars who guarded the canon and kept it alive. As for run-of-the-mill public school teachers, who may have attended normal schools after leaving elementary schools themselves: they were expected to be docile, genteel, and prepared to foster drills and memorization, very often were asked to teach through dictation and reliance on textbooks. Yet as the 19th century went on, some of the most difficult work was accomplished by such teachers, who were relied upon to initiate in-migrants and immigrants into changing society. Nothing was said, however, about the pedagogical implications of the acculturation process, if it was recognized at all. Nor was anything said about teachers forming communities within their schools to talk about the challenges and complexities of initiating newcomers into the New World.

Henry David Thoreau's and Ralph Waldo Emerson's emphasis upon the importance of personal experience and upon finding an appropriate expression for that experience was not related to the plight or development of teachers. Bronson Alcott's work in his short-lived Temple School and the work of those few others who saw the centrality of the teaching act in countering the materiality, the inequities, and the value conflicts in expanding capitalism had little impact on the public schools or public school teachers. Indeed, transcendental visions and quests for personal autonomy were either ignored or considered antithetic by the schoolmen, often primarily interested in social order and social (as well as self) control.

At the middle of the 19th century Horace Mann and other school reformers traveled to Europe to acquaint themselves with the rise of a school system in Prussia and, more importantly, with classroom changes being brought about through the influence of Johann Pestalozzi and teachers associated with his Swiss schools. That meant a dawning interest in the natural growth of children, in classroom learning as at "the mother's knee," and in adapting the pace and content of learning to children's interests and to the concrete particularities of the surrounding world. Bringing such ideas back to teachers' and lyceum meetings in the United States, the reformers introduced a somewhat different climate to classrooms susceptible to a new concern for children. Coming to terms, however, with the demands of the shops and factories, many school people paid far more heed to efficient organization, to monitoring arrangements, and to a concentration of skills without regard for children's curiosity and wonder. Little, if anything, was done to reconcile the call for economy and efficiency with attentiveness to the needs and natures of diverse young people. Where teachers were concerned, there was far more attention paid to the results of their drills and recitations than to the lives and potentialities of the young. Self-generated development on the part of teachers was scarcely considered. Methods of teaching were imposed from without; top-down modes of regulation characterized most schools.

It should be noted, at this point, that the phenomenon of the mass was presenting itself to many American minds at the turn of the 20th century, as it had in Europe some years before. It was in part a function of the expansion of different industries requiring great numbers of workers brought together to work on assembly lines, in vast steel foundries, and in slaughterhouses. It was also in part a response to life in cities with their startling crowds and vast gatherings of people who often seemed undifferentiated. Looking at public schools, many observers saw much to be proud of in the fact that the United States seemed to be the first country to attempt what was thought to be mass democratic education. To consider it in such terms was to shift attention away from the idea of the individual in his/her dignity, distinctiveness, and integrity, long thought to be central in the American view of the world and the being to whom humane education was to be directed. The idea of the mass also seemed to justify the invention of what was to be conceived of as bureaucracy. For a teacher to think of himself or herself as an agent of change or even as someone responsible for the shaping of curricula or the selection of books, the whole environment would have to be transformed. Female teachers were still treated as subordinate even if they were not systematically infantilized and treated, more often than not, as good daughters. The few males in the lower schools were almost always administrators, potential managers, or amateur bureaucrats. Their positions were not granted as much respect as were the positions of churchmen, shopkeepers, bankers, and traders, and there was little likelihood of their leading in such a fashion as to transform. Here and there, a superintendent objected to the dullness, the routine, the lack of enthusiasm for learning; but the repertoire of teachers was limited, and there is no evidence of collaborative inquiry into modes of teaching and modes of leadership. Well into the 20th century, with purposes defined by businessmen and (indirectly) moralistic churchmen, top-down supervision appeared to be the only alternative to total reliance on sometimes minimally literate teachers. There was no time when school administrations thought of consulting teachers, even in conjunction with their university instructors, to gain suggestions about what should be done.

Recalling the almost complete reliance on talk of material success, profit-making, and property, we cannot conceive of official statements of educational purposes without reference to big business and pecuniary triumphs. Certainly, what was called the "big barbecue" in the presumably "Gilded Age" after the Civil War gave rise to images of robber barons, men (usually) who conquered the jungles of New York City, Chicago, and Kansas City in the name of money and power. It has taken literary artists such as Mark Twain, Stephen Crane, Edith Wharton, and Louisa May Alcott and remarkable works such as Herman Melville's *The Confidence-Man* to give us some idea of the depersonalized corruption and the suffering of the powerless under the wheels of what seemed like a vast social machine and to help us even to guess at what was happening to the original visions of possibility. It is difficult not to recall Walt Whitman and his hopes that his poetry could somehow combat the rampant materialism, or his belief (as he put it in his *Democratic Vistas*) that democracy's experiment had turned into a great debacle—"cankered, crude, superstitious, and rotten. . . ." If anyone took that seriously, how might the purposes of education be honestly defined?

There were other images, of course; the beginning of the 20th century saw the rise of what was thought of in political and social terms as "progressivism." That meant multiple movements of reform, inspired by the so-called muckrakers intent on exposing the scandals in business and the cities. It meant the appearance of settlement houses, notably exemplified by Jane Addams's Hull House. It meant the great interdisciplinary studies carried on in Chicago and New York of the economic and sociological arrangements human beings were making in their shared lives. These works, directed to the assumed intelligence of the reader, were optimistic in the sense of believing that if the American public understood the flaws and deficiencies in the society, they would be aroused to do something to repair it. And there were those who still thought that the most significant repairs, morally and educationally, might be brought about by means of teaching and the schools. William James's little book *Talks to Teachers in Psychology* was unusual in the manners in which a philosopher who had not been involved in education thought the practice of teaching significant enough to address teachers in the name of intelligence and energy, and with the hope of change.

There was Francis Parker, moving from a superintendency to establish the Cook County Normal School in Chicago, where he applied his Emersonian vision to the transformation of the elementary school. Play, he said, spontaneity, community, free expression. It had always been an alternative message to teachers, sometimes in dialectical relation to messages about rigor, mastery of skills, and control. When John Dewey came to Chicago from various parts in the teaching of philosophy, he became chair of a Department of Philosophy, Psychology, and

Pedagogy, which (at least symbolically) pointed to a time when pedagogy (or teaching or education) would become a subject worthy of serious study in the contexts of philosophy and the social sciences.

In the Laboratory School connected to the department, experimental and developmental psychology led to studies of child growth. More and more was done with experiential education and the teacher's role in creating situations in which diverse transactions could go on in a stimulating physical and human environment, where questions could be asked, problems solved, friendships made, conflicts resolved. Notable in Dewey's work with what was called the Dewey School was the regular meeting of the teachers with Dewey or whoever served as prinipal. The point was to explore ways to teach to the goal of open-ended growth, critical questioning, and the kind of participant membership required of a democracy. Acutely aware that the young people would find themselves in a world dominated by often unknowable forces, aware that technologies and the unbridled expansion of industry and commerce would present unprecedented problems, teachers themselves (as Dewey saw them) had to be open to the uncertain and the incomplete, to engage with their students in multiple forms of inquiry.

Historians have recognized that Dewey's influence was most directly felt and welcomed in a number of private and progressive schools that ordinarily attracted the children of the white middle class. It was only when some of Dewey's ideas somehow meshed with mainstream educational theories that attention was paid. World War I, quite obviously, distracted attention from the fate and future of the public school. Afterward, in the hectic 1920s—politically conservative, culturally extravagant, morally ill at ease—no one quite knew what the purposes of education should be. Life adjustment, some thought; the cultivation of the skills necessary for the maintenance of a growing capitalist society; the liberation of the young for creativity and self-expression; preparation for citizenship. Some recognized the persistence of the flaws and the sense of emptiness Whitman had discerned, along with later critics of existing society. In *The Great Gatsby* (published in 1925, the same year as Dewey's *The Public and Its Problems*, with its stress on the "social pathology" that existed, the so-called "eclipse of the public," the search for community), Fitzgerald invented a paradigmatic anti-hero in James Gatz, the farmer's son who became Jay Gatsby, the individual forever in quest of the American Dream. His version of that dream is still recognizable, still troubling to those whose projects are teaching school in the diverse public schools: "He was a son of God— a phrase which, if it means anything, means just that—and he must be about His Father's Business, the service of a vast and meretricious beauty"; and, perhaps as a subtext, there is the rendering of the care-lessness of the very rich, the total lack of interest in those who are needy and deprived, creatures of a lower class. Whether implicit or openly declared, this suggested to many what Americans most wanted when it came to the purpose of public schools.

After the devastation of a crashing stock market and an unprec-edented economic crisis, teacher educators at Columbia, Ohio State, Illinois, and a few other centers of reform thinking, identified them-selves with the New Deal and the solidarity it called for at first—soli-darity with those engaged in the building of new institutions. It was, for a brief moment, a time for engagement with trade unions, with the builders of a federal theater, with artists writing guidebooks for each state in the union, with a Civilian Conservation corps that sent the poor and untrained into centers for the saving of the forests, with a National Youth Administration. There was no specific identification of the capacities to be encouraged among schoolteachers, but surely there were many (like the first members of teacher unions) who reso-nated to Teachers College's George Counts (1978), asking whether the schools could change the social order, and to those like John Dewey talking about the need to combat the "economic royalists." Again, for a brief moment, the values of solidarity and collaboration were associ-ated with the teaching act, at least in some places around the nation.

World War II, obviously, changed all that, and the purposes of public education were reaffirmed in terms of preparedness, support for the war effort, and (occasionally) democratic and antifascist commit-ments. After that war, there were climactic changes, certain ones cul-minating in the GI Bill of Rights and the entry of a new teaching popu-lation into the public schools. Also, those postwar years saw the origins of what we now think of as educational research, as tests given those GI's who had been drafted exposed the deficiencies in mathematics and other subjects. In those years after the war, however, there were many incidents of attack on what was thought of as progressive education, with its emphasis on critical questions and participatory experiences. Business and religious interests felt themselves intruded on by what they thought was happening in schools. Given the tensions and the contradictions, given the reminders of what Arthur Bestor (1985) called "educational wastelands," it was difficult to connect what might be identified as educational purposes with a changing conception of pro-fessional development.

In 1957, of course, the success of the Russian rocket *Sputnik* turned people's attention to the need to compete with the Soviet Union in the teaching of the sciences and the mastery of novel technologies.

Liberal arts academies were enlisted in efforts to write appropriate curricula in those and other fields, and the lack of respect for anything called professional development was bitterly dramatized in the phrase "teacher-proof curricula." The increasingly evident lack of respect for teachers was increased by the preoccupation with talent that marked the post–*Sputnik* period. High IQ's were far more important than the needs and potentialities of living children and the multiple situations in which they lived. But then, of course, the moment of the talent search was followed by the decade of protest and demand: the civil rights movement, the antiwar protests, the rejection of bureaucratic controls (and students classified like IBM cards). Just as important were the exposure of the invisible poor, the attempts at a war against poverty, the federal government–enhanced entry into the educational world, the efforts to achieve equity for women and minorities.

Perhaps strangely, among those caught up in the protest movements there was a reinforcement of the sentiments long voiced against classroom teachers. For one thing, there was an identification of schools with other centers of power. Teachers, viewed as functionaries or Mrs. Grundys, were often treated as agents of the governing ideologies, unreflecting individuals kept busy reproducing an unjust culture and way of being. The practices of testing and tracking sustained the conservative roles of the schools, and the teachers were complicit in keeping alive the sorting-out function of the schools. In part because so many teachers (and the culture they purveyed) were white and middle-class, white middle-class students were (consciously and unconsciously) favored in most schools; minority students, it was said, were excluded, ignored, unfairly treated, and pushed out when all else failed. Here and there, "free schools" were created embodying what resembled early progressivism, sometimes in the hope of transforming what was increasingly called the culture of poverty, sometimes to counter the rampant inequalities in most of the systems in the country. The terrible harm done by segregation, the sufferings experienced in desegregating the southern schools, and the phenomenon of white flight in both north and south did not (as they might have done) give rise to what we now think of as professional development. With the exception of the short-lived Head Start centers and the parent groups that grew around some of the free schools and independent schools, little was done to realize the professional status of teachers, and less was done to develop plans involving university and public school faculties in development. It is ironic to recall the ways in which lists of competencies helped to deskill teachers and render the teaching act more and more mechanical and (it must be said) boring. Indeed, in many ways that preoccupation anticipated some of the test-governed curricula now becoming fashionable.

The philosophical and pedagogical problem of reconciling a system oriented to free-market policies and to treatment of young people as human resources rather than as centers of energy and possibility remains open. The growing regard for qualitative research and the uses of ethnography in interpreting what happens and what might happen in the lived realities of classrooms have helped to make visible some of the actualities existing behind the statistics, the test scores, and the policy language. The constructivist recognition is that even little children are in search of meaning, which intensifies as they live and which makes them open to mentoring and coaching in response to curiosity and desire. The new regard for journals has helped, as has the interest in storytelling and the writing of poetry. The ongoing studies of community experiences and the growing understanding that experiences in dialogue, participation in more and more diverse classroom communities have helped more and more educators understand the relationship between the capacities required for democratic living together and the capacities nurtured by reflective teachers open to conversation, open to collaboration, and hospitable to difference.

We cannot pretend that a gulf does not exist between what are officially defined (from the center, from the places where power resides) as educational purposes and what many of us hope for the children and youth in our schools. Violence remains a crucial issue; racism and racist profiling remain crucial, as does the fearful invention called zero tolerance. Censorship remains a threat; uniform objectives and what they require continue to erode the freedom of individual teachers ripe with ideas for teaching and learning, prevented from trying them out in the circumstances that exist.

It is a matter of using imagination in order to be able to perceive the alternatives. It is a matter of inventing metaphors in efforts to reorient the consciousness of those who can only think technically or in terms of measurement, who think of education as a process of matching existing skills and talents (still arranged on a bell curve in too many minds) with the changing demands of the changing technologies. How indeed can the demands of an inequitable, money-groping society be reconciled with the demands of children's growth, of children's diversity? The communities that take shape in schools and colleges, the dialogues set free at last must somehow be made present to a public we can still hope is in the making. To define educational purposes, we know, is to define the kind of culture we inhabit and internalize. In most respects, it is an effort to create that "community in the making" that Dewey (1927) said characterized democracy. We know now that it must be a community in which women's voices are fully audible, in which the multiple voices from the boundaries are given opportunities to sound. This is a century-long struggle, and it just may be that our efforts at professional development will plant new seeds for democracy—and for imagination and thought.

Adrienne Rich (1978) suggests a closing set of metaphors in *The Dream of a Common Language*, poems that speak of something out of reach but sought for, something in some manner extraordinary:

> But there come times—perhaps this is one of them—
> when we have to take ourselves more seriously or die,
> when we have to pull back from the incantations,
> rhythms we've moved to thoughtlessly,
> and disenthrall ourselves, bestow
> ourselves to silence, or a severer listening, cleansed
> of oratory, formulas, choruses, laments, static
> crowding of the wires.

No one, she said, who survives a new language can avoid (at least for Rich) a cutting of the wires. She was calling on her readers to break with bureaucratic talk, media talk, pious talk, with what Dewey (1927) called the "crust of conventionalized and routine consciousness." It is a matter of awakening. It is a matter, gradually, gradually, of attending to the teacher and with the teacher, a matter of keeping open what we can imagine as possibility.

REFERENCES

Bestor, A. (1985). *Educational wastelands: The retreat from learning in our public schools* (2nd ed.). Urbana: University of Illinois Press.

Counts, G. (1978). *Dare the schools build a new social order?* Carbondale: Southern Illinois University Press.

Dewey, J. (1927). The public and its problems. In Boydston, A. (Ed., 1969–91), *The collected works of John Dewey*. Carbondale: Southern Illinois University Press.

James, W. (1983). *Talks to teachers in psychology*. Cambridge, MA: Harvard University Press.

Rich, A. (1978). *The dream of a common language: Poems, 1974–1977*. New York: Norton.

CHAPTER 2

Going Public: The Imperative of Public Education in the 21st Century

CARL D. GLICKMAN
DERRICK P. ALRIDGE

The challenge of fully realizing democracy in 21st-century America will depend heavily on the role that public education and schooling will play in constructing democratic principles among students, the community, and the larger society. American public education and schools will have to respond to several important questions:

- What is the purpose of public education and schooling in the 21st century?
- How best can public classrooms facilitate democratic learning?
- What are some viable strategies for public schools and education to democratize society?
- What is the purpose and goal of the teacher in the public schools, and what role can staff development play in furthering these goals?

In this chapter, we explore these important questions by arguing that public education must play an important role in moving students and communities toward a more democratic society.

THE PURPOSE OF PUBLIC EDUCATION AND SCHOOLING

The chief writer of the U.S. Declaration of Independence was, not coincidentally, one of the first to propose a common education for all children, to be tax-supported. Thomas Jefferson wrote, "If a civilized nation expects to be ignorant and free, it expects what never was and never will be." The idea of democracy in 1776, as proposed by Jefferson, Madison, and others, was to break from the rule of royalty, aristocracy, and the priesthood and form a society in which citizens would rule—the free rather than the king would rule the public domain, thus the word "free-dom" rather than the word "king-dom." (See Arendt, 1963, for a fuller discussion of freedom.) The essential ingredient for governance by the people was to be a common education for all citizens. There was, of course, an obvious contradiction of the idea of democracy in 1776. Citizens of the United States were mostly White men with property. Women, African Americans, Native Americans, and the poor were not included as citizens. The African-American activist and scholar W. E. B. Du Bois (1924) addressed this contradiction when he wrote:

> What do we mean by democracy? Do we mean democracy of the white races and the subjection of the colored races? Or do we mean the gradual working forward to a time when all men will have a voice in government and industry and will be intelligent enough to express the voice? (pp. 257–258)

Contemporary thinkers such as Cornel West have echoed Du Bois's concerns about the current practice and the potential of democratic principles for all people. West (1993), a descendant of slaves who lived during the revolution, wrote, "The greatest experiment in humankind began in 1776 [because] . . . it made the sanctity of each and every one of us . . . at least possible" (p. 8). Thus, the ideals of American democracy have, in time, created a moral consciousness that has been used to include others as citizens, for example, the common school movement, the women's suffrage movement, the elimination of Jim Crow laws and legally segragated schools, and the civil rights movement. For example, the idea of free public education received an important boost during the postbellum era when recently freed African Americans demanded universal, state-supported public education. Realizing that they were entitled to a democratic existence as stated in the Constitution, Bill of Rights, and the 13th Amendment, African Americans during this period believed that education was perhaps the most important means of obtaining their civil liberties. Education, therefore, had most important implications for democracy (see Anderson, 1988).

Education and Schooling

Mwalimu Shujaa (1994) points out the historically fundamental differences between education and schooling by stating that schooling has been intended to perpetuate and maintain existing power relations and institutional structures in society. Education, he notes, is the process of transmitting the knowledge of values, aesthetics, spiritual beliefs, and culture from one generation to the other. While Shujaa's definition provides important insight into a *modus operandi* of an oppressive or liberative society, we borrow from his definition to construct our own. We believe that the practices of public schools must become congruent with beliefs of public education for a better and more inclusive democratic society. For us, public schooling consists of the institutional practices and administrative structures that guide how schools operate to educate their students. Schooling includes practices such as class scheduling, staffing, testing, grouping of students, learning methods, and disciplinary procedures. It provides the environment in which learning will occur (Glickman, 1993). Public education is the knowledge base, epistemological perspective, and teacher, parent, and community modeling that give students the tools that they need to participate in society.

Our ideal of public education is one in which students are engaged in reflections and actions that constantly encourage them to move America toward a "truer" democratic society. A democratic society, we believe, is one in which people of all races, cultures, religions, genders, and sexual orientations have access to what the American founders called unalienable rights. One role of public education, as we shall explain later, is to challenge schools and society to live up to their claims of democracy and to address, head on, issues and problems that have historically impeded the realization of American democracy. We believe that the realization of democracy is a noble cause for public education, which can be found easily in the writings of a group of diverse people from the likes of Thomas Jefferson and Benjamin Franklin to Martin Luther King Jr., and W. E. B. Du Bois to more recent theorists such as Amy Gutmann (1987), bell hooks (1994), and Cornel West (1993).

The Mission and Goal of Public Education

Ideally, all American public schools should have the following mission, consistent with these words (Glickman, 1998c):

> We hold these truths to be self-evident: that all students are created equal; that they are endowed by their creator with certain unalienable rights; that among these are an education that would ensure life, liberty and the pursuit of happiness.

To our minds, the goal of public education is to enable students to become valued and valuable citizens of a democracy, to learn to be free, to have and make choices about their future, and to self-govern themselves individually and collectively. All other outcomes such as jobs, vocations, and intellectual, recreational, and cultural/social/aesthetic pursuits are subgoals of this larger goal and are fully realized in classrooms and schools only when connected to the larger goal. Obviously, to enact this "Declaration of Public Education" is a monumental challenge for teachers and other educators. It involves a core, diverse set of knowledge, skills, and understanding for all students. It ensures that they have the opportunity to pursue individual interests. And it requires that they demonstrate and apply their learning by contributing to a larger community beyond classmates and teachers.

DEMOCRATIC LEARNING

Democracy is as much a theory of learning as it is a political theory. It is a theory that when practiced in classrooms and schools shows astounding results in student achievement and advancement (Aiken, 1942; Meier, 1995; Newmann & Wehlage, 1995). A democracy strives for progress of all its citizens by protecting the general diffusion of knowledge, freedom of expression, a free press, the marketplace of ideas, and the unfettered pursuit of truth. The idea is that the masses, when in an environment that supports open participation and human construction of knowledge, will learn more than if kings, aristocrats, or the wealthy control and determine what they should learn. The idea of people being able to learn best through their own participation is a revolutionary concept about the educability of all humans,who are seen as curious and self-seeking. The job of public educators, thus, is to structure learning environments in developmental ways to support such human capacity to seek for oneself. Paulo Freire (1970) stressed the importance of this type of guided autonomous learning as counter to the "banking" practice of education, which merely "deposits" information into students' minds for the purpose of rote regurgitation. Instead, we suggest that democratic learning encourages students to take an active role in their own learning by giving them greater choices and more autonomy in their acquisition, production, and application of knowledge.

Democratic learning, however, is not without direction and guidance from the teacher. The teacher has the responsibility to use his or her unique attributes—position, experience, age, and wisdom—to guide students to the fundamental aims of a democratic society: learning to be free. Democracy and education, thus, are not separate concepts but two sides of the same coin. Dewey (1916), in the classic work *Democracy and Education,* rightfully claimed that the purpose of education is for democracy, but missed an important dimension of democracy as the most powerful form of learning. Thus, we prefer the term democracy *as* education (see Glickman, 1998a, 1998b, 1998c).

More specifically, democratic learning *is*:

- Students actively working with problems, ideas, materials, and people as they learn skills and content.
- Students having escalating degrees of choices, both as individuals and as groups, within the parameters provided by the teacher.
- Students being responsible to their peers, teachers, parents, and school community to ensure that educational time is being used purposefully and productively.
- Students sharing their learning with one another, with teachers, and with parents and other community members.
- Students deciding how to make their learning a contribution to their community.
- Students assuming escalating responsibilities for securing resources (of people and materials outside the school) and for finding places where they can apply and further their learning.
- Students demonstrating what they know and can do in public settings and receiving public feedback.
- Students working and learning from one another, individually and in groups, at a pace that challenges all.

Let us add a few more qualifiers. There are times in democratic pedagogy when it is perfectly appropriate for teachers to lecture to students. There is no slavish allegiance by teachers to following a certain set of materials, programs, textbooks, activities, or innovations. There is no litmus test of correct democratic pedagogical practices. The current list of innovations—classroom meetings, whole language instruction, cooperative learning, Socratic discussions, project centers, critical thinking, constructivist mathematics, inclusion, technology integration, multi-age grouping, and thematic curricula—all have powerful places in democratic pedagogy, but such innovations do not exclude a teacher's judgment regarding when lecture, drill, direct instruction, phonics instruction, textbooks, imposed discipline, and so on are appropriate. For example, if teacher and students have held previous discussions about the rights and responsibilities of each, then there are times when it is perfectly acceptable for a teacher, after giving reasons, to say, "I want you all to sit down, be quiet, and listen to me!" (The above section is a slightly modified version of Glickman, 1998a, pp. 29–31.)

PUBLIC DEMONSTRATIONS OF STUDENT LEARNING

The impetus to knowing whether a teacher and school are teaching for democratic purpose are the classroom and school standards, and visible assessments that determine how a student can integrate and apply his/her learning to make a contribution to a larger community. Such questions that lead to the development of such public demonstrations are:

1. What should virtually all students know and be able to do prior to leaving my classroom and our school?
2. What should be the product: a portfolio, an exhibit, a project, a demonstration, and/or a presentation?
3. Who should review and assess learning beyond the immediate teacher: other faculty, staff, parents, peers, or other community members?
4. What should be the criteria: for example, a study of a problem, issue, or topic that shows connections among three or more disciplines; the use of basic skills of reading, writing, arithmetic, and speaking; the incorporation of technology; skills of study investigation and problem solving; and application and contribution to a real setting in the school, home, community, state, nation, or world?
5. Finally, how do we judge the quality of the work: by, for example, accuracy of knowledge used; sufficient explanation of issue or problem; clear usage and grammatically correct reading, forms of writing, and speaking; appropriate use of technology as a tool to gaining information and constructing a display; demonstration that application to a real setting is feasible and shows direct and immediate benefits? (See excellent examples of such public demonstrations in Blythe, Allen, & Powell, 1999; McDonald, 1996; Meier, 1995; Wood, 1998.)

Classrooms and schools should be centers of applied knowledge that extend learning to the community and vice versa (Alridge, 1999). This type of communal education taps into the realities of the community and provides students with a laboratory of sorts to conduct research, interact with community leaders, and examine real—neighborhood, state, nation, and world—issues and problems. This *social action* and *communal education* approach, we believe, is an essential component in how public education should promote a more democratic society. Jerome Morris (1999) also has discussed the importance of communal schools in advocating what he has termed communal bonds. In his recent field studies of several schools in St. Louis, Morris found that the community and community school interactions facilitated better learning experience for students, particularly African Americans.

Gloria Ladson-Billings (1994) wrote, in her study of successful teachers of African-American children, that successful schools are responsive to the traditions of one's own community:

> [The school] has one requirement—that its students be successful. The curriculum is rigorous and exciting. The student learning is organized around problems and issues . . . The students have studied cities in ancient African Kingdoms, Europe, and Asia. They are studying their own city. They have taken trips to City Hall . . . Groups of students are working on solutions to problems specific to the city. (pp. 140–141).

The same view of student learning combined with community is seen in the historic teaching methods of Native Americans. Norbert Hill (1993) wrote of the "Indian Way," that

> the universe is the "university." The acquisition of [learning] was largely a by-product of life experiences, including observation and participation in the activities of adults . . . Assistance and guidance, rather than domination and control, were the way of our elders, our greatest teachers . . . An enlightened teacher would encourage students to engage their curiosity through co-generating and participating in a variety of activities." (pp. 171–173)

What is being expressed by Ladson-Billings (1994) and Hill (1993), as well as by Morris (1999), Sonia Nieto and C. Rólon (1995), and others, is that student learning needs to be integral to adult issues of one's neighborhood and larger society. Thus, environmental, economic, social, historic, and civic issues of a larger community become the anchor for student application. For example, when students apply their study of mathematics, science, and reading to solving issues of soil erosion, pollution, the design of a needed suspension bridge, creation of economic development activities, planning new housing, and discovering the lost history of elders, students come to know firsthand how their learning promotes healthier neighborhoods. It is well documented that when students apply their learning in such participatory and contributory ways, their mastery of subject knowledge and skills is much greater than when no such applications are expected or required.

In conceptualizing the role of public education and the connection to issues of community in the 21st century, we must also attend to issues of race, class, gender, and culture that permeate American society and education. Given the recent number of hate crimes, the increase in stratification of the poor from the wealthy, and the growing number of ethnically and culturally diverse groups in the United States, public education must deal with the societal realities of our time and culture. Teachers and schools must assist students to provide real solutions to the problems of the lives of all people in an open, democratic society (see Banks, 1994). Racism, sexism, religious intoleration, and homophobia are a reality—an economic, social, and political one. These issues are controversial and difficult, but they cannot be ignored or merely marginalized if teachers are to promote the type of discourse that is necessary to realize a more democratic society (Delpit, 1994).

THE ROLE OF THE TEACHER AND STAFF DEVELOPMENT

The role of a teacher or school is not to indoctrinate students into a certain perspective or way to think about such social issues, but instead to give students the skills to analyze and think for oneself. This proceeds through professional learning and staff development that open new windows of understanding about students, teaching, learning, purpose, community, and oneself. To move toward more principled democratic learning, a teacher can begin in a number of ways: reading journals, watching videos, seeking information and discussions on websites, and attending classes, presentations, and conferences. A teacher on his/her own might construct a yearly individual personal plan of two components: one, information-gathering; the other, classroom practice. For example,

1. Accessing information about democratic learning, multicultural perspectives, public demonstrations and assessments of students, and school and community bonds.
2. Setting and implementing classroom learning goals with one's own students.

In an experiential manner, a teacher might carefully choose to interact with a group of persons outside of one's own normal friends and colleagues. He/she might visit classrooms, homes, and social/civic settings composed of persons of different ethnicity, religion, economic class, gender, and ideology than oneself. The intent is to learn, use, and appreciate the differences among people and to have such experiences guide working with one's own students and their parents/caretakers.

At another level, one might proceed with professional development plans with colleagues in one's own school, such as being part of a school study group, planning and implementing a school-based program of staff development, observing and coaching each other on jointly agreed classroom changes, having a monthly "critical friends" faculty meeting to share and assess the quality of student work, or being part of a school-wide effort to better define democratic purpose and classroom practice. Participating with equally curious peers at local, state, or national levels in teacher and/or school renewal networks is, further, a powerful way to support, learn, and act.

The following chapters will provide much more detailed references about professional development. The quest to connect education, school, and democracy with the practices of learning is a never-ending challenge. All of these experiences can be exhilarating, at times exhausting, but always satisfying to know that professional and personal learning is an ongoing process. It is why most of us choose to be public educators in the first place.

TO CONCLUDE

Education with a public purpose has several important connotations, including the purpose of education for democratic citizenship, the use of participatory learning and application for students, demonstrations of student learning, and the involvement of the larger public—colleagues, parents, citizens, students—in the life decisions of the school. For an individual or a school to do this work means an openness and vulnerability to criticism, revision, and constant change (Greene, 1973). It means taking the scarce time to rethink, reconsider, reflect, and rework one's craft. To proceed means to find others—both ideological friends and foes—to look at classrooms, to judge student work, and to change curriculum and learning together.

What appears to be a small change in increasing the involvement and participation of students in their learning might in actuality be a huge psychological step for a teacher who has been wedded to past routines. For educators to open their classrooms and the nature of student work to others—colleagues and parents—can be fraught with anxiety. To work in a place where public purpose is encouraged and supported throughout the school by its official leaders through the provision of time and opportunities for professional development is the optimum learning community. But regardless, one who is an educator with a deep concern for public purpose cannot wait for others.

Education alone cannot bring about a totally just and democratic society. However, public education and schooling have historically played an important role in how we view and shape our future society, and its potential for furthering future democratic goals is unquestionable. Given the great diversity that the United States experienced in the 20th century and the reality that the United States is one of the most ethnically diverse countries in the world, it is important that we stop and revisit the ideals of public education. As society becomes more racially, ethnically, religiously, and culturally diverse in this century, we will be challenged to ensure democracy for a plethora of groups with different values and perspectives. We must search for more innovative and inclusive means of ensuring that public education is accessible to all Americans, that the process of schooling promotes democratic education for all, and that the end result of public education is the further development of a more democratic society. This is no small task by any means, but after all, this is central to why we teach.

REFERENCES

Aiken, W. F. (1942). *The story of the eight-year study, with conclusions and recommendations.* New York: Harper and Brothers.

Alridge, D. P. (1999). Conceptualizing a Du Boisian philosophy of education. *Educational Theory, 49*(3), 359–379.

Anderson, J. (1988). *The education of Blacks in the South, 1860–1935.* Chapel Hill: University of North Carolina Press.

Arendt, H. (1963). *On revolution.* New York: Penguin Books.

Banks, J. A. (1994). *Multi-ethnic education: Theory and practice* (3rd ed.). Needham Heights, MA: Allyn & Bacon.

Blythe, T., Allen, D., & Powell, B. S. (1999). *Looking together at student work.* New York: Teachers College Press.

Delpit, L. (1994). *Other people's children: Cultural conflict in the classroom.* New York: New Press.

Dewey, J. (1916). *Democracy and education: An introduction to the philosophy of education.* Old Tappan, NJ: Macmillan.

Du Bois, W. E. B. (1971). *The gift of black folk.* New York: AMS Press. (Original work published 1924)

Freire, P. (1970). *Pedagogy of the oppressed.* New York: Herder and Herder.

Glickman, C. D. (1993). *Renewing America's schools: A guide for school-based action.* San Francisco: Jossey-Bass.

Glickman, C. D. (1998a). Educational leadership for democratic purpose. *International Journal of Leadership in Education 1*(1), 47–53.

Glickman, C. D. (1998b). Revolution, education, and the practice of democracy. *Education Forum, 63*(Fall), 16–22.

Glickman, C. D. (1998c). *Revolutionizing America's schools.* San Francisco: Jossey-Bass.

Greene, M. (1973). *Teacher as stranger.* Belmont, CA. Wadsworth.

Gutmann, A. (1987). *Democratic education.* Princeton, NJ: Princeton University Press.

Hill, N. (1993). Reclaiming American Indian education. In S. Elam (Ed.), *The state of the nation's public schools.* Bloomington, IN: Phi Delta Kappa Society.

hooks, b. (1994). *Teaching to transgress: Education as the practice of freedom.* New York: Routledge.

Ladson-Billings, G. (1994). *The dreamkeepers: Successful teachers of African American children.* San Francisco: Jossey-Bass.

McDonald, J. P. (1996). *Redesigning schools.* San Francisco: Jossey-Bass.

Meier, D. (1995). *The power of their ideas: Lessons for America from a small school in Harlem.* Boston: Beacon Press.

Morris, J. E. (1999). A pillar of strength: An African American school's communal bonds with families and community since *Brown. Urban Education, 33*(5), 584–605.

Newmann, F. M., & Wehlage, G. G. (1995). *Successful school restructuring: A report to the public and educators by the Center on Organization and Restructuring of Schools.* Madison, WI: Wisconsin Center for Education Research.

Nieto, S., and Rólon, C. (1995, November 11). *The preparation and professional development of teachers: A perspective from two Latinos.* Paper presented to the CULTURES conference, "Defining the Knowledge Base for Urban Teacher Education," Emory University, Decatur, GA.

Shujaa, M. J. (1994). Education and schooling: You can have one without the other. In M. J. Shujaa (Ed.), *Too much schooling, too little education: A paradox of Black life in White societies* (pp. 13–36). Trenton, NJ: Africa World Press.

West, C. (1993). *Prophetic thought in postmodern time: Beyond Eurocentrism and multiculturalism.* Monroe, ME: Common Courage.

Wood, G. H. (1998). *A time to learn.* London, UK: Dutton.

CHAPTER 3

Professional Development in Pursuit of School Reform

JUDITH WARREN LITTLE

This chapter takes up school reform as one of the espoused purposes of professional development. Explanations for the success or failure of reform commonly point to the contributions or shortcomings of formal staff development. Reform agendas both focus and justify professional development expenditures, which thus rest not only on the promise of individual teacher growth, but also on a corresponding vision of progress in school improvement.[1]

Nearly a decade ago, I speculated on the likely fit between contemporary reforms and professional development (Little, 1993). I argued that the kinds of pedagogical, curricular, and organizational changes envisioned by reform advocates of the 1980s and early 1990s—embodied in such phrases as "teaching for understanding" and "educating all students to a high standard"—could not readily be expressed in terms of specific, transferable skills and practices. To make headway on ambitious but broadly defined aims and principles would require adequate opportunities to learn (experiment, consult, evaluate) that were embedded in the routine organization of teachers' workday and work year. That is, such reforms would require less of a conventional training model and more of a consultation, problem solving, and program development model (see Ball & Cohen, 1999).

Since that time, I have spent several years investigating the trajectory of reform in schools engaged in programs of whole-school change.[2] The principal occasion for this work came in the form of a state-funded school restructuring demonstration program created to engender "powerful teaching and learning for all students." As public officials recited at the time, school restructuring was intended to "raise the bar *and* get everyone over it." Toward that end, schools were granted supplemental resources and urged to reinvent themselves in all respects—from school-level governance arrangements to curriculum, instruction, and assessment. Profiles of the individual schools convey aspirations, strategies, and change trajectories similar to those described by observers of whole-school restructuring elsewhere (for example, Louis & Kruse, 1995; Muncey & McQuillan, 1996; Newmann & Associates, 1996). Our inquiries yielded a familiar tale: overall, change was modest in scope and depth, uneven within and across schools, and slow to unfold. Like other observers of reform, our research team uncovered wide variations in the capacity and will for whole-school change, both within and across schools.

Despite the schools' uneven record of accomplishment, these case studies deepened our understanding of the ways in which teachers' capacities and dispositions matter to the success of large-scale reform initiatives. Without attributing progress solely to wise choices regarding professional development, it remains the case that we uncovered the most supportive learning environments for students in those schools—or more often, in pockets within schools—where teacher development was also valued and supported. Conversely, the most impoverished learning conditions for students (especially for low-achieving students) persisted where professional development was relatively peripheral to the restructuring efforts. At issue here is the fit between the school's reform aspirations and the individual and collective capacity and orientation of the school's staff.

These studies also brought us a new and unexpected appreciation for what it means to teach in a reform-active environment. Advocates of comprehensive school reforms anticipate that ambitious restructuring initiatives will motivate instructional improvement, stimulate the formation of a teachers' professional community, and enable a better fit between organizational structure and effective teaching practice. Yet by the end of the schools' five-year experiment with restructuring, we were inclined to join many teachers in wondering aloud, "Is reform good for good teaching?" Teachers who had embraced the overarching goals of restructuring—educating all students, reducing achievement disparities linked to family background, enlivening the classroom experience, forging more supportive relationships between teachers and students—were often disappointed by the fruits of their efforts and humbled by the difficulty of pursuing change on a school-wide scale. Some left their schools or left teaching altogether.

A mounting body of evidence suggests certain paradoxes: reform both stimulates teacher enthusiasm *and* results in burnout, expands some learning opportunities *and* erodes others, intensifies professional bonds *and* foments professional conflict. Chronicles of whole-school reform convey the intensity and turbulence of reform efforts. Laraine Hong (1996) titles her firsthand account *Surviving School Reform*, while Muncey and McQuillan (1996) speak to the "resistance and reform" that intertwine in sites affiliated with the Coalition of Essential Schools.

These two strands of discovery—about the *significance* of reform for teachers and teaching on the one hand, and about teachers' individual and collective *capacity* for reform on the other—serve as the organizing points for this chapter. They are cast here as questions:

- What is the significance of reform as a context for teaching and teachers? That is, how does working in a reform-active environment affect teachers' practice, professional growth, and commitment?
- How can professional development equip teachers, individually and collectively, to make good on the promise of reform? That is, what contributions does professional development make to the capacity of teachers and schools to reform?

Reform advocates and researchers have turned their attention primarily to the second set of questions—the questions of individual and collective capacity for reform. Drawing on insights from our recently completed study, I argue that our understanding of teachers' stance toward and engagement in school reform will be deepened by taking simultaneous account of both organizing questions.

THE SIGNIFICANCE OF REFORM FOR TEACHING AND TEACHER LEARNING

In proposing that we attend to the significance or meaning of reform, I take my point of departure from the perspective of teachers' lives and work. In doing so, I emphasize aspects of teaching and teacher development in reforming schools that may be obscured by the dominant focus on specific reforms and their implementation.

First Things First: The Ongoing Work of Teaching

Even in the most reform-active times and places, reform is only part of the picture of daily life and work. Teachers engage with any given reform at a particular place and time: at a specific moment in a teaching career; in the midst of a teaching assignment with particular students and subjects; in the company of particular colleagues; and in a school that may be well or weakly led. In our analysis so far, three aspects of teachers' lives and careers stand out especially in helping explain responses to reform and related participation in professional development.

First, reforms have the potential to enhance or threaten the intellectual, moral, and emotional satisfactions of classroom teaching. They do so most directly by targeting changes in classroom practice. A veteran high school mathematics teacher who dramatically changed her teaching observes the successes she is having with students (including those who had never before succeeded in math) and the corresponding pleasure she is finding in her teaching:

> I think I've been through a lot of growth, personal change, because this is 26 years of teaching now and I taught my first 18 years or so exactly the way I was taught, which is—you can picture the scene. Umm . . . and to change . . . that was not any automatic overnight thing for me at all. . . . I think when people get involved doing things like that, you just get so much renewed strength as a teacher. You are excited again. I was at a point after my first 10 years, kind of like, is this all there is? You know, I had every problem in the book memorized. And I loved the kids, but I wasn't finding anything for me. And you would find cute little activities now and then to do. But it wasn't anything significant for me. (Math teacher, North Meadow High School)

Not all teachers greeted the proposed changes in classroom practice with enthusiasm. Indeed, some objected to what they saw as a new instructional orthodoxy. A high school teacher complains:

> One of the things I resent the most is the hidden agenda to get rid of lecture/discussion learning and go more towards "student centered." . . . Look, I recognize that certain teachers can use cooperative learning and groups and other activities and make a class come alive—but most can't!! I can make my class come alive with lecture and discussion! (Teacher, Zapata High School, S96)

New out-of-classroom responsibilities also stand to affect the rewards of teaching. While such added responsibilities sometimes enabled teachers to pursue personal interests (like a fascination with technology), they also diminished the time and attention available for classroom teaching. As one middle school teacher described it, "I'm doing two jobs. I teach and I do the technology [for the school], and to be honest, my curriculum is suffering a little bit in my classroom."

Second, reforms have the potential to unite or divide colleagues, or to generate or interrupt friendships and other bonds of professional community. Reform activity typically entails a greatly increased level of teacher interaction and collaboration, especially in whole-staff forums and in newly configured teaching teams or programs. The two quotations below cannot convey the complexity of this domain, but do illustrate something of its range:

> I think the [restructuring] money helps, but deep down it's that we say, "Hey, as a group, look how much farther we can go when we put our heads together." You know, myself, I feel so cleansed and refreshed after a day together. And we might spend the whole six hours bashing heads over philosophical issues. But that's okay because you could come away from it saying, "Wow! We're moving. We're thinking. We're not just isolated. We're in it together." [Science teacher, interview, Hacienda High School]
>
> This school is definitely polarized and administration offers very little leadership or vision. . . . The important decisions affecting this school's future are made by "veteran" teachers who carry union power and make no attempt to alter their approaches and views of teaching. I honestly believe that it is impossible to have a successful learning climate on a campus where half of the school is involved in traditional teaching and the other half is involved in small learning communities. These are completely opposing philosophies . . . [Humanities teacher, survey comment, Rose High School]

Finally, reforms have the potential to consume teachers' private lives and strain family relationships. Teachers describe greatly increased personal commitments of time, emotional and intellectual energy, and real work (developing curriculum, writing reports, collecting unaccustomed kinds of student data, participating in meetings, traveling). With rare exceptions, as when teacher leaders may be granted a reduced teaching load, new work piles on top of all the other labors required for classroom teaching. An elementary teacher writes:

> The enormous amount of personal time one must spend at workshops, inservice, compiling data, producing reports is

totally unacceptable with time away from family. Finally, the last 2 years have been the most troubling and disturbing years of my life. There is no doubt in my mind that if we were not a restructuring school I would not have been put through what has happened to me. (Teacher, survey comment, Harrison Elementary School)

Where teachers experience a happy fit between reform initiatives and these three aspects of their teaching lives, they tend to become visible as reform enthusiasts. However, such a happy fit seems elusive, especially over long periods of sustained innovation. At issue here is how teachers interpret the significance of reform in the context of the ongoing obligations and opportunities of teaching.

Interpreting Reform

However reform proposals are portrayed in documents or by their advocates inside and outside the school, they are subject to individual, collective, and institutional interpretations. Responses to reform constitute an ongoing interpretive act that for teachers is personal, interactive, and continuous. All of this interpretive work in some way answers the question "What does this mean for me (or us)?" It operates to explain and justify a stance toward proposed change, and a disposition toward teacher learning associated with such change. Among the teachers in our restructuring schools, interpretation of reform took up four problems.

The Worth of Reform—Is this good for me, for us, for my students? The promise of whole-school change required a foundation of whole-school agreement about the central goals and strategies of restructuring. Teachers assessed the merit of reform rationales and proposals, sometimes revising their initial judgments as broadly defined ideas took more and more specific form over time.

Although most schools were able to achieve agreement on broadly defined educational goals, they found agreement much harder to come by at the level of grade-level and subject standards (what's important for students to learn, and what counts as good work). They often found themselves divided in their interpretation of the school's problems or their explanations for student failure, and thereby in their views of precisely what changes, if any, were in the best interests of students. Philosophical divisions manifested themselves in teacher-by-teacher differences in classroom practice and teacher–student interactions. They showed up in staff meetings and in the messages communicated to students by teachers, administrators, counselors, and others. Dividing lines among teachers seemed most firmly drawn over the meaning of "high expectations for all students" and over the role of teachers in reaching low-achieving students or students who were alienated from school. In some cases, divisions among staff increased over time, as broad provisions of the initial restructuring plan began to take shape in ways that affected the daily work of individual teachers, administrators, and counselors.

In schools or groups that achieved some measure of unity, we tended to find provisions for working out these complicated matters openly and at a level of detail close to practice. Such provisions included forums for open debate, investigation, and problem solving; planning strategically for managing turnover and the introduction of newcomers; and means of addressing explicitly the tensions between a teacher's individual autonomy and obligations to the school or group. An English teacher at Dewey Middle School acknowledges that teachers differ in what they believe it means to "serve kids well," and explains that the school uses its staff meetings and in-service events to deliberate the meaning of high expectations and to examine their own assumptions about students:

> It's always good to have department meetings and other types of meetings so that people can exchange ideas. I think a lot of people have changed over the years. We also had . . . a workshop [this year] on "dysfunctional rescuing," which is [thinking] that because a child comes from a certain area of disadvantage, they have to be treated differently or the curriculum has to be watered down, and that they shouldn't be challenged as much as others. So in order to fight that, we had that type of workshop so that people would examine what they do in the classroom. It doesn't help to rescue a child in that way, because it's going to affect them later on. (English teacher, Dewey Middle School)

The Scope of Reform. Teachers consider the intended scope and reach of reform, interpreting its aims and strategies in relation to their own values, beliefs, practice, and circumstances. (See also Drake, Spillane, & Hufferd-Ackles, in press; Putnam & Borko, 2000; Richardson & Placier, in press). In doing so, they assess the degree to which pursuing reform would entail fundamental change in teaching ideas, practices, and relationships. In some instances, they saw the proposed changes as enabling them to make better use of existing knowledge and experience. At the middle and high school levels, this was particularly apparent in the responses of some English, social studies, and science teachers to lengthened instructional periods. One of the most vivid expressions of "good fit" comes from a middle school English teacher who describes how her involvement in the California Writing Project and in an informal group of women writers has made a difference in her ability to help all her students develop interest and facility in writing. Drawing expertise and confidence from sources of expertise and professional community outside the school, she eagerly embraces the idea of extended instructional periods:

> I was very much supportive of the block [schedule] change. Some teachers had a real hard time with that, saying, "How do we entertain them for ninety-eight minutes"? And I was going, "Oh, boy, ninety-eight minutes!" (Humanities teacher, Dewey Middle School)

Yet as this comment suggests, not all teachers in this school felt well prepared to make good use of the new schedule. In other schools as well, such structural reorganization left teachers feeling the need to alter their teaching but uncertain how to proceed: "Well, one of the things that makes me feel guilty is that I feel with the 90 minute block I should have more variety in my lessons than I do" (Math teacher, Hacienda HS).

The Feasibility of Reform. However worthy a reform idea, teachers remain sensitively attuned to its pragmatic requirements. With one eye on the existing imperatives of classroom teaching and one eye on a changing horizon, teachers calculate the sheer feasibility of reform— and they do so continuously as the reform unfolds. A factor in these restructuring schools was the state's comparatively low investment in public education. In a climate where resources were scarce, schools sought any revenue stream that would bolster the school's basic program. The resulting tendency toward entrepreneurial activity ("getting grants") contributed to piecemeal efforts and a short-term project mentality in some sites. Indeed, some teachers viewed restructuring less as a program of school or classroom change than as a resource windfall. Meanwhile, those who sought genuine change had to confront the multiple demands on the discretionary resources that the restructuring grant supplied. Altogether, restructuring resources paid mainly for what might be considered basics—professional staff time, computer equipment, and other instructional resources. At the same time, relatively few resources (11% of all grant funds over 5 years) were devoted to professional development, a category that might be seen as more directly associated with efforts to produce dramatic improvement in teaching and learning.

The Authority Behind Reform. In considering the merit, scope, and feasibility of selected reform proposals, teachers also assess the formal authority with which the reform advocates speak and act. Where does the reform originate, and what is the impetus behind it? What latitude do individuals, groups, and schools enjoy in deciding whether or how to take up a given reform? What are the consequences associated with succeeding or failing? Our restructuring schools had competed for funds as part of a voluntary program of school restructuring. The state acted principally as the source of resources and as a proponent of ideas with a decidedly progressive cast. Local reform advocates in the demonstration schools were in a position to persuade and sometimes to pressure, but the consequences were largely internal to participating schools. The policy landscape has now changed. In the evolving climate of standards, accountability, and testing, teachers and administrators must increasingly contend not only with the coercive authority of the state, but also with what some teachers see as a massive shift in reform logic and in underlying assumptions about teaching and learning.

Teachers adopt a stance toward reform drawing not only on reformers' claims but also on what they know about their expertise and experience, the principles and values that govern their teaching, the pragmatics of context, and the judgments of colleagues they trust and admire. The potential contribution of professional development to the pursuit of reform in turn rests on teachers' overall stance toward reform proposals and the origins of that stance.

TEACHER LEARNING AS A RESOURCE FOR REFORM

Long-term observers of educational innovation and school reform have argued that reform might more productively be seen as a problem of learning than as a problem of implementation. Even given widespread endorsement of a reform idea, progress toward that reform also appears to rest in crucial ways on the capacity of teachers, both individually and collectively. Indeed, teachers' individual accounts of their restructuring experiences pointed vividly to issues of knowledge, experience, and confidence. The discussion that follows focuses particularly on the capacity that resides in individual and collective knowledge, experience, and commitments; it does not take up the ways in which capacity also entails other human, material, and organizational supports for teaching and teacher learning. (See Elmore & Burney, 1996; King & Newmann, 1999; Lieberman, 1995; Newmann & Associates, 1996; and Wilson & Berne, 1999.)

Learning Demands Associated with Reform

Whether implicitly or explicitly, directly or indirectly, restructuring proposals introduced new expectations for teachers' knowledge and practice. The case study schools proposed a range of strategies: multiage classrooms, 90-minute instructional blocks, interdisciplinary teaching, cooperative learning, alternative methods of student assessment, and new uses of technology are all cases in point. Teachers offered detailed accounts of the learning demands that emerged as restructuring unfolded. These accounts highlighted new expectations that affected virtually every aspect of teachers' work.

First, restructuring envisioned *classroom teaching* marked by integrated or interdisciplinary curriculum, more varied and flexible instruction, multiple forms of assessment, new uses of technology, more broadly supportive relationships with students, and more uniformly high levels of academic expectation. Second, it called upon teachers and others to engage in *collegial work* in a more collective and public way, sometimes in areas that proved complex and contentious. Restructuring directly affected the overall professional culture by bringing greater collegial and public scrutiny to the practices of teaching and learning, seeking more widespread agreement on teaching priorities, and spawning leadership roles premised on expected changes in teaching (see Little, 1995, 1996). Finally, restructuring engaged teachers in new forms of *governance and decision making*, altering their relationships with administrators and parents, making the boundaries between school and community more permeable and the relationships in some ways less predictable.

The Pace of Reform and the Pace of Learning

For the most active participants, restructuring was something of an emotional, intellectual, and professional roller coaster. Reform enthusiasts recounted the early days of reform activity as a period of professional stimulation, renewal, and challenge. Advocates of restructuring were genuinely excited about the possibilities associated with new approaches to teaching and learning, and new ways of working together with colleagues. Over time, fatigue tempered their excitement, especially as gains were slow to materialize and staff members found themselves in conflict over the best course of action. That is, the restructuring experience yielded both personal renewal and burnout, with talk of burnout increasing over time. By the fourth year of restructuring, nearly half of teachers surveyed reported feeling burned out by restructuring. A sizable proportion, especially in the middle schools (38%) and high schools (43%), said they would be likely to accept a job in a more traditional school if one were offered. The emotional exhaustion and depersonalization that are marks of burnout arguably make it hard to develop and sustain the culture of inquiry that many believe will be needed to support a restructured school.[3]

Administrative and public expectations for rapid pace, broad scope, and visible outcomes of change exacerbate the difficulties surrounding teacher learning in a context of reform. At issue here is whether such intensity is conducive to deep questioning of assumptions and certainties, or whether it drains individuals of the energy and concentration needed to learn. Reform environments tend to be volatile, fast-paced, and public, while learning may require sustained concentration, gradual development, and opportunities for relatively private ("safe") disclosure of struggles and uncertainties.

In effect, the demands on knowledge and practice were substantial and simultaneous. Even in schools where a large proportion of the teachers had taken part in crafting the restructuring plan and where support for its core tenets ran high, teachers were taken often aback by the learning demands that emerged over time. Not all the difficulties that schools encountered in pursuing reform could be resolved by opportunities for professional growth, but it seems reasonable to assess the headway that might be made by investing more consistently and strategically in teachers' opportunity to learn.

Learning Opportunities in the Context of Reform

Schools differed in the way they thought about professional development and in the uses they made of the resources available to them. Most schools introduced new organizational arrangements that were conducive to teacher learning. Specifically, they formed teacher teams with designated blocks of common planning and professional development time. They devoted school-wide staff development days, summer institutes, or staff retreats to topics related to the reform goals (for example, organizing systematic reviews of samples of student work).

They made use of external sources of expertise and assistance (for example, affiliation with the Coalition of Essential Schools or participation in one or more of the California Subject Matter Projects). Most schools subsidized individual teachers' participation in conferences or other activities, paying for release time, conference-related travel or fees, or stipends.

Compared to the ease with which they anticipated the structural and programmatic possibilities for professional development, schools were far less prepared to tackle the resources or constraints for teacher learning that are deeply embedded in a school's professional culture. On the one hand, teachers in nearly all schools described a generally supportive professional climate among staff. Nearly all of the nearly 1,100 teachers surveyed (90%) say they can count on their colleagues at least some of the time to support them in trying new ideas, and nearly all (93%) report that they are able to turn to their colleagues for good advice. Most teachers (88%) reported some kind of teacher collaboration, although the meaning of "collaboration" varied greatly among schools.

On the other hand, we find substantial evidence that collaborative progress often stalled when teachers uncovered strongly held and opposing views about teaching practice and student performance. Reform advocates in each school—especially those in teacher leadership positions—expressed a profound appreciation for the tenacity of established traditions in teaching. Among themselves, they acknowledged the "re-culturing" that must accompany restructuring, but they had little preparation or standing to deal with the issues they encountered.

At issue here is the extent to which schools were able to mobilize resources to support a constellation of learning opportunities for teachers, while also cultivating the kind of professional culture conducive to struggle. The elementary school portrayed by Laura Stokes in Chapter 9 of this volume offers one "existence proof" of such a school. In this school, teachers meet as a whole staff to review student work and other evidence designed to help everyone understand overall patterns of student learning. Within grade-level groups, teachers design action research projects that bring inquiry closer to the classroom. Finally, voluntary study groups offer a relatively private environment in which teachers can examine their own assumptions and teaching practices. Each opportunity enables some kinds of learning that the others do not; together, the opportunities build individual and collective capacity for improvement. In our own case study schools, randomly sampled from the universe of funded schools, we found no such whole-school exemplars, though we did find impressive instances of well-supported teacher learning in pockets within schools and sometimes in teachers' professional activities outside the school. Altogether, we uncovered a rather eclectic configuration of activities. To a greater or lesser extent, they embodied four broad conceptions of professional development:

Professional Development as Inspiration and Goal-Setting. Reform leaders placed great emphasis on rallying and sustaining school-wide endorsement, or "buy-in," for reform goals and strategies. Accordingly, they devoted a relatively large share of professional development time to activities and discussions designed to inspire and persuade. The relationship between such activities and teacher learning remains uncertain. At its best, this strategy supplied teachers with a "big picture" of student experience and performance that inspired them to rethink their own practice. A high school English teacher attests that he found unexpected and lasting value in

> sitting around the table with [the previous principal] in the first year of restructuring, with other teachers, and thinking back to powerful learning experiences in my life. Realizing that those powerful learning experiences had to do with—and this is the main thing that I've learned over the last few years—had to do with times when I was involved with something real. . . . So that's what I'm always looking for now in my class. (Teacher, North Meadow High School)

But beyond a certain threshold, teachers question the utility of such "team-building" and "empowerment" strategies, especially at the expense of time spent delving into matters of curriculum, instruction, and assessment.

> [Getting] involvement and empowerment of all of us requires a lot of time. To me, it's not worth it. I would rather see the time go into reading the framework for history, which I need. (Teacher, Harbor Middle School)

Professional Development as Knowledge and Skill Development. This conception embodies the most familiar face of professional development, and it was visibly evident in the plans and resource allocations of the restructuring schools. Schools established specific school-wide priorities for professional development that matched their priorities for curricular and instructional change. Teachers at Dewey Middle School maintain that the school's substantial achievements would not have been possible without "all the professional development," particularly long-term involvement with university-based partnership projects centered on language arts, math, and science teaching. Teachers in North Meadow High School's math department took advantage of the discretionary resources associated with restructuring to pursue a department goal—increasing students' participation in upper-level math courses. They credit their out-of-school professional development, in the company of other reform-oriented math teachers, with enabling them to act on their premise that new ways of teaching math would result in greater student participation and success:

> It's just the fact that we realized that teaching Algebra in the traditional method was not as successful as it should be and our failure rate, you know, was unsatisfactory. And so we had to look for another avenue and . . . there's no reason why more of them could not be successful in Algebra if it was presented in a different way. (Math teacher, North Meadow High School)

School-wide priorities sometimes presented a substantial challenge to individuals' felt sense of preparation. Some middle and high schools asked that teachers tackle interdisciplinary teaching assignments, exciting some teachers and disturbing others. Elementary schools combined two or more grade levels or introduced "cycles" in which teachers stayed with a class for two years. Nearly all schools enrolled a growing population of students with a first language other than English. At Olive Grove Elementary, one teacher describes her initial reluctance to teach a second-language population of Hmong-speaking children and to the additional preparation it would require. Now, after two years' participation in a special project developed by two nearby universities, she says she is no longer "fumbling along with ESL," adding, "I've learned a lot . . . I'm enjoying it, I love it, so I'm glad I got coerced or pressured or whatever."

Other problems of fit arise when schools propose new approaches to curriculum and teaching with little corresponding support. One example comes from an elementary-grade teacher whose school had elected to employ more systematic and varied approaches to the teaching of writing, but failed to back the plan with a consistent level of professional development support:

> Some of us had a "one-day wonder shot," and some people had three weeks of training. Some of us just kind of said, "Okay . . . we've got our folders," and other people were just really excited

about it. So we were at all different levels of expertise. (Teacher focus group, Olive Grove Elementary School)

Professional Development as Inquiry. Emerging research on teacher learning underscores the importance of professional development that focuses on learning in and from practice, and that concentrates on the combination of knowledge of subject, knowledge of teaching, and knowledge of particular groups of students (see especially Ball & Cohen, 1999). The teacher development and educational change literatures are replete with appeals for reflective practice, and the architects of the restructuring initiative pushed hard to introduce the idea of a "culture of inquiry." Consultants to the restructuring schools developed instruments and routines ("protocols") that would structure reviews of student work and other evidence related to student learning. In regional and statewide meetings, they spoke of the professional norms and technical expertise it would take to open up a discussion of how student learning was affected by schooling processes and teaching practices. Some schools, like the one described by Stokes in Chapter 9, placed this conception at the center of a professional development strategy. Other schools devoted occasional meetings to the review of student work, supplying teachers with more of a "big picture" of student performance:

> It was really interesting to see on the exit interviews [with the 8th graders] . . . all this data we collated and spent time looking at. And, there were a couple of interesting learnings that came out of that—like how well the ESL kids were doing was kind of surprising. (Teacher, Harbor Middle School)

Such occasions generally stopped well short of analyzing teaching practice and its possible relationship to the evidence of student learning on display. Some teachers argued for inquiry that would get more directly at teaching practice:

> I think a lot of us slip into complacency . . . and we say, yeah, I have this system in my head and I just know [how I grade], without sitting down and saying what is it exactly that you grade and what are our criteria and what is it that makes an A grade in your class? . . . I think it needs to be a focus of the whole school, frankly. I think it just needs to be a focus. . . . I think it would be much more complicated for each of us, if we were forced to sit down and analyze why we do what we do in

the classroom and why we give that grade. . . . We're not forced
to do that. (English teacher, North Meadow High School)

Professional Development as Collaboration and Community.
Reform leaders placed substantial faith in the generative power of
teacher collaboration, and made efforts to marshal time and other resources to support it. Most brought teachers together in collaborative
arrangements that entailed regularly scheduled time together and
shared responsibility for students or curriculum. Some committed substantial amounts of funding to teachers' collaborative time; a restructuring coordinator in one large high school reports having "paid for
14,000 hours of collaboration time" over a four-year period. It is most
certainly true that these collaborations sometimes resulted in new
teacher learning as teachers worked together on curriculum, student
assessment, and other tasks. Overall, however, the professional development potential that resides in collaboration and community remained relatively underdeveloped in the restructuring schools.

First, reform leaders took little account of the role played by teachers' established professional communities within the school as a resource for or impediment to reform. This is not to say that they could
not detect some of the differences in professional culture among these
groups (referring, for example, to "innovative" or "dysfunctional"
teams or subject departments), but that they did not conceive of them
as a focus of reform strategy or a locus of teacher learning.[4]

Second, schools appeared to have had little access to professional
development that employs professional community as a vehicle for
teachers to acquire greater depth in substantive areas of curriculum
instruction and assessment. The available literature portrays a small
but growing number of programs that combine deep, sustained attention to specific domains of teaching practice with an effort to build
professional community among a group of participating teachers.[5] A
high school math teacher attests to the power of such long-term collective engagement with matters of mathematics teaching. One feature of her professional development experience was revealing gaps in
her own mathematical knowledge in the context of a group of teachers all grappling together with both the mathematics content and their
approach to math instruction:

> There is a unit . . . that focuses on chi square. And you should
> have seen all of us. We all took some stat class in college,
> and we don't teach this. We are so uncomfortable with

statistics. . . . And all of us were able to, at our training—we really bonded with our group. We called it our class, that we went through our four years of training with [teachers] who were from all over the state. We all had different degrees of strength in mathematics. But we had to get comfortable with each other and really put it on the line. Hey, we don't really all know everything here. We are all going to approach these problems differently. And recognize that there is a parallel to what our kids would go through. But there were many times when we were terrified!

For a variety of reasons (access, perceived demand on time, adequate resources), such intensive activities were uncommon among teachers in these restructuring schools. Further, the schools' formal relationships with external "partner" organizations more often tended to focus on assistance with whole-school change processes than on expertise and relationships built around the demands of classroom teaching.

Finally, teachers' individual ties with the professional community outside the school remained nearly invisible as an influence on teachers' will and capacity for reform. Schools subsidized conference participation, but otherwise took little note of teachers' levels of participation in professional growth activity or the ways in which a teacher's web of professional relationships beyond the school might affect individual or collective choices and progress. The math teacher quoted above views her out-of-school professional community as an integral part of her teaching life and the source of ideas that she in turn brings into her department:

I don't know how teachers find out what's going on out there if you don't get out! And I have always believed in going to conferences and being a member of organizations and reading their journals and newsletters. . . . So I have always been in touch that way. But you have got to get out! (Math teacher, North Meadow High School)

This teacher's department colleagues are also active participants in external math teaching communities, and credit their participation with equipping them to teach math in ways that have increased student enrollment in upper levels of mathematics. Their story stands out as an exception. Overall, both the possibilities and the obstacles that reside in teachers' professional community went largely unattended.

Expanding Opportunities for Teacher Learning

In principle, the four conceptions of professional development suggest a constellation of supports for teacher learning and the improvement of practice. In practice, the professional development activity in these restructuring schools remained relatively episodic, fragmented, and weakly connected to practice. Further, the first conception—professional development as inspiration to reform—dominated the use of officially designated time. Virtually all the schools, to a greater or lesser extent, concentrated on rallying school-wide support for goals, and then indulged in something of a leap of faith regarding individual capacity and will. Reform leaders organized professional development events to expose teachers to alternative instructional practices, and expressed hope that teachers or groups would be sufficiently inspired and informed to change. Investments in sustained inquiry at the level of teaching practice were far more meager, with inquiry activities infrequent and often superficial or formulaic.

With few exceptions, professional development opportunities lagged behind the new learning demands presented by restructuring. The sheer scope of the restructuring agenda sometimes made the demands on teaching practice difficult to specify. Further, the comprehensive reform agenda resulted in numerous, competing demands for scarce staff development time.

> We've only had a couple of staff development [events] on technology, and I know why we haven't. . . . There's a lot of other demands on our staff development days. . . . The big problem is that there are so many demands on curricular areas, restructuring—things that we have to do to. (Teacher, Harbor Middle School)

Although reform leaders were able to justify each individual activity by its relationship to the larger reform goals, the combined effect was a professional development agenda that appeared diffuse and fragmented. Relatively few teachers reported having substantial influence over the content of staff development activity. In six of the nine intensive case study schools, a sizable percentage of staff (from 29% to 57%) characterized staff development events as often being "one-time workshops with no follow-up."

Finally, in the context of a high-visibility demonstration project, teacher learning opportunities were often displaced by accountability demands. Teachers tell how designated staff development time came to be used for documenting restructuring progress. A focus group of middle school teachers offered these comments:

> *T1:* We committed, at least, I think two [staff development] days, last year, in terms of documenting stuff to justify the grant. It doesn't seem to be really anything to help us move forward.
>
> *T2:* [The time] is needed to document what we're doing and all that, but at the same time, for us to keep moving forward, it's almost like, "Stand still while you qualify what you've done." Then they say, "What have you done here?" So, we've eaten up the time when we're supposed to be moving forward.
>
> *T3:* All this time and effort is being spent for some kind of bureaucrat to justify something [at the state level], and it doesn't seem to be benefiting teachers, the kids, or the community, you know, this school community.

CONCLUSION

At the turn of the 21st century, policymakers and public leaders show an increasing tendency to portray teachers' work as the work of reform—and more specifically, the reform of classroom teaching in ways that result in more uniformly high levels of student achievement. Investments in teacher development are proposed and justified on the basis of their contributions to "teacher quality," defined as teachers who will be up to the task of teaching to the academic standards defined by states and school districts. Researchers have followed a parallel path, with investigations that increasingly center on teachers' responses to and implementation of various reform initiatives.

In this chapter, I have argued that we will enhance our understanding of reform trajectories and outcomes by considering not only teachers' *capacity* for reform, but also the *meaning or significance* that teachers attach to specific reform initiatives. Those meanings arise in part from teachers' interpretations of reform and its entailments, and in part from the multiple, ongoing obligations of classroom teaching and other professional work.

By attending to the significance of reform in those terms, we place ourselves in a position to anticipate a reform trajectory while questioning whether and how particular reforms stand to improve teaching. By tackling the corresponding question of individual, collective, and organizational capacity for reform, we acknowledge the urgency associated with the educational problems to which reforms are targeted—especially the persisting inequities in educational opportunities and outcomes—and the human and material resources it will take to remedy them.

NOTES

1. Over the years, observers of school change have regularly identified professional development as an underdeveloped resource for successful innovation and reform; for example, see McLaughlin and Marsh (1979) and King and Newmann (1999). Schlechty and Whitford (1983) argue that formal professional development, while typically promoted and justified as a resource for change, also serves institutional interests in stability and continuity, while Popkewitz (1991) challenges the assumption that reform necessarily entails progress.

2. Altogether, these investigations have encompassed three separate rounds of case study work. This chapter relies on data collected for the School Restructuring Study (SRS), coinciding with the final three years of a state-funded restructuring program. Funded by the Stuart Foundation and Hewlett Foundation, the study examined the restructuring choices made by 36 elementary, middle, and high schools, and the significance of those choices for students and teachers. Ongoing analysis of these data has been supported in part by the Spencer Foundation. All schools and individuals have been supplied with pseudonyms. For a more detailed description of the study design and a summary report of findings, see Little and Dorph, 1998.

3. For a comprehensive discussion of research on teacher burnout, see Vandenberghe and Huberman (1999), especially the chapter by Maslach and Leiter; on the various responses to conflict among teachers' collegial groups, see Achinstein (1998).

4. For a detailed analysis of the significance of departmental community and reform progress at the high school level, see Little (1999). For related analyses of the differences between "traditional professional community" and "teacher learning community," see Talbert (1995) and McLaughlin and Talbert (in press).

5. Such projects have often originated in universities and have incorporated a long-term research agenda. Nationally known examples include both the Cognitively Guided Instruction project and the QUASAR project in the area of elementary and middle school mathematics (Fennema et al., 1996; Stein, Silver, & Smith, 1998). Subject matter networks have long afforded teachers an opportunity to deepen or broaden subject teaching knowledge within a community of teachers with similar interests and teaching responsibilities (Lieberman & Wood, this volume; Greenleaf & Schoenbach, 1998).

REFERENCES

Achinstein, B. (1998). *Ties that bind: Conflict within teacher professional communities.* Unpublished Ph.D. dissertation, Stanford University.

Ball, D. L., & Cohen, D. K. (1999). Developing practice, developing practitioners: Toward a practice-based theory of professional education. In L. Darling-Hammond & G. Sykes (Eds.), *Teaching as the learning profession: Handbook of policy and practice* (pp. 3–32). San Francisco: Jossey-Bass.

Drake, C., Spillane, J. P., & Hufferd-Ackles, K. (in press). Storied identities: Teacher learning and subject matter context. *Journal of Curriculum Studies.*

Elmore, R., & Burney, D. (1996). Staff development and instructional improvement: Community District 2, New York City. In L. Darling-Hammond & G. Sykes (Eds.), *Teaching as the learning profession: Handbook of policy and practice* (pp. 263–291). San Francisco: Jossey-Bass.

Fennema, E., Carpenter, T. P., Franke, M. L., Levi, L., Jacobs, V. R., & Empson, S. B. (1996). A longitudinal study of learning to use children's thinking in mathematics instruction. *Journal for Research in Mathematics Education, 27,* 403–434.

Greenleaf, C. L., & Schoenbach, R. (1998). *Close readings: A study of key issues in the use of literacy learning cases for the professional development of secondary teachers.* San Francisco: Strategic Literacy Initiative, WestEd.

Hong, L. K. (1996). *Surviving school reform: A year in the life of one school.* New York: Teachers College Press.

King, M. B., & Newmann, F. M. (1999, April). *School capacity as a goal for professional development: Mapping the terrain in low income schools.* Paper presented at the annual meeting of the American Educational Research Association, Montreal.

Lieberman, A. (Ed.). (1995). *The work of restructuring schools: Building from the ground up.* New York: Teachers College Press.

Lieberman, A., & Wood, D. (in press). When teachers write: Of networks and classrooms. In A. Lieberman & L. Miller (Eds.), *Teachers caught in the action: Professional development in practice* (Chapter 11, this volume). New York: Teachers College Press.

Little, J. W. (1993). Teachers' professional development in a climate of educational reform. *Educational Evaluation and Policy Analysis, 15*(2), 129–151.

Little, J. W. (1995). Subject affiliation in high schools that restructure. In L. S. Siskin & J. W. Little (Eds.), *The subjects in question: Departmental organization and the high school* (pp. 172–200). New York: Teachers College Press.

Little, J. W. (1996). The emotional contours and career trajectories of (disappointed) reform enthusiasts. *Cambridge Journal of Education, 26*(3), 345–359.

Little, J. W. (1999, April). *Teachers' professional development in the context of secondary school reform: Findings from a three-year study of restructuring schools.* Paper presented at the annual meeting of the American Educational Research Association, Montreal.

Little, J. W., & Dorph, R. (1998). *Lessons about comprehensive school reform: California's School Restructuring Demonstration Program*. Berkeley: Graduate School of Education, University of California, Berkeley.

Louis, K. S., & Kruse, S. D. (1995). *Professionalism and community: Perspectives on reforming urban schools*. Thousand Oaks, CA: Corwin Press.

Maslach, C., & Leiter, M. (1999). Teacher burnout: A research agenda. In R. Vandenberghe & M. Huberman (Eds.), *Understanding and preventing teacher burnout* (295–303). Cambridge: Cambridge University Press.

McLaughlin, M. W., & Marsh, D. D. (1979). Staff development and school change. In A. Lieberman & L. Miller (Eds.), *Staff development: New demands, new realities, new perspectives*. New York: Teachers College Press.

McLaughlin, M. W., & Talbert, J. E. (in press). *High school teaching in context*. Chicago: University of Chicago Press.

Muncey, D. E., & McQuillan, P. J. (1996). *Reform and resistance in schools and classrooms: An ethnographic view of the Coalition of Essential Schools*. New Haven: Yale University Press.

Newmann, F. M., & Associates (1996). *Authentic achievement: Restructuring schools for intellectual quality*. San Francisco: Jossey Bass.

Popkewitz, T. S. (1991). *A political sociology of educational reform: Power/knowledge in teaching, teacher education, and research*. New York: Teacher College Press.

Putnam, R. T., & Borko, H. (2000). What do new views of knowledge and thinking have to say about research on teacher learning? *Educational Researcher, 29*(1), 4–15.

Richardson, V., & Placier, P. (in press). Teacher change. In V. Richardson (Ed.), *Handbook of research on teaching* (4th ed.) Washington, DC: American Educational Research Association.

Schlechty, P. C., & Whitford, B. L. (1983). The functions of staff development. In G. Griffin (Ed.), *Staff development, 82nd yearbook of the National Society for the Study of Education* (pp. 62–91). Chicago: University of Chicago Press.

Stein, M. K., Silver, E. A., & Smith, M. S. (1998). Mathematics reform and teacher development: A community of practice perspective. In J. Greeno & S. Goldman (Eds.), *Thinking practices*. Hillsdale, NJ: Lawrence Erlbaum Associates.

Talbert, J. (1995). Boundaries of teachers' professional communities in U.S. high schools: Power and precariousness of the subject department. In L. S. Siskin & J. W. Little (Eds.), *The subjects in question: Departmental organization and the high school* (pp. 68–94). New York: Teachers College Press.

Vandenberghe, R., & Huberman, M. (Eds.). (1999). *Understanding and preventing teacher burnout*. Cambridge: Cambridge University Press.

Wilson, S. M., & Berne, J. (1999). Teacher learning and the acquisition of professional knowledge: An examination of research on contemporary professional development. *Review of Research in Education, 24*, 173–209.

CHAPTER 4

Beyond Certainty: Taking an Inquiry Stance on Practice

MARILYN COCHRAN-SMITH
SUSAN L. LYTLE

Over the last several decades, what some people refer to as a "new image" of teacher learning, a "new model" of teacher education, and even a "new paradigm" of professional development has emerged (Cochran-Smith & Lytle, 1999a; Darling-Hammond, 1994; Grimmett & Neufeld, 1994; Hawley & Valli, 1999; Lieberman & Miller, 1991; Little, 1993; McLaughlin, 1993; Stein, Smith, & Silver, 1999). For prospective teachers, teacher learning is no longer seen as a one-time process of "teacher training" wherein undergraduates are equipped with methods in the subject areas and sent out to "practice" teaching. Similarly, for experienced teachers, teacher learning is no longer seen as a process of periodic "staff development" wherein experienced teachers are congregated to receive the latest information about the most effective teaching processes and techniques. New images of professional development are informed by research about how teachers think about their work (Clark & Peterson, 1986), and emphasis has shifted from what teachers do to what they know, what their sources of knowledge are, and how those sources influence their work in classrooms (Barnes, 1989).

The general orientation of the new approach to professional development is more constructivist than transmission-oriented—the recognition that both prospective and experienced teachers (like all learners) bring prior knowledge and experience to all new learning situations, which are social and specific. In addition, it is now generally understood that teacher learning takes place over time rather than in isolated moments in time, and that active learning requires opportunities to link previous knowledge with new understandings. It has been widely acknowledged that professional development needs to be linked to educational reform (Loucks-Horsley, 1998) and needs to focus on "culture-building," not skills training (Lieberman & Miller, 1994). It is also generally agreed that professional development that is linked to student learning and curricular reform must be deeply embedded in the daily life of schools (Darling-Hammond, 1998; Elmore & Burney, 1997) and must feature opportunities for teachers to inquire systematically about how teaching practice constructs rich learning opportunities for some students (Ball & Cohen, 1999; Little, 1993) but may limit access and learning opportunities for others (Cochran-Smith & Lytle, 1993).

Very broadly speaking, this new vision of professional development is shared by many of those responsible for designing, implementing, and researching programs, projects, and other initiatives that are intended to promote teacher learning. Some even suggest that there is a new consensus about what it takes for effective professional development (e.g., Hawley & Valli, 1999). We would like to argue, however, that "the new professional development" is much less monolithic and consensual than is now being proposed. In fact, just beneath the surface, new visions of professional development look very different from one another, depending upon underlying assumptions and goals, including underlying images of knowledge, practice, and teacher learning. In this chapter we briefly describe three contrasting sets of assumptions that animate some of the most prominent and visible initiatives for professional development. We suggest that one of these is most in keeping with a democratic agenda. Along these lines, we propose that a legitimate and essential purpose of professional development is the development of an inquiry stance on teaching that is critical and transformative, a stance linked not only to high standards for the learning of all students but also to social change and social justice and to the individual and collective professional growth of teachers.

CONTRASTING CONCEPTIONS OF PROFESSIONAL DEVELOPMENT

We have argued in detail elsewhere (Cochran-Smith & Lytle, 1999a) that although the surface contours of the new professional development are similar, there are at least three significantly different conceptions of teacher learning that drive many of the most prominent and widespread initiatives intended to promote teacher learning and professional development. These three derive from differing ideas about knowledge and professional practice and how these are related to one another in teachers' work. Although competing in fundamental ways, these three conceptions coexist in the world of educational policy, research, and practice and are invoked by differently positioned people in order to explain and justify quite different ideas and approaches to improving teaching and learning. Although they are considerably different, however, the lines between the three are not perfectly drawn, and the language that emanates from them to describe various policy initiatives for teacher learning is not mutually exclusive.

This is the case in part because there are no particular methods of teacher education and no particular organizational arrangements for improving teachers' practices or altering curriculum that follow directly or necessarily from any of these three conceptions of teacher learning. Rather, professional development initiatives are driven primarily by interpretations and ideas—even if these are unexamined and tacit— and not simply by methods and practices. For example, some of the most widespread methods of preservice teacher education—mentoring, reflection, and teacher research/action research—carry multiple meanings and are connected to agendas that are quite different from one another. By the same token, some of the most prominent strategies for promoting professional development—inquiry groups, school-wide projects, coaching, and collaborations with universities—are constructed quite differently and serve very different purposes.

We have made distinctions among three prominent approaches to professional development by unpacking their differing images. The first approach is what we refer to as "knowledge-*for*-practice." Here it is assumed that university-based researchers generate what is commonly referred to as formal knowledge and theory (including codifications of the so-called wisdom of practice) *for* teachers to use in order to improve practice. The second approach to professional development is what we think of as "knowledge-*in*-practice." From this perspective, some of the most essential knowledge for teaching is what many people call practical knowledge, or what very competent teachers know as it is embedded in practice and in teachers' reflections on practice. Here it is assumed that teachers learn when they have opportunities to probe the knowledge embedded *in* the work of expert teachers and/or to deepen their own knowledge and expertise as makers of wise judgments and designers of rich learning interactions in the classroom.

In this brief chapter, we want to look more closely at the third approach, which we refer to as "knowledge-*of*-practice, and particularly at the concept of "inquiry as stance."[1] This concept is based on a three-year study of the relationships among inquiry, knowledge, and professional practice in urban inquiry communities and on our experiences as university-based teachers and researchers working with student teachers and experienced teachers over the last 20 years. We suggest that "inquiry as stance" permits closer understanding of knowledge–practice relationships as well as how inquiry produces knowledge, how inquiry relates to practice, and what teachers learn from inquiry within communities. We believe that this construct may also offer promising directions for thinking about the purposes of professional development, and may point to some of the most interesting but difficult questions related to teacher learning as we enter the 21st century.

The assumptions underlying professional development understood as knowledge-*of*-practice are different from those implicit in knowledge-*for*-practice and knowledge-*in*-practice. Unlike the first two, this third understanding of the relationship of knowledge and practice in professional development cannot be understood in terms of a universe of knowledge that divides formal knowledge, on the one hand, from practical knowledge, on the other. Rather, it is assumed that the knowledge teachers need to teach well is generated when teachers treat their own classrooms and schools as sites for intentional investigation at the same time that they treat the knowledge and theory produced by others as generative material for interrogation and interpretation. In this sense, teachers learn when they generate local knowledge *of* practice by working within the contexts of inquiry communities to theorize and construct their work and to connect it to larger social, cultural, and political issues.

When professional development is defined as teachers working together to construct knowledge-*of*-practice, both knowledge generation and knowledge use are regarded as inherently problematic. That is, basic questions about knowledge and teaching—what it means to generate knowledge, who generates it, what counts as knowledge and to whom, and how knowledge is used and evaluated in particular contexts—are always open to question. From this perspective, knowledge-making is understood as a pedagogic act—constructed in the context of use, intimately connected to the knower, and although relevant to immediate situations, also inevitably a process of theorizing. From this perspective, knowledge is not bound by the instrumental imperative that it be used or applied to an immediate situation, but rather that it may also shape the conceptual and interpretive frameworks teachers develop to make judgments, theorize practice, and connect their efforts to larger intellectual, social, and political issues as well as to the work of other teachers, researchers, and communities. The basis of this knowledge–practice conception is that teachers across the professional life span play a central and critical role in generating knowledge of practice by making their classrooms and schools sites for inquiry, connecting their work in schools to larger issues, and taking a critical perspective on the theory and research of others. Teacher networks, inquiry communities, and other school-based collectives in which teachers and others conjoin their efforts to construct knowledge are the major contexts for professional development in this conception.

The idea behind knowledge-*of*-practice is *not* that practitioners' research provides all the knowledge necessary to improve practice, or that the knowledge generated by university-based researchers is of no use to teachers. Nor are we suggesting that, using roughly the same strategies as university-based researchers, school-based teacher researchers add to the knowledge base a new body of generalizations based on their perspectives inside schools and classrooms. In other words, our assumption is not that expert teachers and others who are studying them (collaboratively or otherwise) generate a new or supplementary kind of formal knowledge about expert practices in teaching. Rather, implicit in the idea of knowledge-of-practice is the assumption that through inquiry, teachers across the professional life span—from very new to very experienced—make problematic their own knowledge and practice as well as the knowledge and practice of others and thus stand in a different relationship to knowledge.

INQUIRY AS STANCE

In the remainder of this chapter, we explore what it means to think of the purpose of professional development as the development of an inquiry stance on teaching that is critical and transformative and to contrast this conception with others. In everyday language, "stance" is used to describe body postures, particularly with regard to the position of the feet, as in sports or dance, and also to describe political positions, particularly their consistency (or the lack thereof) over time. In the discourse of qualitative research, "stance" is used to make visible and problematic the various perspectives through which researchers frame their questions, observations, and interpretations of data. In our work, we offer the term *inquiry as stance* to describe the positions teachers and others who work together in inquiry communities take toward knowledge, its relationships to practice, and the purposes of school-ing. We use the metaphor of stance to suggest both orientational and positional ideas, to carry allusions to the physical placing of the body as well as to intellectual activities and perspectives over time. In this sense, the metaphor is intended to capture the ways we stand, the ways we see, and the lenses we see through as educators. Teaching is a com-plex activity that occurs within webs of social, historical, cultural, and political significance. Across the life span, an inquiry stance provides a kind of grounding within the changing cultures of school reform and competing political agendas.

Inquiry as stance is distinct from the more common notion of inquiry (or action research or teacher research) as a time-bounded project within a teacher education program, or one of a number of "proven-effective" strategies for staff development. Taking an inquiry stance means teachers and student teachers working within commu-nities to generate local knowledge, envision and theorize their prac-tice, and interpret and interrogate the theory and research of others. Fundamental to this notion is the idea that the work of inquiry com-munities is both social and political—that is, it involves making prob-lematic the current arrangements of schooling; the ways knowledge is constructed, evaluated, and used; and teachers' individual and collec-tive roles in bringing about change. To use inquiry as stance as a con-struct for understanding professional development, we believe that we need a more nuanced conception of knowledge than that allowed by the traditional formal knowledge–practical knowledge distinction; a more complex conception of practice than that suggested in the aphorism that practice is practical; a richer conception of learning across the profes-sional life span than that implied by concepts of expertise that differen-tiate expert teachers from novices; and a politically informed concep-tion of the cultures of communities as connected to larger educational purposes and contexts. In the remainder of this chapter, we outline the dimensions of the construct of inquiry as stance, and point to some of the significant issues that are raised when we regard the purpose of pro-fessional development as developing such a stance.

BEYOND THE FORMAL KNOWLEDGE–PRACTICAL KNOWLEDGE DISTINCTION: GENERATING LOCAL KNOWLEDGE-OF-PRACTICE

Some approaches to professional development emphasize formal knowledge (of subject matter, learning theory, and so on) as a basis for improving practice, while others focus on the importance of teachers' practical knowledge (decision making, dealing with practical dilemmas, and so on). Although, as we mentioned above, these views are strikingly different in some ways, both derive from the assumption that the knowledge needed to teach well fits into a universe of knowledge types that subdivides into the categories of formal knowledge and practical knowledge, a distinction that is often made in discussions about what teachers need to know and be able to do (Fenstermacher, 1994; Richardson, 1994).

The formal knowledge versus practical knowledge distinction is a dualism that has been part of epistemological discussions for years. However, in many instances, even when scholars have claimed to accept the possibility of "new epistemologies" (e.g., Fenstermacher, 1994; Huberman, 1996), they have continued to impose on these new conceptions the distinctions and conventions of the old, as we have argued in more detail elsewhere (Cochran-Smith & Lytle, 1998). What is happening in critiques of this kind, as Smith (1997) has astutely pointed out, is what has often happened when new voices and modes of discourse push their way into existing conversations about ways of knowing: Those located squarely inside the dominant epistemological and methodological paradigms use established terms, conventions, standards, and definitions to evaluate, and essentially dismiss, alternative ones.

It is possible and indeed quite useful to talk about knowledge of teaching in ways that break with the traditional formal knowledge–practical knowledge distinction. In fact, we have found that teachers' work in inquiry communities generates knowledge of teaching that may be thought of as both *local* and *public* (Cochran-Smith & Lytle, 1998; Lytle & Cochran-Smith, 1992). Our local–public conception does not posit two kinds of knowledge analogous in any way to the distinction made between practical and formal knowledge. Rather, borrowing from Geertz (1983), we use the term *local knowledge* to signal both a way of knowing about teaching and what teachers and communities come to know when they build knowledge collaboratively. In his volume of essays on interpretive anthropology, Geertz talks about the difficulties involved in representing emic or insider knowledge and meaning perspectives. He suggests that ultimately anthropologists cannot really represent local knowledge, or what native inhabitants see, but only what they see through, that is, their interpretive perspectives on their own experiences.

Representing teachers' local knowledge is similarly complicated. Using the phrase *local knowledge*, however, foregrounds the processes (not the products) of knowledge construction as they are expressed and integrated with daily life in schools and classrooms, and emphasizes the link of knower to that which is known and the context in which it is known. In this sense, constructing local knowledge is understood to be a process of building, interrogating, elaborating, and critiquing conceptual frameworks that link action and problem-posing to the immediate context as well as to larger social, cultural, and political issues. Implicit in this process is a set of questions that functions as lenses for seeing and making sense of practice, broadly construed: Who am I as a teacher? What am I assuming about this child, this group, this community? What sense are my students making of what's going on in the classroom? How do the frameworks and research of others inform my own understandings? What are the underlying assumptions of these materials, texts, tests, curriculum frameworks, and school reporting documents? What am I trying to make happen here, and why? How do my efforts as an individual teacher connect to the efforts of the community and to larger agendas for school and social change? When inquiry communities attempt to present and represent local knowledge of practice, their efforts invoke complex and provocative questions of ethics, access, and research methods that merit careful attention.

BEYOND THE EXPERT–NOVICE DISTINCTION: INQUIRY COMMUNITIES ACROSS THE LIFE SPAN

The knowledge-*for*-practice and the knowledge-*in*-practice approaches to professional development pivot on the notion of expertise in teaching and its role in the improvement of practice. This notion reflects a methodological approach that is prominent in cognitive psychology and often used to study differences between expert and novice performances in a variety of areas. From the perspective of knowledge-*for*-practice, the expert teacher is one who knows the knowledge of the formal knowledge base generated or codified by university-based researchers. Here, the expert teacher is expected to constantly update her knowledge of the knowledge base and adeptly follow the demonstrations and models of others. From the perspective of knowledge-*in*-practice, on the other hand, the expert teacher is defined as one who is able to articulate and make explicit the knowledge implicit in wise action and also to articulate this knowledge for novices or less accomplished teachers. Novice teachers, on the other hand, are expected to learn practices by imitating the strategies of their more competent colleagues. In each case, professional development is seen as a process of moving away from the status of novice to that of an expert.

Implicit in the construct of inquiry as stance is a richer conception of teacher learning across the professional life span than that implied by the expert/novice distinction. Learning from teaching through inquiry assumes that beginning and experienced teachers need to engage in similar intellectual work. Working together in communities, both new and more experienced teachers pose problems, identify discrepancies between theories and practices, challenge common routines, draw on the work of others for generative frameworks, and attempt to make visible much of that which is taken for granted about teaching and learning. From an inquiry stance, teachers search for significant questions as much as they engage in problem solving. They count on other teachers for alternative viewpoints on their work. In a very real sense, the usual connotation of "expertise" is inconsistent with an image of teacher as lifelong learner and inquirer. Expertise implies certainty and state-of-the-art practice. Lifelong learning, on the other hand, implies tentativeness, and practice that is sensitive to particular and local histories, cultures, and communities. The expert–novice distinction serves to maintain the individual in-the-head model of professional development that highlights individual differences among teachers. An across-the-life span perspective on professional development makes salient the role of communities and their intellectual projects over time.

When teachers work in inquiry communities, they enter with others into "a common search" for meaning in their work lives (Westerhoff, 1987). When groups of teachers come together as researchers, they need sufficient chunks of time in which to work and sufficient longevity as a group over time. When the pace of a community's work is unhurried and members of the group make a commitment to work through complicated issues over time, then ideas have a chance to incubate and develop, trust builds in the group, and participants feel comfortable raising sensitive and risky self-revelation. Over time, communities that support inquiry develop their own histories and in a certain sense their own culture—a common discourse, shared experiences that function as touchstones, and a set of procedures that provide structure and form for continued experience.

In communities where inquiry is a stance, not a project or strategy, groups of teachers and student teachers engage in joint construction of knowledge through conversation and other forms of collaborative analysis and interpretation. Through talk and writing, they make their tacit knowledge more visible, call into question assumptions about common practices, and generate data that make possible the consideration of alternatives. Part of the culture of inquiry communities is that rich descriptive talk and writing help make visible and accessible the day-to-day events, norms, and practices of teaching and learning and the ways different teachers, students, administrators, and families understand them. In this way, participants conjointly uncover relationships between concrete cases and more general issues and constructs.

From an inquiry stance, teacher leadership and group membership look very different from how they might look when teachers are "trained" in workshops or staff development projects. Taking an inquiry stance on leadership means that teachers challenge the purposes and underlying assumptions of educational change efforts rather than simply helping to specify or carry out the most effective methods for predetermined ends. When inquiry is a stance on teaching, learning, and schooling, there is an activist aspect to teacher leadership. From this perspective, inquiry communities exist to make consequential changes in the lives of teachers and, just as importantly, in the lives of students and in the social and intellectual climate of schools and schooling.

BEYOND THE IDEA THAT PRACTICE IS PRACTICAL: CRITICAL FRAMEWORKS FOR CHANGE

In teaching, the term *practice* has typically been used to refer to doing, acting, carrying out, and/or performing the work of the profession. Often this term is juxtaposed with the terms *theory* and *research* to suggest both relationships and disconnections—as in the common phrases *putting theory into practice* and *translating research for practice*, and in the complaints that something is *too theoretical, not practical enough*, or, quite to the contrary, *only practical* and even *anti-intellectual*. These phrases seem to equate practice with that which is practical (Britzman, 1991) or useful, immediate, functional, and concerned with the everyday. From the perspective of inquiry as stance, however, neither the activity of teaching nor inquiry about teaching are captured by the notion that practice is practical. Rather, teaching and thus professional development are centrally about forming and re-forming frameworks for understanding practice: how students and their teachers construct the curriculum, co-mingling their experiences, their cultural and linguistic resources, and their interpretive frameworks; how teachers' actions are infused with complex and multilayered understandings of learners, culture, class, gender, literacies, social issues, institutions, histories, communities, materials, texts, and curricula; and how teachers work together to develop and alter their questions and interpretive frameworks, informed not only by thoughtful consideration of the immediate situation and the particular students they teach and have taught, but also by the multiple contexts within which they work.

Our concept of inquiry as stance is intended to capture the nature and extent to which those who teach and learn from teaching by engaging in inquiry interpret and theorize what they are doing. More generative than regarding practice as primarily practical is the idea of "teaching as praxis," which emphasizes that teaching involves a dialectical relationship between critical theorizing and action (Britzman, 1991; Freire, 1970). The key idea here is that teachers theorize all the time, negotiating between their classrooms and school life as they struggle to make their daily work connect to larger movements for equity and social change.

When inquiry is a stance on teaching, it is assumed that professional development is inextricably linked to larger questions about the consequences and ends of professional development: What are or should be the purposes of professional development? Who makes decisions about these purposes and consequences? In what ways do particular initiatives for professional development challenge and/or sustain the status quo? What are the consequences of teachers' learning for students' learning? What part does professional development play in school reform? How is professional development connected to larger social, political, and intellectual movements? The most significant questions about the purposes and consequences of professional development are connected to teacher agency and ownership.

When wholesale participation in specific professional development programs is mandated at the school or school system level, or when it is scripted in certain ways, it becomes a substitute for grassroots change efforts. When teachers work from an inquiry stance, they sometimes begin to challenge and then alter or dismantle fundamental practices such as tracking, teacher assignment, promotion and retention policies, testing and assessment, textbook selection, school–community–family relationships, administrator roles, personnel decisions, and school safety, not to mention to raising questions about what counts as teaching and learning in classrooms. Sometimes teachers begin to reinvent their own job descriptions. They critique and seek to alter cultures of collegiality; ways that school or program structures promote or undermine collaboration; ratios of teacher autonomy to teacher responsibility; norms of teacher evaluation; relationships among student teachers, teachers, and their university colleagues; and the ways power is exercised in teacher-to-teacher, mentor-to-teacher, and school–university partnerships.

There are starkly different kinds of professional development initiatives that feature what is referred to as inquiry—some that are readily integrated into the existing social and institutional arrangements of schools and school systems, and others that are not. From the perspective of inquiry as stance, professional development is associated more with uncertainty than certainty, more with posing problems and dilemmas than with solving them, and more with the recognition that inquiry both stems from and generates questions. In many situations, "questioning" and "challenging the system" are rather difficult to explain as the consequences of inquiry-based professional development, and yet these may be precisely the kind of consequences that lead to more democratic schooling and to the formation of a more just society.

It is our hope that the concept of inquiry as stance and our critique and comparison with other conceptions of professional development will help to support a different kind of discourse about what it means when variously positioned reformers and policymakers advocate that teachers today need to know more and need to be engaged in the "new" professional development. As we hope we have made clear, there are contrasting interpretations of what the new professional development means. The idea of inquiry as stance is intended to argue that professional development for the next century should be understood not primarily as personal and professional accomplishment, but as a lifelong stance and a long-term collective project with a democratic agenda.

NOTES

Acknowledgment. Preparation of this chapter was supported in part by a major grant from the Spencer Foundation to Marilyn Cochran-Smith and Susan L. Lytle for "Teacher Inquiry and the Epistemology of Teaching."
    1. We have been developing the language and concept of *inquiry as stance* over a period of years, based on the dialectic of our work with teachers and student teachers in urban inquiry communities. See Cochran-Smith and Lytle, 1999a, 1999b, as well as two publications in preparation (Cochran-Smith & Lytle, forthcoming; Lytle & Cochran-Smith, forthcoming).

REFERENCES

Ball, D., & Cohen, D. (1999). Developing practice, developing practitioners: Toward a practice-based theory of professional education. In G. Sykes &

L. Darling-Hammond (Eds.), *Teaching as the learning profession: Handbook of policy and practice* (pp. 3–32). San Francisco: Jossey-Bass.

Barnes, H. (1989). Structuring knowledge for beginning teaching. In M. Reynolds (Ed.), *Knowledge base for the beginning teacher* (pp. 13–22). New York: Pergamon Press.

Britzman, D. P. (1991). *Practice makes practice: A critical study of learning to teach.* New York: State University of New York Press.

Clark, C., & Peterson, P. (1986). Teachers' thought processes. In M. Wittrock (Ed.), *Handbook of research on teaching* (pp. 255–296). New York: Macmillan.

Cochran-Smith, M., & Lytle, S. (1993). *Inside/outside: Teacher research and knowledge.* New York: Teachers College Press.

Cochran-Smith, M., & Lytle, S. (1998). Teacher research: The question that persists. *International Journal of Leadership in Education, 1*(1), 19–36.

Cochran-Smith, M., & Lytle, S. (1999a). Relationships of knowledge and practice: Teacher learning in communities. In A. Iran-Nejad & C. D. Pearson (Eds.), *Review of research in education* (Vol. 24; pp. 251–307). Washington, DC: American Educational Research Association.

Cochran-Smith, M., & Lytle, S. (1999b). The teacher research movement: A decade later. *Educational Researcher 28*(7), 15–25.

Cochran-Smith, M., & Lytle, S. (forthcoming). *Inquiry as stance.* New York: Teachers College Press.

Darling-Hammond, L. (1994). *Professional development schools: Schools for developing a profession.* New York: Teachers College Press.

Darling-Hammond, L. (1998). Teacher learning that supports student learning. *Educational Leadership, 55*(5), 6 11.

Elmore, R., & Burney, B. (1997, August). *Investing in teacher learning: Staff development and instructional improvement in Community School District #2, New York City.* New York: National Commission on Teaching and America's Future.

Fenstermacher, G. (1994). The knower and the known: The nature of knowledge in research on teaching. In L. Darling-Hammond (Ed.), *Review of research in education* (Vol. 20; pp. 3–56). Washington, DC: American Educational Research Association.

Freire, P. (1970). *Pedagogy of the oppressed* (M. B. Ramos, Trans.). New York: Seabury Press.

Geertz, C. (1983). *Local knowledge: Further essays in interpretive anthropology.* New York: Basic Books.

Grimmett, P. P., & Neufeld, J. (1994). *Teacher development and the struggle for authenticity: Professional growth and restructuring in the context of change.* New York: Teachers College Press.

Hawley, W. D., & Valli, L. (1999). The essentials of effective professional development: A new consensus. In L. Darling-Hammond & G. Sykes (Eds.), *Teaching as the learning profession* (pp. 127–150). San Francisco: Jossey-Bass.

Huberman, M. (1996). Focus on research moving mainstream: Taking a closer look at teacher research. *Language Arts, 73*(2), 124–140.

Lieberman, A., & Miller, L. (1991). Revisiting the social realities of teaching. In A. Lieberman & L. Miller (Eds.), *Staff development for education in the nineties: New demands, new realities, new perspectives* (pp. 92–109). New York: Teachers College Press.

Lieberman, A., & Miller, L. (1994). Problems and possibilities of institutionalizing teacher research. In S. Hollingsworth & H. Socket (Eds.), *Teacher research and educational reform* (pp. 204–220). Chicago: University of Chicago Press.

Little, J. W. (1993). Teachers' professional development in a climate of educational reform. *Educational Evaluation and Policy Analysis, 15*(2), 129–151.

Loucks-Horsley, S. (1988). Effective professional development for teachers of mathematics. In Eisenhower National Clearinghouse (Ed.), *Ideas that work: Mathematics professional development* (pp. 2–9). Columbus, OH: Eisenhower National Clearinghouse for Mathematics and Science Education.

Lytle, S., & Cochran-Smith, M. (1992). Teacher research as a way of knowing. *Harvard Educational Review, 62*(4) 447–474.

Lytle, S., & Cochran-Smith, M. (forthcoming). *Rethinking teacher learning: Inquiry as stance.*

McLaughlin, M. (1993). What matters most in teachers' workplace context? In J. W. Little & M. McLaughlin (Eds.), *Teachers' work* (pp. 79–103). New York: Teachers College Press.

Richardson, V. (1994). Teacher inquiry as professional staff development. In S. Hollingsworth & H. Sockett (Eds.), *Teacher research and educational reform* (pp. 186–203). Chicago: University of Chicago Press.

Smith, J. (1997). The stories educational researchers tell about themselves. *Educational Researcher, 26*(5), 4–11.

Stein, M., Smith, M., & Silver, E. (1999, Fall). The development of professional developers: Learning to assist teachers in new settings in new ways. *Harvard Educational Review, 69*(3), 237–269.

Westerhoff, J. H. (1987). The teachers as pilgrim. In F. S. Bolin & J. M. Falk (Eds.), *Teacher renewal* (pp. 190–201). New York: Teachers College Press.

PART II

Contexts, Strategies, and Structures for Professional Development

CHAPTER 5

Teacher Learning at the Intersection of School Learning and Student Outcomes

JACQUELINE ANCESS

This chapter presents a model and perspective of teacher learning and its connection to school learning and student outcomes. Based on an analysis of three cases of high-performing high schools, the chapter demonstrates that teacher learning does not occur in a vacuum; rather, it is inextricably connected to school culture, instructional mission, and organization, as well as teachers' knowledge and the learning and achievement of students.

INTERNATIONAL HIGH SCHOOL

International High School, located in New York City, serves 450 9th through 12th grade new-English-language-learner immigrant students who have been identified as being at-risk. The school's mission is to foster social responsibility, intellectual development, and the "linguistic, cognitive, and cultural skills necessary for [students'] success in high school, college, and beyond" (International High School at LaGuardia Community College, 1985).

In order to achieve this mission, teachers developed a pedagogy that included a trimester organization, 70-minute periods, team teaching, heterogeneous grouping, an ESL approach to English language learning, an interdisciplinary approach to curriculum, a career educa-

---

This chapter derives from *The Reciprocal Influence of Teacher Learning, Teaching Practice, School Restructuring, and Student Learning Outcomes.* (June 2000). *Teachers College Record, 102* (3), 590–613.

tion program that features three semesters of internships in the community, activity-based instruction, and collaborative learning that brings together in small groups students who speak different languages, giving them a reason to have to help, teach, and learn from one another and to speak English, which is the language of public discourse.

With the encouragement of his principal, David Hirschy, a veteran high school physics teacher who previously had taught in traditional settings, convinced three colleagues and the school's assistant principal to join him in the creation of an innovation called the Motion Program five years after the school began in 1995. As described in an earlier study (Ancess & Darling-Hammond, 1994a), the Motion Program teachers developed a self-contained, interdisciplinary theme-based cluster—a sort of temporary mini-school—with a group of students who met all day every day for the duration of a single trimester. During the course of the program, the five-member teaching team took responsibility for the students' total education. The Motion faculty had the autonomy and authority to make decisions about scheduling, students' assignment to classes, curriculum, instructional strategies, assessment, discipline, and the social needs of students. Their meetings to assume these responsibilities occurred during the weekly 90-minute block already in place for the school's regular faculty meetings.

Motion teachers designed three courses that constituted the curriculum for the program: literature, integrated math/physics, and Project Adventure, an indoor ropes course modeled on Outward Bound. Motion curriculum emphasized the development of students' critical and creative capacities, peer collaboration, and cross-disciplinary activities on the theme of motion.

The Motion faculty developed a "fail-one-fail-all" grading policy in which students received a single letter grade that combined all three courses in the cluster. The policy required students to pass all the Motion courses, and teachers to come to consensus on students' grades. Because the policy discouraged students from making private bargains with themselves to do less, marginal, or failing work in courses in which they were struggling, teachers discovered that it produced higher course pass rates in difficult subject matter than any of them had individually experienced when teaching solo. Despite students' resistance to the policy, no students failed the Motion cluster. In instances where students could have opted for a failing grade, they chose instead an incomplete and elected to take the cluster of courses again. The Motion faculty developed an assessment system to closely monitor students' progress through group exhibitions; individual student portfolios; self, peer, and teacher written evaluations; and individual evaluation conferences with a committee of teachers and peers.

Several factors led Hirschy to initiate this innovation. He had long been eager to increase articulation between math and science, believing that many students avoided physics because they were intimidated by the mathematical background they thought the course required. If the mathematics students needed for success in physics could be integrated into the course, perhaps they would find physics more accessible. After several years at International, Hirschy concluded that the traditional lockstep approach required for the New York State Regents physics course was ineffective with his diverse, new-English-language-learner students. In International's heterogeneously grouped classes, where students possessed various levels of skill, content knowledge, and experience with science instruction, Hirschy had to construct at least three different levels of lessons and assessments. But even Hirschy's multiple preparations left him frustrated with what he felt were unacceptable student success rates. Nor were students achieving the Regents physics course goal of learning the same content at the same rate.

After attending a summer institute to learn cooperative learning models, which were especially successful with minority students, Hirschy was eager to apply the model at International. Simultaneously, he wanted his students to experience the excitement, joy, and inquisitiveness he had observed in his wife's kindergarten students. The Motion Program, explained Hirschy, seemed to be a strategy that would enable him to consolidate these multiple goals. It could enable him, along with his colleagues, "to create a total educational experience [that would] broaden the context for students' learning and deal with the whole person," Hirschy said. It was Hirschy's hope that the cluster would become a vital learning community.

Seventy-five students enrolled in this trimester-long program, spending all of their time each day with the five-member Motion team. After a second trimester of the program, data revealed that student attendance exceeded the average for the school, and that all of the 150 students enrolled had passed the Motion course. Hirschy and the math instructor observed that students worked on projects for as long as 2 ½ hours without a break. The extended responsibility for students and the opportunity for teachers individually and collectively to know students well enabled the staff to apply more appropriate and intensive interventions in a more timely fashion to students who needed them. Students did not fall through the cracks. These results were constant over the next three years.

Motion's first-year results stimulated a desire in International's principal, Eric Nadelstern, to restructure the school into self-contained clusters modeled on the program. He arranged for Hirschy and his colleagues to present their results to the IHS faculty and proposed restructuring International as a set of clusters prototyped on Motion. Despite Hirschy's status as Teachers Union representative and the credibility of the Motion team, the faculty rebuffed the principal's proposal. Nonetheless, two other IHS teachers adapted the Motion model to form an interdisciplinary course on another theme.

Hirschy and his colleagues, who supported the principal's hopes to restructure the school into self-contained, interdisciplinary thematic clusters, continued to present Motion's results to the faculty, adding presentations by students and then distributing samples of student work, which the faculty examined. The quality of the students' work, along with their presentations on their Motion experiences, their preference for the close family atmosphere the cluster structure provided, and their belief in its capacity to generate better-quality performance, impressed the staff. Other faculty were especially impressed by the authenticity of students' responses to questions they asked. When Nadelstern broached the topic of restructuring at the end of the second year of Motion, the majority of faculty members, by now persuaded of Motion's benefit to students, no longer objected to the idea of restructuring, but admonished him to slow his pace. Nadelstern backed off.

Then, in 1993, eight years after the creation of IHS, a majority of the faculty voted to restructure the school into six self-contained, autonomous, interdisciplinary teaching teams and adopt the fail-one-fail-all grading policy. A handful of teachers who had voted against the change had the option to transfer from the school, but chose to remain. After faculty self-selected their cluster teammates, all those who opposed the reform found themselves unchosen. Nadelstern clustered them together as a team so that he could support their development and so that their opposition would not burden other teachers. The new structure aimed to make International more intimate and to increase students' achievement.

After the first year of restructuring, the course pass rate for the entire school was up 5%. The school restructuring generated faculty learning that resulted in changes in administrative roles, teacher accountability, student assessments, and standards for student performance. Nadelstern explained how the cluster structure made him and his assistant principal more accessible to support teachers' professional development and their efforts to promote students' intellectual growth. Because they now dealt, said Nadelstern, "with six teams rather than fifty individual teachers," they assessed the work of teams and the capacity of their interdependency to produce effective classroom instruction. With their supervisory responsibilities streamlined, they joined teams as teachers in order to model effective pedagogy for teams with less experienced teachers, to contribute their knowledge and skills in team conversations, and to provide encouragement and instructional support to the cluster of teachers who had opposed the new organization. Such interventions provided students with access to effective teaching and teachers with access to professional development designed to improve the delivery of services they were providing to their students.

Teachers interviewed asserted that the cluster structure provided them with more opportunities to assess the degree of students' intellectual engagement and affiliation. They also asserted that the self-contained student grouping and the lower faculty–student ratio of the clusters increased the time and opportunities for access between faculty and students. And they further asserted that the increase of faculty interaction within the cluster, coupled with a high degree of autonomy and control over their working conditions, increased their opportunities to find diverse ways to take individual and collective responsibility for the progress and achievement of all students in the cluster.

Evidence of increased teacher accountability affecting student learning opportunities emerged at the close of the first year of restructuring. When one team was disturbed by the rate of course incompletes, which was higher than for other clusters, they assigned themselves as mentors to each student who had an incomplete, even though none of the students was any longer in their cluster. In effect, they committed themselves to working on their own time with former students in order to help them complete the work so that they could pass the cluster.

As the faculty began to examine student achievement more closely, their interest in exploring the idea of a coherent school-wide assessment system began to develop. Over the next three years the individual clusters developed multiple forms of authentic assessments, and a faculty committee worked on developing school-wide coherence.

Hirschy asserted that the restructuring helped teachers support higher standards. As students completed activities in the Motion curriculum, teachers sought feedback on the supports needed for high-level performance. Through interactions with students, the Motion teachers realized that many did not have any images of what constituted excellent work. As a result, the team developed a collection of student work that served as diverse and concrete benchmarks of excellence. Motion students were able to sift through a file of former students' work to see what excellence looked like. Other clusters added courses, such as reading, that students needed in order to perform at higher levels.

The curricular and structural autonomy of the new organization also contributed to increased levels of intellectual challenge to students. As students raised questions in the content areas, teachers encouraged their investigation. Student investigations led teachers to suggest that the students develop activities that could teach their peers the lessons they had learned. Some of this peer-produced curriculum was regularly incorporated into the program.

Faculty learned individually and collectively that increased control over the conditions of their teaching and student learning could increase their control over the quality of student performance. More teachers learned from their own and their colleagues' practice how to increase the intellectual challenge for students; they expanded their repertoire of social and academic intervention skills; and they learned how to design curriculum that sustained high levels of student engagement. They learned that their analysis of the alignment of curriculum, instruction, assessment, and student performance could not only impact student achievement, but could also improve their capacity for effective practice. They learned to look to their own practice as a powerful source of learning.

THE URBAN ACADEMY

The Urban Academy (UA) is a 15-year-old New York City "second chance high school," which many of its 100 students redefine as their "last-chance school." UA has been described by its deputy superintendent as "a school where bad kids go and become good. And if they go back to their former schools, they become bad again." Ninety percent of UA students have had at least one unsuccessful experience in one or more of 35 other high schools. Sixty percent of the students transfer in from comprehensive neighborhood high schools notorious for their violence and high failure and low graduation rates; 20% come from vocational or high-performing academic public high schools such as Bronx Science; and 20% are from private and parochial schools. Ten percent enroll directly from junior high school. Of the high school transfers, 20% come to UA after a superintendent's suspension for violence or weapons possession, and 25% have been "asked to leave" their former schools for reasons of poor attendance or academic failure.

The UA faculty report that students' prior school history includes one or a combination of these attributes: chronic cutting, dropping out, suspension because of violence against another student or a teacher, failing grades, patterns of not completing assignments, and depression. All UA teachers confirmed that upon entry, students lack perseverance, time management skills, and the habits of work necessary for school success. They have poor academic skills, and 10% have never read a book to completion.

Despite the academic and social history of their students, the UA faculty have ambitious goals for them. They aim to collaboratively "build the students' facility to: explore ideas, conduct research, evaluate information, discuss ideas respectfully, develop new sources of fact and opinion, and present and defend their findings" (Urban Academy, 1991, unpaginated). UA's priority is to prepare students for success in college and responsible participation in society.

In order to prepare students for success in college, UA collaborates with local colleges so that UA students can enroll in their courses alongside the colleges' own students. At the inception of the college initiative, UA history teacher Avram Barlowe was assigned the role of UA liaison to the local Borough of Manhattan Community College (BMCC) in order to support eight students in their first college course and for UA faculty to learn about students' responses to the experience. Barlowe's teaching schedule was adjusted so that he could oversee the students enrolled in the course. Early on, he learned that the students needed support to manage their college assignments. He began attending the college course along with the students and met regularly with the instructor to explain students' learning and behavior needs, analyze the students' responses, discuss what the instructor wanted them to do, and suggest ways of structuring assignments. Back at the Urban Academy, Barlowe transformed what was scheduled as an advisory class composed of college-attending UA students into the BMCC Homework Lab, where he helped the students analyze and complete the BMCC assignments.

Barlowe's restructured schedule enabled him to learn firsthand what students needed for success in a college experience and to immediately apply those learnings to his teaching practice in order to influence students' possibilities for achievement. The flexibility and authority Barlowe had enabled him to invent the BMCC Homework Lab and teach students the skills they needed to succeed—the skills necessary for doing college assignments. These included outlining, drafting papers, revision, time management, and perseverance. Barlowe christened the BMCC Homework Lab a "supply side course [because] it teaches students how to do the assignments for another teacher." Barlowe supplied the students with the kinds of interventions, skills, supports, and monitoring that middle-class parents routinely provide for their children and that give them access to institutions of higher learning. Barlowe contends that the lab helped a higher percentage of students meet deadlines and achieve significantly higher grades. All of the students passed the BMCC college course. The course also enabled UA to expand the college opportunity to more students. Seven years later, UA collaborates with four local colleges, which enroll nearly three times the number in the first UA group to take the college course. Now, each year, 20% of UA's population is enrolled in college courses that include history, writing, literature, science, math, and world languages.

The BMCC lab class had a broad impact on the organization of instruction and on curriculum offerings at UA. At weekly staff meetings, Barlowe discussed the students' responses to their college courses and the issues that emerged in the BMCC lab course. When his UA colleagues realized that the labs were enabling students to perform to higher standards, they were eager to attach lab courses to demanding courses they were teaching. They recognized the lab as an intervention that could enhance both their teaching and students' learning opportunities. The UA schedule was restructured in order to attach labs to courses that required students to read extensively and write analytic papers. In 1994, five UA courses had labs attached to them: *Civil Rights: History of the Movement, American History, The Economics of Money, Misfits in Literature, Children's Books: Are They for Children?,* and *Issues,* a course in which students analyze and debate current events. Additionally, a weekly Homework Lab was scheduled for after school so that students could get help with homework assignments.

English and math teachers designed a second variation on the lab course: a content skills lab that expanded students' learning opportunities. In Reading Lab, students were supported to develop a "reading habit," which the UA faculty believes is necessary for college success. Students also sharpen their literary analysis skills. In Math Lab, students can master basics such as fractions, decimals, percents, and proportions at the same time they are taking another, higher-level mathematics course. As a result of this change, more students have access to high-stakes mathematics curriculum. Course-taking and passing rates over the duration of the study bear this out: 72% of UA students took courses in trigonometry, advanced algebra, and pre-calculus, and 90% of these students passed at least one class.

Faculty members interviewed explained that labs increase students' access to courses with complex content by teaching them the demands of rigorous coursework while simultaneously providing them with the habits necessary to meet rigorous demands. Students interviewed confirmed that assertion. One young man, who had been expelled from his former school for throwing a chair at a teacher, said:

> I didn't think I'd ever have confidence in writing papers. But now, like I'm slowly gaining confidence in writing because these teachers will sit down and help me. They will tell me what's bad and what's good.

Another student, who had dropped out of her zoned high school prior to enrolling at UA, commented:

> I picked up a lot of good habits. My work habits are improving and I'm slowly edging my way towards that big research paper. I'm kinda scared sometimes, but I think I've improved my chances. I feel more confident about applying to colleges that I wanna go to now, that I wouldn't last year or the year before that.

The success of the lab courses led to further restructuring as UA abandoned their advisories for organizational tutorials for all students. Organizational Tutorial provides those organizational supports students need to successfully complete the assignments in their classes, such as the conventions of writing (e.g., proper use of quotations), the organization skills for constructing a coherent paper, perseverance for revision, research writing skills, and the struggle for finding their voice—figuring out what they want to say and crafting ways in which to say it.

The evolution of the advisory into the Organizational Tutorial reflects the staff's matured capacity to efficiently consolidate into one mechanism those supports necessary for student achievement: social, emotional, and academic support. Students' needs for close, enduring relationships with caring and supportive adults who know them well is met implicitly in the context of the Organizational Tutorial, the ostensible purpose of which is the improvement of student performance.

HODGSON VOCATIONAL TECHNICAL HIGH SCHOOL

Paul M. Hodgson Vocational Technical High School is one of three 9th through 12th grade vocational high schools in Delaware's New Castle County Vocational School District. Hodgson's restructuring has occurred over a number of years on several fronts, including organizational; instructional, curricular, and assessment; teacher roles; organization of students and student support services; and decision-making processes. As described in an earlier study (Ancess & Darling-Hammond, 1994a), Hodgson, prior to restructuring, had a nine-period day and students were streamed into five tracks, from advanced placement to special education. Hodgson aimed to fulfill the stereotypical expectations of vocational schools: employment preparation for students who were thought to "lack the capacity" for college. Although special education students were fully mainstreamed in career programs, they remained in self-contained classes for academics. The faculty was organized hierarchically, with authority descending from principal to assistant principals, to departmental chairs, to discipline deans, to teachers. Restructuring changes included

1. The establishment of a steering committee of teachers and administrators to oversee school governance
2. The decision to become a Delaware Re:Learning school and to join the Coalition of Essential Schools (CES)
3. The development of specialized committees to oversee diverse school initiatives such as the integration of academic and vocational curriculum and learning and student assessment
4. The formation of interdisciplinary teams for each grade
5. The introduction of activity-based learning initiatives in the academic program
6. The development of performance assessments in the academic program
7. Student advisories
8. A senior project as the first step toward graduation by exhibition.

Restructuring was stimulated by a combination of internal and external factors aimed at rethinking the school goals and practices, focusing more on students' learning needs, and raising academic expectations. Over the period of a year, Hodgson principal Steve Godowsky sponsored morning and afternoon faculty "conversations" on education at the school. These conversations became the forum for educational debate among Hodgson staff and the wellspring for the school's restructuring efforts. They produced a critical core of teachers who became committed to and then led school-wide changes. Among the first outcomes of these conversations was the formation of a faculty committee to explore the possibility of developing a senior project that would integrate learnings from career and academic programs and require students to demonstrate their mastery of these learnings.

A district-wide voluntary desegregation initiative catalyzed school-wide detracking, heterogeneous grouping in academic classes, and special education inclusion in English and American history classes. Hodgson faculty agreed to adopt recommendations of the Southern Regional Education Board (SREB) to set higher academic standards and provide learning opportunities for vocational school students to increase their chances for academic success. These included academic and vocational education integration and advisories that would provide extra attention.

Although the organizational and instructional restructuring at Hodgson departed from the traditions and culture of the school, the curricular and assessment reforms were rooted in and built on them. This made for a compatible coupling that used teachers' experience and expertise while simultaneously requiring and generating new professional learning and practice. Beginning with the goal to raise students' academic expectations and performance standards and using the strategies of academic and vocational integration and the CES idea of graduation by exhibition, a committee of Hodgson academic and vocational teachers developed a performance-based Senior Project that required students to synthesize their academic and vocational learnings, skills, and knowledge. The Senior Project requires students to

1. Produce a research paper that expands their knowledge and abilities on a topic that interests them in their shop major
2. Design and construct a product connected to their research
3. Give a half-hour–long public, formal oral presentation before a committee of three teachers in order to demonstrate their knowledge and understanding of the topic, the research, and the product.

The customized organization of the Senior Project required the restructuring of teachers' roles and the development of new teaching practices, including Senior Project student advisor. Advisors met regularly and individually with each of their advisees, supervised their progress, ensured that tasks were completed on time, oversaw revisions of work, rehearsed their oral presentation, coordinated with two other teachers on their advisees' Senior Project committee, mentored them throughout the project's year-long duration, guided their use of the other teachers as resources, encouraged expanded learning experiences such as interviews with out-of-school experts, and provided interventions when necessary. The other teachers on the committee also met individually with the student, read and commented on the several drafts of the research paper, or supported the development of the product. These roles were radically different from what isolated, stand-up, direct-instruction academic and vocational teachers were used to.

Teachers learned these new roles through experience. For example, advisors learned to provide a structure for students to work independently. They developed mechanisms such as a time line of tasks to prevent students from work pileups. They learned to demand higher levels of self-challenge from students by negotiating with them to develop more complex Senior Project topics and by helping them to revise their work. Several teachers brought these experiences to the Senior Project Evaluation Committee, which, in response, created mechanisms such as a standardized timeline and a task check-off form to refine the project's functioning. Additionally, because teachers shared their experiences mentoring students and learned what to expect and demand from students and how to effectively respond to their anxieties and needs, each year students' topics grew in sophistication and their work improved in quality.

The role requirements for teachers also blurred content-area boundaries, particularly for vocational teachers who were uncomfortable expanding their educational reach into the foreign territory of academics. Although the shop teachers were comfortable assessing the Senior Project products and guiding revisions, they were not comfortable assessing drafts of the research paper, even though they were required to review only the shop content. English teachers assessed the drafts for proper conventions and mechanics, but lacked the expertise to evaluate the content.

In contrast, the curriculum and exhibition components of the Senior Project drew from successful Hodgson practices and traditions. The career/shop-based research paper was adapted by the English department from the traditional literature-based research paper that students had been expected to write in senior English. Although the paper's content was a shop topic, students were nonetheless held to a rigorous standard of a thorough research process. The Senior Project research paper required students to learn and demonstrate appropriate understanding of research conventions such as the proper format for their citations and bibliography. It required them to use multiple sources of data and to represent their findings in multiple formats, including prose, charts, tables, and photographs. Finally, the paper had to be typed. The English Chair explained that the connection between the paper and the product was natural because students were curious about the real-life application of their research.

The paper's success with the full range of Hodgson students, including mainstreamed special education students, made it popular with both English and vocational teachers, with the result that there was strong school- and district-level support for making it a component of the Senior Project and creating a one-semester technical writing course to allow English teachers to teach students how to write the Senior Project paper while they were engaged in the Senior Project. The content of the Technical Writing course drew on teachers' learning of what research and writing skills students needed in order to successfully execute the Senior Project paper. Because what students were learning had immediate, authentic, and personal application, students' motivation to learn these research and writing skills was heightened. Eventually, teachers compiled a bank of Senior Project papers that became exemplars of what was expected of students and what their peers had produced.

As teachers observed and evaluated students' performance of Senior Project tasks, they increasingly learned what students needed to know and be able to do to perform well. This knowledge enabled teachers to adapt their curriculum and expand students' learning opportunities, particularly in writing, in the earlier grades. Academic and vocational courses in grades 9 through 11 added research components and project-based curricular units. In order to help students develop oral presentation skills, teachers of an 11th grade course called *American Experience* required students to produce a videotaped oral biography. Ninth grade interdisciplinary teams introduced both research papers and oral presentations in shop and English classes. Two years after what teachers described as an intensive emphasis on writing beginning in the 9th grade, Hodgson ranked first in the state on the Delaware high school writing assessment.

The exhibition component of the Senior Project drew on the vocational education tradition of performance-based evaluation and applied it to academic learning. In their shop classes, students were used to being evaluated on their production of real products, and teachers were familiar with performance assessment instruments. Drawing on a voc-ed rubric used for competitions, Hodgson teachers developed a rubric for the Senior Project that guided their evaluation of the oral presentations. The application of exhibitions to the Senior Project confirmed the belief of many teachers that performance assessments could more accurately demonstrate their students' academic knowledge and skills than the more conventional short-answer, multiple-choice, norm-referenced tests used to measure students' learning.

As academic teachers saw the quality of the Senior Project exhibitions, some began to incorporate more projects and activities into their curriculum. In social studies/English classes some teachers provided opportunities for mock trials, simulations, and role-playing of important historical events and persons. These performances also became assessments of students' learning.

Teacher learning about student learning became a lever for pedagogical reform. In a math integration initiative stimulated by district funding to improve students' mathematics performance, teachers learned how to create access to normally intimidating content by operationalizing their belief that vocational education could provide a context for improving learning in math. Math teachers visited shop classrooms and while there, they taught math that corresponded to shop units so that students learned math when they needed to know it for their shop projects. In this fashion, students approached roofing as angle and measurement problems, flower arranging as geometry, and photo enlargement as problems in proportion. In their own classrooms, math teachers began to use shop references to teach math—when teaching the slope of a line in algebra, they could refer to the pitch of a roof—increasing students' access to mathematics.

The math integration project was facilitated by changes in the school organizational structure that made professional collaboration possible between shop and math teachers, who got to know one another and learned about student learning and their colleagues' work through classroom visits, joint conversations, and curriculum development. After the initiation of the math integration reform, the math scores on the Delaware math assessment increased 13% over the previous year (New Castle County Vocational Techical School District, 1994, p. 2).

Hodgson's reformed governance structure, in which teachers sat on curriculum committees that developed instructional policy, meant that teachers applying pedagogical reforms in their classrooms could be and indeed were in a position to decide the instructional policies they would apply. The new organizational structure enabled them to use their observations and understandings about students' responses to the reforms to refine them and to shape policy school-wide. Teacher policymaking resulted in the school's adoption and the district's approval of the Technical Writing course and the Senior Project as a graduation requirement.

Teachers and the school learned what organizational structures, what student and teacher learning opportunities, and what curriculum and teaching strategies could produce higher levels of academic achievement for students. They validated and learned how to implement a predominant pedagogical belief that their students need to learn academics and can develop intellectually through a concrete approach to content that is more often restricted to vocational education. The organizational restructuring enabled the faculty to apply their knowledge of how students learn to their practice. And they began to shape pedagogical policy from the lessons of their practice.

Almost immediately, student outcomes began to change. In addition to Hodgson's top ranking on the Delaware writing assessment, the college admission rate for Hodgson students increased within a two-year period from 25% to 44%, which is 12.5% higher than the national average for vocational high school students *planning* to attend college (National Center for Education Statistics, 1995, p. 40).

CONCLUSION

This study finds that there is a reciprocal influence among teacher learning, school or organizational learning, and student outcomes. Specifically, organizational learning at the study schools meant a continuous cycle of broad-based faculty understanding of their own and their colleagues' learnings, their application of the lessons learned to their own practice, and the adaptation of the school's organizational and pedagogical structures so that they support the changes demanded by the new knowledge.

Teacher learning can be characterized as problem solving or inquiry that starts with teachers' particular goals for their students; theories about their particular students as learners, especially as relates to the particular goals; and theories about what conditions are necessary for the students to achieve the particular goals. Hirschy theorized that many students were intimidated by physics because they were intimidated by mathematics. He also theorized that the teaching practices and curriculum he had used in the past were inappropriate for many of his current students and for the class's heterogeneous organization of students. Keeping the students and their configuration constant, he had a vision of the organizational conditions for learning and the outcomes he aspired to: a cluster organization that increased teacher autonomy and responsibility for students' total education and joyful student engagement, and a physics course integrating mathematics in a supportive context that would make physics more accessible.

Barlowe theorized that his students lacked the study and organization skills and a support structure necessary for college success. He theorized that interventions redressing these deficits would increase students' chances for college success. The enactment of the lab course, his intervention, led to his theory of "supply side teaching." His goal was to produce students who could be successful in college.

Hodgson faculty theorized that their students had not performed at high levels academically because they had not been taught in the way that they learn. They theorized that adapting successful vocational practices—which they also theorized would capture the way the students learn—to the academic sphere would improve academic performance. They saw their students expanding beyond the boundaries of conventional vocational education and stereotyped identities and entering the academic and intellectual domains.

Implicit in each goal and theory were the identification of a problem or set of problems to be solved and the solution that teachers chose. These were applied in the pursuit of the goal. The teachers developed and implemented new knowledge and practice that drew on their school's culture and their knowledge of their students, successful practice, and their content area. Because teachers had the opportunity to create new knowledge and to apply it to their school's daily life, they had the opportunity to create and recreate their school culture and community each day, helping it to achieve a closer correspondence to its values and vision and increasing their investment in it.

In each case teachers made changes in their teaching practice and school and curricular organization. Except in Barlowe's case, the teachers' initial solutions extended beyond a single classroom and changes in teaching practice. The initial solutions of Hirschy and Hodgson were simultaneously organizational, curricular, and instructional. The changes in organization and structure presented new, often unanticipated and unintended pedagogical challenges, which then catalyzed new teacher learning and pedagogical changes. There emerged a reciprocal relationship between individual teacher learning and change and organizational learning and change. As Lieberman pointed out in an informal conversation, this is learning by changing. It is important to note that in all three cases, teachers had the authority and autonomy to pursue the pedagogical and organizational changes, and the support of their principals and a critical core of peers to implement them.

In this study, student outcomes, the quality of student performance, influenced organizational and individual teacher learning and teaching practice in powerful ways. Student performance mapped against their teachers' goals for them was the most powerful catalyst for teacher learning. It defined the content and determined the direction of teacher learning. Barlowe, Hirschy, and the Hodgson faculty who were dissatisfied with the performance of their students brought their knowledge of their students to the problem of improving student performance and acquired new knowledge and developed strategies to apply it to their situation. As the teachers involved in the innovations implemented them and reflected on their impact on student learning and achievement, they learned more about what pedagogical and organizational structures worked to improve student performance.

Teachers' learning about student learning and achievement led to further pedagogical and organizational changes. In each case the teachers shared student outcomes and their practice with other faculty in school wide forums designed for public sharing. Over a period of several years, evidence of improved student outcomes and opportunities for teachers to examine students' work and performance were the most powerful catalysts and incentives for the entire faculty at each school to adopt these organizational and pedagogical changes on a school-wide basis and to counteract faculty resistance to structural and pedagogical change. In each school a constellation of nine conditions made these changes possible:

1. Incentives for teacher inquiry
2. Opportunity for teacher inquiry
3. Teacher capacity for leadership in innovation and inquiry
4. Respect for teacher authority
5. Flexible school structure
6. Responsive and supportive administration
7. Time
8. Resources
9. Regulatory flexibility

In this study, teachers engaged in a process of inquiry for which there was no road map other than their intuitive knowledge base, their practitioner experience base, their pedagogical content knowledge, their knowledge of their students and content area, and their clear understanding of the student learning outcomes they were seeking, all of which provided significant signposts but no well-standardized path on how to get where they wanted to go. This was well-informed, highly organized discovery learning in the service of problem solving to achieve particular student learning goals, but discovery learning nonetheless, and risky because the trial and error of discovery learning gives no guarantee of what results will occur from this labor-intensive, time-consuming journey. In an era of narrowly defined, standardized-test–driven accountability, such risks can be dangerous to a teacher's career and to a school's existence, but as shown here, they can also break open a future for children.

REFERENCES

Ancess, J., & Darling-Hammond, L. (1994a). *Teaching, learning, and assessment for new English learners at International High School.* New York: NCREST, Teachers College, Columbia University.

Ancess, J., & Darling-Hammond, L. (1994b). *The senior project: Authentic assessment at Hodgson Vocational-Technical High School.* New York: NCREST, Teachers College, Columbia University.

International High School at LaGuardia Community College. (1985). *The International High School mission statement.* Long Island City, N.Y.: Author.

National Center for Education Statistics. (1995). *Trends among high school seniors, 1972–1992.* Washington, DC: U.S. Department of Education.

New Castle County Vocational Technical School District. (1994). *New Castle County Vocational Technical School District performance report.* Wilmington, DE: Author.

Urban Academy. (1991). *Why? The Urban Academy brochure.* New York: Arthor.

CHAPTER 6

Teachers Engaged in Evidence-Based Reform: Trajectories of Teachers' Inquiry, Analysis, and Action

MILBREY W. MCLAUGHLIN
with JOEL ZARROW

This chapter draws on one initiative's experience with evidence-based reform to describe a trajectory of teachers' engagement and comfort with inquiry and how evolving patterns of inquiry are associated with different questions, different forms of evidence, and capacity for change at both school and classroom levels. This descriptive analysis highlights ways in which policy can affect teachers' inquiry skills and taste for evidence and considers the forms of knowledge they find useful as they seek to make change at their school and in their classrooms.

The Bay Area School Reform Collaborative (BASRC), a 5-year reform effort involving schools throughout the 118-district Bay Area region supported by the Hewlett-Annenberg Challenge, seeks to "reculture" schools in ways that support whole-school change.[1] BASRC aims to change the way schools do business. Merrill Vargo, BASRC's executive director, likes to ask people to complete the sentence: "The problem with schools today is . . ." BASRC's design for reform finishes the sentence with "their culture" and posits a missing element in schools' cultures as evidence-based decision making centered on a focused reform effort. BASRC's overall strategy uses a school-based cycle of inquiry to inform school reform efforts, and marshals diverse forms of knowledge to support teachers' learning and change.

The cycle of inquiry required of BASRC schools is intended to help schools pose, investigate, and respond to questions about policies and practices and has six steps (See Figure 6.1). The first two steps have to do with selecting and narrowing a question for investigation. The next step is to identify measurable goals. This step recognizes that setting specified targets as a measure for success is critical in determining the success or failure of an action. The fourth and fifth steps include creating and implementing a particular action—connecting knowing and doing. The sixth step is to collect and analyze results from data generated by the action taken. Finally, the cycle connects back to the first step as the problem statement is refined in light of new evidence. Simply put, BASRC's cycle-of-inquiry aims to inform schools about what they are accomplishing in terms of their focused reform effort and consequences for students.

The initiative also attends to the learning skills teachers will need in order to carry out a cycle of inquiry. In an effort to foster teachers' capacity and comfort in generating knowledge of practice, teachers

Figure 6.1. The Cycle of Inquiry

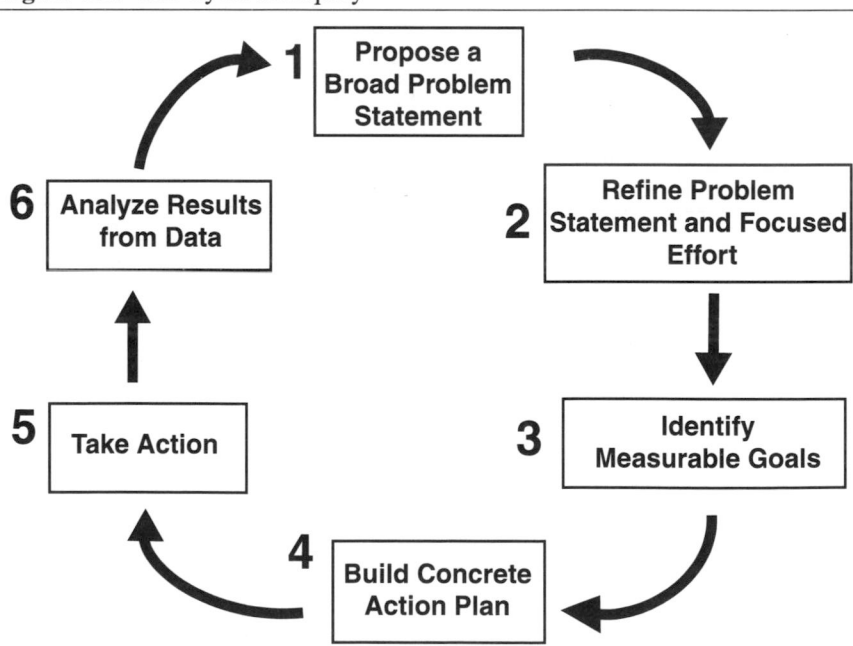

receive training in asking probing questions, developing an account-ability framework to guide their school's cycle of inquiry, and construct-ing standards against which to measure their school's progress in their focused reform effort. They practice these skills in many BASRC events. For example, regional meetings of hundreds of Bay Area teachers, ad-ministrators, parents, support providers, and funders were convened to score schools' portfolio applications for BASRC Leadership School status. Subsequently, regional preparation and reviews of Leadership Schools' Reports of Progress immersed teachers in use of rubrics to evaluate process on five dimensions of whole-school change.

A number of teachers told us that evaluating the portfolios with teachers from around the Bay Area "was the best professional develop-ment I have ever had." One said, for instance, "Just reading about other schools and using that rubric forced us to use it well. It taught me about standards and accountability, skills I could take back to my school." Through summer institutes for faculty teams from Leadership Schools, BASRC gave teachers tools in other areas important to their success in carrying out a cycle of inquiry—how to run a meeting, how to facili-tate a discussion, and how to deal with the "politics of data."

PATTERNS AND PROCESSES OF INQUIRY

Looking at activities and consequences associated with the cycle of inquiry, we see different patterns and processes within BASRC Lead-ership Schools. When the initiative began in 1996, only a few teachers or schools were relatively sophisticated in their thinking about inquiry-based reforms; many teachers wondered out loud, "What's data?" Few schools had experience with the school-based cycle of inquiry and accountability of the sort or in the spirit BASRC required—they were experienced in accounting for compliance's sake, but not for inform-ing their own community of practice. Points along an "inquiry trajec-tory" emerge as teachers and their school community wrestle with how to do a cycle of inquiry and what use they can make of the evidence it generates.

Taking First Steps: What's Data?

For some Leadership Schools, BASRC involvement comprised the faculty's first efforts to think about whole-school change—either in substantive or strategic terms—or to consider systemic inquiry as some-thing within teachers' purview. First steps were apparent, especially in secondary schools, where faculty rarely thought in whole-school terms, but rather in terms of departments, student academic placements, or grade levels. The evidence and inquiry BASRC requires of its Leadership Schools was both foreign and threatening to many teachers. "Why are we doing this data collection stuff?" one teacher asked as she began her involvement with BASRC and was introduced to expectations for assessment and analysis. "We're not methodologists," said another. This teacher, like many if not most of her colleagues, knew nothing about how to develop standards for assessment, how to go about systematic inquiry into the consequences of practice, or even how to construct the indicators that would be most meaningful to practice and action. For many if not most of the BASRC Leadership Schools, their BASRC involvement was their first venture into looking at evidence about their school-level practice. These schools struggled with questions about appropriate indicators for their focused effort, sources of data, and strategies for data collection.

In schools building the capacity to implement a cycle of inquiry, teachers expressed concern about the robustness of their findings. As one teacher explained, a lack of inquiry skills hampered their efforts to uncover findings that they would feel comfortable using to guide future actions. "I'm a teacher, not a researcher," he said. "The farthest I got was taking a methodology class in sociology umpteen-zillion years ago." A high school teacher commented, "I'd be blown out of the water if we were to get anything that's close enough to reliable data that would lead anybody else in this school to want to change their practice." The confidence threshold to make changes to practice based on findings from the cycle of inquiry was high in Leadership Schools, especially where faculty were inexperienced as data collectors or analysts. Teachers wanted to feel more comfortable using a cycle of inquiry before trusting the data.

In schools taking their first steps in a cycle of inquiry, teachers made tentative, usually difficult and painful efforts to think about what evidence and inquiry at the school level would mean or require. Teachers at this point on an inquiry trajectory attended BASRC workshops on accountability and standards, but often found them inadequate in the light of their inexperience and anxiety about what they would do concerning inquiry at the school level.

A major element frustrating the inquiry process in "first-step" schools, in addition to skills and experience with data, was the normative climate typical of American schools, one that makes teachers' work and student outcomes largely a private matter, and casts demands for evidence as something done *to*, not *for*, the school. A related factor was the perception that responsibilities for inquiry were just an add-on to their already hectic workday. Facing a host of other demands, teachers expressed a reluctance to spend time on reflection. As one teacher put it, "I feel like saying, 'Leave me alone. I don't want to deal with the reflection. I have work to do.'"

Getting Comfortable with Inquiry

We see norms about evidence and uses of data changing from the culture of privativism observed as teachers and schools began an inquiry trajectory, to openness on faculty's part to consider new ways of looking at their practice at the school level. Teachers in schools beginning to engage inquiry in substantive ways remark on what they have learned about the power of data to illuminate their own practice and student accomplishments school-wide.

> We are starting to ask what are our data and inquiry strategies really telling us about our children? What do we want to know about our children? We have finally been able to ask ourselves: What do we really want them to know about and be able to do when they go out the door at the end of the year?

Teachers in schools at this point on the trajectory were having some of their first conversations about data, using new language, and working to generate evidence of practice as a faculty. In many of these Leadership Schools, teachers tell us that this was the first time that "every single teacher" had some form of assessment data for his or her class, and that for the first time, baseline data were collected across the school. Teachers also point to the changed lens they have now: "I never could see what a good school this is because I was so into my own classroom. I never had the broad picture. And until I saw that, when I could really sit down and see the whole school, that's when the light went on."

This year, BASRC emphasized the importance of identifying the achievement gap between white students and students of color. Analysis of a representative sample of 40 1999 Reviews of Progress [ROPs] prepared by BASRC Leadership Schools indicated that approximately 77% of schools reported disaggregating student achievement data to uncover racial/ethnic disparities in student achievement. Of those schools not doing so, the majority were serving primarily low-income students of color, where making such a distinction was less useful. While the differences in achievement among racial/ethnic subgroups is not news to people working in schools, the focus on data has made this stark reality more explicit and difficult to ignore. A high school principal commented about the ability of data to make the staff at his school confront this critical issue:

> There are people even on our campus that will not accept that [the gap in achievement] without seeing the data. That's why the data are really powerful, because it doesn't allow you to say, 'Nah, no. . . .' There's no escaping and looking for arguments for not accepting the accountability. That's the power of the data. It's like this little quote, "In God we trust. Everyone else, bring the data."

In line with BASRC's two questions for a cycle of inquiry—evidence of student progress toward grade-level achievement and evidence that practices are closing the achievement gap among students—Leadership Schools report more attention to specifying concrete benchmarks for student achievement. Forty-eight percent of sampled Leadership Schools' 1999 Reviews of Progress, for example, identified explicit targets for increasing student achievement scores, especially for students of color. For example, a case-study elementary school noticed that students of color were disproportionately failing to reach the district's reading comprehension benchmark. They targeted an 8.5% improvement in reading comprehension for that year, and by 2002, they want 90% of all students reading at or above grade level. By making improvement goals explicit, the school will be able to better assess if it is on the right path. Those schools that did not establish a specific target for improvement tended to set more general goals of improving the academic performance of a particular subgroup of students. At a staff retreat kicking off the beginning of the year, a high school principal explained to the staff the difference between the approach for the upcoming year compared to the prior year: "We haven't always described what we want to do in terms of measurable goals. We've had mission statements that have said what we are aiming at, but now, I think, what we are directed to do is say what the results are actually going to be." The more focused attention on performance benchmarks provided schools with a more explicit indicator of progress.

BASRC assisted schools in moving to this point in an inquiry trajectory in two important ways. One was political; we saw how BASRC affiliation helped faculty deal with the politics of data.

> The data part of this has been hard for our school . . . a real challenge . . . we have some teachers who will pass any child who breathes. We have to be very creative in how we look at

data ... BASRC is a real help [as a shield]. BASRC says "data, data, data."

BASRC's requirements about evidence and accountability allowed teachers to make objective fact of problems or issues that before had been seen as personal and subjective evaluation, when they were seen at all—most especially problematic evidence about particular classrooms or student groups. Teachers commented on how BASRC's status as "outsider" and BASRC requirements for Leadership Schools enabled their schools to wade into the difficult waters of equity, outcomes, and ties to practice.

BASRC also provided important technical help to schools uncertain about what to do and confused about such issues as adequate benchmarks of progress. A reform coordinator at an elementary school points to the comments BASRC personnel gave the school after reading last year's Review of Progress:[2] "They told us that we needed to identify which students, by specific subgroups, that were not meeting standards, why they were not— the specific obstacles—and then what support teachers needed to remove those obstacles." In addition, she reported that the school needed to become clearer on what measures they would need to use to know if their new strategies worked. Schools using the assessments for the second year were able to track marginal change from year to year; schools in their first year were able to generate baseline indicators of student achievement from which to measure future progress.

Where schools began to see the value in site-level data, most remarkable to us was the shift in teachers' discourse. The language of inquiry and data thread through faculty conversations. Teachers use evidence-based standards comfortably, and we hear new standards brought to evaluation and planning sessions. For example, this snippet of conversation among members of the leadership team at a BASRC school reflects a serious effort to take a hard look at data and learn from it:

Do all students meet or exceed the standards? What plan should we make to figure out who isn't or is and why? We need to understand how to say a particular student meets or does not meet the standard. We should be able to explain why one child got a particular stamp on their head and another did not. If standards aren't understood by teachers, then it's a problem for our school.

We would not have heard this conversation among this faculty the year before, when they were grappling with how to address new expectations for accountability and decision making associated with their Leadership School status. We hear this discourse as evidence of the emergence of a "community of explanation," where teachers share language and understandings about the meanings of evidence and social facts (see Freeman, 1999).

In some "beginning inquiry" schools, these conversations have started to make their way into changes in practice at school or classroom levels. However these schools were the exception. The problem most pressing in terms of knowledge generation and use in beginning inquiry schools is the character of the community of practice in the school. Many reform-minded faculties in these schools wrestled with rifts in their community; not all teachers bought into the "whole-school" character of the reform. Moreover, in some schools—most especially high schools—reform leaders acknowledge that not all of their colleagues really believed that "all students could perform at challenging standards," a central tenet of BASRC's whole-school reform vision. These faculty debated in fundamental terms the significance of data showing achievement gaps among their students.

In these schools, the community of explanation is only emergent, since teachers viewed the same disappointing data about student performance in different ways—some see it as a warrant to reexamine practice, and others view it as evidence about students' abilities and motivation. Yet in schools such as these, the sites and sources of teachers' knowledge and learning are moving, if only in tentative ways, inside the school. Outside knowledge resources remain important to teachers' thoughts about how to change, but energy in these communities focused more at this stage on establishing priorities for data collection and reform.

Moving to a Culture of Inquiry

A third pattern of relations among knowledge, learning, and change could be called "moving to a culture of inquiry." Some Leadership Schools entered the initiative already comfortable with inquiry and experienced with school-level reform.[3] But for most of the Leadership Schools where we found faculty comfortable with using evidence from their own inquiry to rethink their practices, we saw significant learning on the part of individual teachers and the faculty as a whole as a result of their BASRC participation. We also found faculty struggling with their inquiry processes, but around different issues than were schools less experienced with inquiry. In some of these schools, the most important learning was about inquiry itself. For example, at the end of their first cycle of inquiry a high school faculty realized that they had chosen the wrong measures to assess their focused effort. In their second year, they returned to questions of indicators and evidence, but with concrete experience about internal validity to guide their decisions.

In this and other schools, we saw that the cycle of inquiry often was not as sequential as a "cycle" image might imply. Faculty had to revisit first questions before proceeding to data collection and analysis. Faculty gained confidence and competence as data collectors and analysts. One teacher said, for instance: "It's hard to know what is good evidence. But the more you do it, the more you are able to identify what's good evidence."

An elementary school teacher's remark speaks volumes about the new knowledge and skill teachers have acquired through BASRC, in this instance the reading assessment tool of "running records":

> It will be interesting to compare running records across teachers to see whether the evaluations are reliable—we all need to be speaking the same language and looking at kids' work in the same way . . . next year we want to get people to the table understanding data . . . it will be a "so what" year. We have been working on collecting data to take action.

In many schools, we see that the results of their inquiry process have led to new understanding about practice in their school and classrooms. For example, an elementary school faculty looking at student work samples based on BASRC rubrics saw examples of "high levels" of instruction in some classrooms, but also identified issues of coordination within and across grade levels. Based on this knowledge, the faculty took steps to "evaluate where our kids are and what we are going to do to move them forward." A high-poverty elementary school faculty was surprised to discover unequal patterns of achievement among student groups when they disaggregated their data as BASRC required. The principal told us:

> Since we're disaggregating our data more and more, we have a picture of . . . the characteristics of our kids who aren't doing well . . . one of the reasons it took us a while to look at it [here] is that we're highly diverse and yet we're not. We're diverse because of the kids of color . . . but we're not really diverse in terms of nonpoverty . . . and so we didn't look at it.

Teachers' new knowledge of their practice motivated more inquiry and commitment in some instances. Faculty in a number of Leadership Schools told us that "there is a lot of buy-in [to reform] from doing these assessments." Teachers formerly resistant to collecting baseline data, or to engaging in the assessment effort at all, are energized by seeing growth in their students as well as by identification of concrete problem areas for the school to grapple with. What had been generic problems became more concrete—they took on names and faces. These problems also became more amenable to action as teachers began to agree about the nature of the issues facing the school and a range of possible responses. Teachers in schools comfortable with new learning skills and norms of discourse readily admit that such conversations did not and could not have taken place prior to their involvement with BASRC—nor could have expressions of collective responsibility for all students in the school.

This teacher's comment makes apparent, for instance, how teachers' problem-solving skills developed though the BASRC rubrics can affect faculty discourse and attention:

> We gave a writing sample to all students last fall. All staff learned how to score it. From that experience, all teachers, even art teachers, realized how important writing is. It was interesting to hear history teachers debate with the art teacher about whether [student work] was a 3 or a 4 [on a rubric of 1 to 4, with 4 being high].

An elementary school made substantial progress in their students' achievement once they disaggregated scores by ethnicity and reevaluated the literacy programs they were using. In two years, the school's Limited English Proficient students moved from 44% scoring at grade level on a reading comprehension test to 73% achieving at or above grade level. In this and other Leadership Schools, we find positive signs that changes in practices at school and classroom levels are reflected in student achievement. Compared to other Bay Area and California schools, Leadership Schools showed significantly greater gains in their students' standardized achievement scores (SAT9) from 1998 to 1999. The majority of BASRC Leadership Schools are improving their students' performance on SAT9 relative to their own prior performance: 77% of elementary schools, 64% of middle schools, and 59% of high schools showed gains from 1998 to 1999 (Center for Research on the Context of Teaching, 1998, 1999).

Faculties at this place in an inquiry trajectory have begun to internalize norms of inquiry and habits of evidence. Teachers ask for data to support decisions and inform discussions about practice. By their language and action, faculty in schools described by these relationships between knowledge, learning, and change appear to have become communities of explanation (Freeman, 1999).

Becoming a School-Based "Learning Community"

In a few of the Leadership Schools we see a fourth pattern of relations between knowledge generation, use, and change and position on a trajectory of teachers' inquiry and action. In these schools, the cycle of inquiry has begun to mature into an accepted, iterative process of data collection, analysis, reflection, and change. These schools function as learning communities, and themselves constitute teachers' essential site and source of learning. They appear to be "recultured" in the way BASRC's theory of change envisioned. The whole school is both the site of inquiry and the focus for change; the community of explanation incorporates most of the faculty, not just a smaller group of reformers. Discourse about students' standards-based achievement and expectations about evidence are commonplace rather than exceptional.

Knowledge of "best practice" is both sought and filtered through knowledge of student outcomes and evidence of links to practice. Teachers' new knowledge about how students do across groups and across grades enables them to see ways in which they need to improve, and the kinds of resources they need to begin making those improvements. One teacher commented, for example, that the links between their focused effort on literacy and their students' work have allowed them to "see connections" they had not seen before. Likewise, an elementary school faculty discontinued its use of a popular reading program and moved to a writing-focused literacy effort when they looked at their students' poor performance on writing subtests. Teachers in such schools have become particular and demanding in terms of what their school needs by way of knowledge resources from the outside, and in what form they should be provided. Knowledge of their practice has made them more powerful as consumers.

We observe a number of other things in schools where teachers are comfortable with and have come to rely on inquiry. We see that teachers' generation and use of school-level evidence often comes before systematic production of knowledge about classroom-level outcomes. A hunch based on this observation is that the collective experience of inquiry at the school level may stimulate more inquiry at the classroom level. Teachers' involvement with and acceptance of inquiry at the school level both lends cachet to the norms and mental attitude teachers need to do the work in their own classrooms, and provides the experience, skills, and comfort necessary to ask tough questions of one's own practice—and to share the results.

We also see how school-level inquiry adds meaning to classroom-based inquiry. One Leadership School experienced with action research prior to their involvement with BASRC quickly saw how this classroom-based research needed to be situated in school-level inquiry if it were to add up to coherent knowledge for school decision making. The principal points directly to the strategic relationship between these two forms of evidence:

> Whatever's happening in the classroom that a teacher is doing in terms of action research . . . has to be linked to overall school goals. Because one of the dangers of doing action research is you can have a whole bunch of teachers doing that kind of work and it will look classroom-by-classroom real specific. However, if they don't have any relationship to each other and there's no relationship to overall school goals, the value of it will have very different kinds of results. And also what we find is that for action research you need some people to be involved in some common problem-solving issues [part of the cycle of inquiry]. If there's no one doing something in common, there's nobody to help you debrief and talk deeply about what you might be doing.

In a few Leadership Schools such as the one this principal leads, school-level inquiry is making its way into classroom-based inquiry and change. For example, a high school science teacher who had long assumed that the disappointing achievement of many students in his culturally diverse classes was a consequence of indifference or laziness was provoked by literacy data collected at the school level to take a look at his own class through that lens. What he found forced him to fundamentally reevaluate his practice. He discovered that a significant number of students in his science classes read at a level insufficient to grasp the material. However, teachers' systematic collection and analysis of their classroom data to inform both their practice and school-level decision making is not yet routine in any BASRC Leadership School.

In schools comfortable with inquiry, we also find instances of teachers using inquiry tools to address issues that confront the school. For example, in the face of concern about the relationship between the assessments the state was soon to require and those the school was using to assess their progress, a teacher did research on the overlap, congruence, and conflict between them. She found "potentials for overlap and a different way of looking at this" and so turned a problem into an opportunity for the school to deepen its work. This teacher's response to a challenge signals an inquiry stance new to the school and extraordinary in most communities of practice.

The inquiry and action we see in Leadership Schools comfortable and confident with learning from their own site and practice contrast to the norms of privacy and individualism characteristic of schoolteaching (Lortie, 1975). They mark a changed school culture, and generate a number of questions based in institutional traditions. Why would site-level data about problematic patterns of achievement among students encourage teachers to face up to their own effectiveness and look at the gap in their classrooms between intention and accomplishment? Why would teachers expose their own uneven student results to their colleagues?

COMMUNITIES OF TEACHER LEARNERS

We find some answers to these questions in the character of the school's community of practice and relations among teachers. Teachers' comments and our observations of faculty meetings and planning sessions point to the emergence of a significantly different community of practice in many Leadership Schools. These new communities of practice have formed around the knowledge resources associated with BASRC—new skills and capacities, new knowledge of the school as an educational setting—and the community itself serves as a resource to generate new practices and invent ideas for reform.

These communities of practice have become communities of explanation by virtue of their collective inquiry; they also are learning communities where reflection about current practice and habits of inquiry prompts change at schools and classroom levels. They are communities of teacher learners where learning and change are a social process of active participation in inquiry (Rogoff, 1994; Wenger, 1998).

BASRC Leadership Schools suggest how patterns of knowledge use and learning define and are defined by the culture of the school's community of practice and how BASRC's strategies shaped this culture. We see five interrelated elements of the school's community of practice that influence whether or how teachers participated in and benefited from a cycle of inquiry and signaled teachers' position on a trajectory of evidence-based reform.

Clear and Shared Goals

In schools where we find teachers using data about their students and about the consequences of school-level policies such as course assignment to inform their decisions about directions for their school and external resources that would be most useful, we find that a majority of the faculty have clear and shared goals for their students and their performance as a faculty. We also see clear links to BASRC tools and "curriculum." BASRC-stimulated conversations about priorities for their school's reform effort, insistence on evidence to support their strategy, portfolio application, and design of a cycle of inquiry promoted clarity and buy-in on school goals. These BASRC activities also stimulated active communication within the faculty, across grade levels and departments. Faculty communication continued to address these classroom-specific concerns, of course, but in addition regularly engaged whole-school issues, most especially patterns of student performance and faculty responses to disparities by students' ethnicity. Table 6.1 shows principals' reports of changes in school culture and discourse associated with BASRC involvement. An overwhelming majority of Leadership School principals say that BASRC has stimulated teacher discussion and consensus about teaching and learning.

Table 6.1. Leadership School Principals' Report of Changes Associated with BASRC Involvement ($n = 63$)

	Strongly Disagree				Strongly Agree
High standards for all students	0%	0%	10%	62%	28%
Teachers' consensus on desired student learning outcomes	0%	0%	10%	53%	37%
Teachers' consensus on needed areas for whole-school change	0%	0%	3%	52%	45%
Teacher leadership	0%	0%	10%	47%	44%
Staff discussions of teaching and learning	0%	0%	5%	49%	46%
Working with outside change agents to support reform goals	0%	0%	12%	53%	35%
Use of data as a basis for decision making	0%	0%	8%	50%	42%

Data come from a Winter 1999 survey of all 86 Leadership School principals.

Inquiry Stance

Communities of teacher learners explicitly adopted what Cochran-Smith and Lytle (1999) call an *inquiry stance* toward their own practice as well as toward their broader workplace environment. A number of principals commented on change in this aspect of the school community. One said, for example: "I see my staff asking one another more questions. They check things out from the resource lab. A teacher will walk in to get materials, have a dialogue with the teachers and before you know it, one will be stopping by another's classroom." Similarly, 92% of Leadership School principals report change in the use of data for decision making (see Table 6.1). BASRC Support Providers (organizations of people that provide technical assistance to schools) also see new, stronger communities of practice forming in Leadership Schools. One said, for example:

> What difference do I see in BASRC schools? The main difference I see is that those schools and the district, to a lesser extent, are slowly turning towards gathering and using evidence in a formal accountability system. I think teachers, individuals, have been turning that way. . . . And it's been neat to get a whole school community to pay attention and give [data and consequences] that level of priority.

In school communities adopting an inquiry stance, we found instances where "problems" were transformed from "social facts" to subjects for inquiry and problem solving. This transformation was most apparent in high school faculty, where explanations for poor student performance moved from those based on beliefs about students' attitudes, backgrounds, or capacities to the "fit" between what their students needed to learn and achieve and what was provided them. Faculty wrestling with rethinking student performance in their school find themselves looking at student data in new ways. Said one middle school principal, for example:

> The place we want to be is to have student achievement at such high levels that when you disaggregate our data, you don't see anything significant about [group differences]. And since we're disaggregating our data more and more, we have a clearer picture of the characteristics of our kids who aren't doing well. That's the heart of what equity means for us.

Learning Skills

Communities of teacher learners possessed and used a number of resources. They developed the learning skills necessary to pursue inquiry and analyze evidence; they had a growing body of knowledge about aspects of their practice and continued to add to that understanding. These skills and knowledge were broadly distributed across the faculty community, not merely the assets of an isolated subgroup of teachers.

Communities of teacher learners also had built a store of knowledge about "best practices" and were able to distinguish on technical grounds among alternative practices available to them. They knew not only what kinds of resources best suited their school, they also knew where to build or rebuild their own core technical capacity. This technical knowledge, combined with knowledge of their school site and classrooms, combined to make teachers adept at evaluating the kind and quality of knowledge for practice available to the school, and was central to what Donald Schon called the "reflective transfer" of knowledge from outside the school (Schön, 1983).

Boundary Spanners

Communities of teacher learners were communities open to the environment. In one or another form, they had boundary spanners, individuals active in the context outside the school who brought new ideas as well as challenges into the community. In most of the Leadership Schools, these individuals held the BASRC-funded position of reform coordinator.

Broadened Community Boundaries

Finally, some communities of practice changed their borders to include students and parents in new ways. We see instances where teachers have involved parent groups in discussions of data and their implications, for example. One school held a series of sessions to introduce parents to the inquiry skills they had learned themselves, such as how to understand the results of standardized tests, how to consider disaggregated data, and ways to see links to practice. A few Leadership High Schools have invited student voice into their professional community. In one school, for example, student focus groups tackled questions about their experiences as learners in the school, and factors that supported or frustrated their success. Students carried out a content analysis of the transcripts from these sessions, and then briefed the faculty on them. Faculty plans for revision in course assignment, classroom practice, and community outreach reflect this student input.

These elements of the communities of teacher learners we encountered among BASRC Leadership Schools were mutually reinforcing and deeply interdependent. Technical skills alone did not enable a community of practice to be learners, or teacher learners to make productive change in their practice. Teachers required common values about inquiry, goals for their school, and shared conceptions of "good" work and a "good" colleague.

High levels of social participation are signal to communities of teacher learners in BASRC Leadership Schools (see Rogoff, 1994; Wenger, 1998). We saw how communication and coordination among teachers extended the shared understanding, or community of explanation, that generated both action and inquiry. A number of teachers commented, for example, on how the diverse perspectives within their community enable them to see gaps in understanding that would otherwise be invisible. One said, for example:

> I know that I'm not perfect, but my standards are higher because of my colleagues. Also, I found out that there are many different ways to do something amazingly well . . . [through our teacher community] I found out that a person who writes a whole lot differently from me can be amazingly successful . . . and although I found out that I need to improve a lot I also found a couple of ways that work.

Communities of teacher learners use active participation to forge common ground about the meaning of the evidence they generate, and agreements about a course of action at both individual and organizational levels. Further teachers' quests for shared goals and common perceptions of the facts of the matter involve both individual accommodation and learning. Individual teachers' learning and inquiry stance, in this sense, are part and parcel of their involvement in reflecting on and inquiring into the practices of their school community. A middle school teacher put it this way:

> By sticking together, someone comes up with something and we try it. When you start in this [teaching] business you are isolated and think in the box. [Because of the teacher community in my school,] I have learned to think outside the box. We have hit a lot of curves, but we feel like we are a group that can

work through them. When you talk together it is a powerful problem-solving group. There are things to be gained from this [community of practice] that cannot be gained from working alone.

Many teachers attribute the stronger teacher learning communities at their schools to the tools and processes they learned at BASRC's Summer Institutes, most especially skills in facilitation, reflective dialogue, and conflict resolution—pragmatic skills important both to generating new knowledge and understanding about practice and to making effective use of the knowledge resources available to members of the Bay Area School Reform Collaborative.

LESSONS ABOUT EVIDENCE-BASED REFORMS AND TRAJECTORIES OF INQUIRY

This chapter draws upon our evaluation of BASRC to suggest elements of a descriptive theory of how teachers engage in inquiry and use evidence to consider change at school and classroom levels, and how the trajectory of inquiry is associated with elements of BASRC's vision and strategy.

Patterns of Inquiry and Knowledge Use

Looking atBASRC Leadership Schools, it is evident that inquiry and knowledge use are *path-dependent.* We notice that the knowledge teachers seek to improve their practice builds on what they know and can do. Wesley Cohen and Daniel Levinthal (1990) use the term "absorptive capacity" to signal the critical role prior knowledge plays in an organization's ability to use external knowledge to remain vigorous and stay ahead of the competition. Their conception of how organizations identify and use knowledge corresponds with our observation that what teachers already know mediates between external knowledge and teachers' capacity to use it effectively—or even to recognize relevant external knowledge resources.

This view of knowledge use and the role of situated evidence about student outcomes makes it evident why "solutions" cannot be "imported" into schools or classrooms with any significant effect. Without foundational, situated knowledge of links between practice and outcomes, teachers lack effective hooks to pull new ideas into their workplace. In other words, what teachers know about their own practices, and about their school as an educational environment, shapes fundamentally what and how much they can learn from knowledge for practice.

These diverse but interrelated images of knowledge complicate policy investments in teachers' knowledge, since they implicate both the evidence and knowledge of best practice, and their necessary interrelationship. A successful school reform effort, in this view, would need to enable teacher inquiry in order for teachers to learn what they need to know to initiate, deepen, and sustain change.

Communities of Practice

A description of relations in a community of practice also illuminates age-old problems of knowledge use. Change agents and reformers have long been frustrated that teachers too often make little or only superficial use of the knowledge resources available to them. Knowledge resources evidently are not self-enacting, nor do they necessarily engender learning. And learning does not necessarily lead to productive change in practice. What happens to knowledge brought into or produced by a community of practice depends fundamentally on the character of that community and relations among its members.

BASRC's experience highlights the many ways in which a community of practice is both the site and source of learning, reflection, and new knowledge about practice. It also illustrates the situated character of the community of explanation created at a school. In each of the Leadership Schools where we found a community of teacher learners, we found a community of explanation—we heard language and understandings particular to and shared by that community.

One important implication of the central role we see for communities of practice is their centrality to reformers' visions of how to stimulate and sustain change. Policies need to consider how strategies can provide occasion, tools, and resources for building a community of teacher learners. BASRC's design is remarkable in that it provides teachers with the tools they need in order to learn how to learn, to forge new conversations and accommodation among faculty, and with a "focused effort," the work essential to constructing shared goals and understandings. Few reform policies keep communities of practice in their vision or acknowledge the pivotal role of a community of explanation to knowledge use, learning, and change.

Another important implication of the situated character of these communities is that they cannot simply be regrouped or combined with other communities without attention to the (re)building of shared understanding and language. Policies aiming to bring different communities of explanation together—be they different school communities or more obviously diverse communities such as researchers and practitioners, policymakers and practitioners, or knowledge providers and knowledge users—must attend at the outset to building common understandings. BASRC accomplished some of this in its first years through the Portfolio Review process, where parents, educators, researchers, business people, and others first spent time together calibrating their responses to schools' portfolios and talking about why they saw the same evidence in divergent ways. Only after some level of mutual understanding was achieved did the group move on to their common work. Teachers' assessments of these Portfolio Reviews as "the best professional development I've ever had" lay in the process of participation and joint sense-making it entailed. These evidence-based strategies for developing shared understandings and standards for good work not only created new communities of explanation among individuals based in other ones, they also played a critical role in generating a *regional* understanding of the goals and elements of school reform in the Bay Area. BASRC experience illuminates the trap of de facto assumptions about common language and explanations across communities of practice. Simply convening stakeholders from different organizational or institutional communities may be efficient, but likely will accomplish little by way of learning and progress absent opportunity for them to first have conversations about their different perspectives and understandings.

A related lesson: BASRC's experience also suggests how teachers' participation in multiple communities of practice/explanation can promote more durable structures for knowing and learning. Teachers from Leadership Schools who have participated in conversations throughout the region have been able to hear multiple perspectives on practice and reform and integrate them into their own. Participation in multiple stakeholder groups enables teachers to take them into account as they go about work in their own school communities. Access to multiple communities makes teachers' own understandings more durable because they are more cosmopolitan and so less vulnerable to external shocks to their beliefs such as new or contradictory ideas about practice.

Conceptions of Effective Teacher Professional Development

BASRC's experience and the practical theory of teacher learning it suggests implicate the conceptions of professional development underlying reform proposals. For one, they stand in direct contrast to professional development or school reform policies that frame teachers' learning as solely an individual matter. We see in BASRC Leadership

Schools that learning is a social process, where the process in critical ways comprises the product, and where the knowledge generated by the community is more than a sum of individuals' learning. Communities of practice generate knowledge and understanding that are different in kind from that produced by individuals alone. Likewise, individuals' learning is a matter of their participation in a community of practice engaged in reflection and inquiry. Observations of relations among teachers and forms of knowledge in BASRC schools suggest a different perspective for policy, one rooted in communities of practice as sites and sources of teachers' learning.

Further, teachers' responses to and experience with the learning opportunities associated with BASRC add two important elements to deliberations about "What is effective professional development?" We see in BASRC a potentially powerful response to the fragmented professional development hodgepodge teachers experience, and a different way to move beyond dichotomous dickering over the value of opportunities offered outside the school or situated inside it. In the best of cases, BASRC enabled teachers to integrate outside knowledge resources for practice with learning efforts animated by knowledge generated by school-based inquiry. BASRC's strategy of a focused effort and cycle of inquiry directed both external and internal knowledge resources and the use teachers made of them. In Leadership Schools where teachers have created a culture of inquiry, BASRC made possible a system of professional knowledge and learning that stands in contrast to the non-system that exists in most school settings. Leadership Schools' experience advises reformers about how policy can foster coherent links between external resources and internal capacity.

The patterns of knowledge use and teacher learning evident in BASRC Leadership Schools also accent a missing element in the emerging consensus about what constitutes "good" professional development. Putnam and Borko (as quoted in Wilson & Berne, 1999, p. 176) condense common understandings about effective professional development into four "truisms":

1. Teachers should be treated as active learners.
2. Teachers must be empowered as professionals.
3. Teacher education must be situated in classroom practice.
4. Teacher educators should treat teachers as they expect teachers to treat students.

BASRC's experience finds this listing of professional development "mantras" (ibid.) substantively and strategically incomplete. Missing from the roll call are *data and evidence* about practice and policies at school and classroom levels. The communities of practice evident in some Leadership Schools demonstrate how knowledge of and evidence about *school-level* outcomes activates teachers' inquiry into classroom practices and refashions external knowledge into resources particular to the particular school context. The trajectory of inquiry, knowledge use, and change emerging in BASRC Leadership Schools shows how evidence can animate and guide teachers' reflection on and reinvention of their practices. It also positions school-level evidence about student outcomes and their connections to practice in a transformative spot for professional development and school reform—mediating the knowledge that comes into the school and provoking the generation of knowledge at the classroom level. Knowledge of this stripe, it appears, galvanizes and makes meaning of other forms of professional knowledge, and so occupies a pivotal role in what teachers learn, how they learn it, and the action that results.

NOTES

1. The Bay Area School Reform Collaborative (BASRC) was formed in the spring of 1995 as part of the nationwide Annenberg Challenge. BASRC became the Hewlett-Annenberg Challenge, funded jointly by the Hewlett and Annenberg Foundations, which provided 50 million dollars to Bay Area public schools to be matched by public and private funds over a five-year period. The Collaborative established by BASRC currently includes 86 Leadership Schools, each of which receives grants of up to 150 dollars per student for three to five years after completing a rigorous, evidence-based, peer-reviewed portfolio process. Leadership Schools use these grants to fund support provider services, time for school inquiry and professional development, and other resources in support of their focused reform effort.

2. BASRC requires all Leadership Schools to prepare an annual Review of Progress to document progress on their focused efforts, consequences for students, teachers' instructional practices, and school-level choices that affect teaching and learning.

3. Many of these schools had received funds under an earlier California reform effort in 1978 that was a significant BASRC ancestor in its focus on inquiry and whole school change: Senate Bill 1274.

REFERENCES

Center for Research on the Context of Teaching. (1998, 1999). *Assessing results: The Bay Area School Reform Collaborative*. Stanford, CA: School of Education, Stanford University.

Cochran-Smith, M., & Lytle, S. L. (1999). Relationships of knowledge and practice: Teacher learning in communities. In Ashgar Iran-Nejad & C. David Pearson (Eds.), *Review of Research in Education*, Vol. 24. Washington, DC: American Educational Research Association.

Cohen, W. M., & Levinthal, D. A. (1990). Absorptive capacity: A new perspective on learning and innovation. *Administrative Science Quarterly*, 35, 128–152.

Freeman, D. (1999, July) Towards a descriptive theory of teacher learning and change. Paper given at the International Study Association on Teachers and Teaching (ISATT) Conference. Dublin, Ireland.

Lortie, D. (1975). *School teacher*. Chicago: University of Chicago Press.

Rogoff, B. (1994). Developing understanding of the idea of communities of learners. *Mind, Culture and Activity*, 1 (4), 209–229.

Schön, D. A. (1983). *The reflective practitioner*. New York: Basic Books.

Wenger, E. (1998). *Communities of practice*. New York: Cambridge University Press.

Wilson, S. M., & Berne, J. (1999). Teacher learning and the acquisition of professional knowledge: An examination of research on contemporary professional development. In A. Iran-Nejad and P. D. Pearson (Eds.), *Review of Research in Education*, Vol. 24. Washington, DC: American Educational Research Association.

CHAPTER 7

School–University Partnership as a Venue for Professional Development

LYNNE MILLER

School–university partnerships are unique organizations. In some ways, they are like networks (Lieberman & Grolnick, 1996; Lieberman & Wood, Chapter 11, this volume) in that they connect practitioners who share common interests and concerns about education. However, school–university partnerships have some noteworthy characteristics that distinguish them from subject-matter or reform networks.

- They extend beyond the world of public schools and classrooms. They insinuate themselves into the life of the university, holding higher education to the same scrutiny and expectations as K–12 settings. Encompassing two distinct systems, they seek to leverage change in both. In many ways, they function as "third cultures." Neither schools nor universities, they create their own norms, values, expectations, rules, and roles that support reciprocity, equality, open conversation, and purposeful actions.
- They are regional, multi-focused organizations. As place-bound alliances, they find their constituent base within a specific geographic area. Though they may be connected to national reform initiatives, they answer to local concerns and issues. Often they develop regional responses to state initiatives and policies. They tend to work several agendas simultaneously rather than focusing on one content domain or endorsing and promoting one reform agenda.

The Southern Maine Partnership, where I serve as Executive Director, is such an organization and serves as reference point for this chapter. From its example, we can develop insights about the nature of school–university partnerships, what they are, how they develop and sustain themselves, and how they promote growth and change in the two institutions that they embody.

ABOUT THE SOUTHERN MAINE PARTNERSHIP

The Southern Maine Partnership is a membership organization that has linked schools and universities in the work of reforming themselves and each other for 15 years. It is currently made up of 34 public school districts and 3 institutions of higher education. Located at the University of Southern Maine, the Partnership has grown from a group of six school districts and one university to a collaboration that represents one-third of the public school students and teachers in the state and involves neighboring institutions of higher education. The Partnership is a regional alliance with national ties that is dedicated to the complex task of influencing both universities and schools in southern Maine.

Membership is open to school districts and higher education institutions, rather than to individual schools, departments, or faculty. Districts join by submitting a letter that is addressed to the member superintendents, who make the final decision about admission. The letter describes the district's improvement efforts and how joining the Partnership would deepen its own work and also contribute to the work of others. Further, the letter documents school board approval of membership and a commitment to pay annual dues of $1,300. Higher education partners follow a similar process when they join. The University of Southern Maine is the most active of the Institution of Higher Education (IHE) members, providing major support for personnel and operations. Membership dues support basic operations, the publication of a monthly calendar and occasional newsletter, preparations for meetings and seminars, and featured guests and speakers. External grant funding supports a myriad of activities in both schools and higher education. When a school district or university becomes a member of the Partnership, it makes the following commitments:

- To participate in Partnership conversations, activities, and projects
- To contribute to the professional knowledge of K–12 and university educators

- To share information, practices, and insights about teaching, learning, assessment, schooling, and the education of educators
- To contribute to and distribute Partnership communications to staff and, when appropriate, to a broader community audience
- To make appropriate financial and human resource contributions
- To maintain connections to member institutions through shared work
- To incorporate Partnership work into local improvement efforts and to incorporate local improvement efforts into Partnership work

The Partnership operates in the context of a local-control state, where districts, school boards, and town councils and meetings have considerable discretion over curriculum and assessment. Maine has recently adopted a set of standards, called the Maine Learning Results, that are meant as guidelines rather than mandates. There is a statewide assessment, given at grades 4, 8, and 11, but this is not a high-stakes test and is not tied to promotion or graduation requirements. Rather, each district is given the *responsibility* for developing its own Comprehensive Assessment System, based on the Learning Results but geared to local values and expectations. The Comprehensive Assessment System is supposed to be in place by 2003; it will be the vehicle by which each district guarantees the value of its high school diploma.

Since it strives to be a field-based organization, the Partnership keeps a lean central office staff that includes a half-time Executive Director who holds a faculty appointment, two full-time professional staff who were previously teachers in Partnership schools, and one full-time administrative assistant. When funding permits, we are able to hire people from the field to serve on special assignment. Currently we have one parent/school board member and three teachers involved in funded project work, which is largely based in schools. Over a dozen university faculty are now actively involved in some aspect of Partnership work, either in schools or at the university.

A distinguishing feature of the Partnership is that it does not have a fixed vision. Rather, its vision evolves over time, as the work evolves, responding to the emergent issues, concerns, and needs of the members as well as to the demands of the context. This is not to say that the Partnership lacks conviction or that it navigates without a moral compass. To the contrary, the Partnership is firm in its values of participation, reciprocity, democracy, and collaborative inquiry. It has never deviated from its commitment to serve schools and universities by improving practice and by enabling good policy. What does change, however, is how purpose is defined and iterated over time. For instance, in the 1980s, the Partnership's letterhead had as its tag line an adaptation of John Goodlad's thinking about partnerships. It read, "The simultaneous renewal of schools and the education of educators." A second printing of the letterhead proclaimed the Partnership's commitment to "linking school renewal and teacher development." In the first instance, there was a link between institutions; in the second, a connection between processes. Now there is a more concerted focus on outcomes. The Partnership currently advertises itself as promoting "the development of educators and educational settings that fulfill the promise of public education; that is, providing a guarantee of equitable choices and futures for all students" (Southern Maine Partnership, 1999). This last iteration of purpose seeks to define ends rather than means. It states clearly the goals of a university/school collaboration and the intended consequences of school renewal and teacher development. Vision has matured as the organization matured, each new iteration bringing the work into sharper focus and setting a clearer path for the Partnership to follow.

In this light, it may be helpful to view the Partnership as an amoeba or as being amoebaean in form and function. The noun *amoeba* derives from the Greek *amoibe,* and means "change." The English adjectival form, *amoebaean,* means "responsive; answering or responding to each other, as the responsive readings of a church service or the successive strophes of a verse dialogue" (*Webster's,* 1974). The Partnership embodies both definitions; it responds and it changes. Like the simple organism, it depends on a nucleus of clear values for its continued survival. These values allow the organism to move out into its environment, alter its form, and constantly be renewed and rejuvenated. And like responsive song or dialogue, the Partnership acknowledges the reality of multiple voices.

CORE TASKS OF SCHOOL–UNIVERSITY PARTNERSHIPS

School–university partnerships have four core tasks:

1. To establish firm bases in two distinct cultures, school and university
2. To cross institutional boundaries in order to respond to needs in the field
3. To ensure inclusive decision making
4. To create new venues for educator development

Below, I explain each core task and how the Southern Maine Partnership has gone about meeting it.

Establishing Firm Bases in University and K–12 Settings

Because a school–university partnership involves complex relationships among diverse institutions over time, it has to find ways to maintain durable footholds at all levels of engagement. For the Southern Maine Partnership, footholds have been established and maintained at the level of the university, district, school, and classroom.

The University. In the Southern Maine Partnership, the mainstay in higher education has been the University of Southern Maine (USM). The other two higher education institutions, the Maine College of Art and the Southern Maine Technical Institute, reach out to public school teachers and students through early study options and teacher institutes and workshops. Because they do not have degree programs for educator development, they do not participate as fully as the university in the total Partnership agenda. As the founding higher education member of the Partnership, USM has been unwavering in its support. It views the work of the Partnership as integral to its mission and goals and routinely demonstrates its commitment. For example, the position of Executive Director is a fully financed, tenure-line appointment in the College of Education and Human Development that provides half-time release from teaching. In addition, the College contributes clerical and administrative support, provides adequate office space, offers access to computer and phone lines as well as to printing and mailing services, and handles all grant processing and reporting. The dean encourages and rewards faculty involvement in Partnership activities and includes a Partnership delegate in his Advisory Council. Partnership professional development activities are eligible for earning university course credit. The president and provost of the university include the accomplishments of the Partnership in their annual reports to the trustees and to the public, and they encourage involvement from cross-campus faculty in K–12 education. All of these commitments help ensure that the Partnership maintains a secure position in the university.

The District. At the district level, commitments come in various forms. There are the obvious obligations to pay dues and secure school board approval. Perhaps more important is the personal engagement of the superintendents. A formal Superintendents' Group, which also includes the three deans, meets five times a year. Serving as the main governing body of the Partnership, it discusses and approves iterations of purpose and regularly reviews activities and progress. In addition, a Superintendents' Seminar was formed as an offshoot of the formal group. This is a smaller group of superintendents who meet four times a year for the purpose of reading, reflection, and collective action around a specific topic. Since its inception, the Seminar has concentrated on the issue of democratic practice and policy. Just recently, Seminar members agreed to sponsor a pilot program for teachers in the induction years, having as a group decided that it is important to socialize new teachers to the norms of democracy and inclusion that the districts espouse. This New Teacher Induction Program required additional financial and time commitments, which the participating superintendents were eager to provide. By making this level of commitment, the superintendents further ensured that Partnership membership remains integral to each district's staff development work.

Also at the district level, curriculum directors and teacher leaders participate in what is called the Curriculum Think Tank. This is a group that meets monthly to pool resources in curriculum and assessment development. Through these sessions, curriculum leaders not only identify and solve problems together, they also develop a common vocabulary and vision for their work. The Think Tank is now in the process of designing a Partnership-wide template that will inform local efforts to meet the state-mandated requirement for local Comprehensive Assessment Systems. Since Think Tank members are closer to the ground than the superintendents in implementing district curriculum and assessment policy, their continuing engagement and commitment are essential to the Partnership's viability and usefulness at the district level.

The School and Classroom. At the school level, the principal is key to maintaining an investment in the Partnership. Regular principal meetings have long provided opportunities for building this backing. Here administrators are able to gather together to share information, insights, and strategies, and to form alliances across district boundaries. In some years, the meetings have been open to all levels; in others, they have been focused on either elementary, middle, or secondary schools. Currently, the Partnership is using an issues-oriented approach, concentrating on topics such as how to use staff meetings for professional development and how to provide feedback on teaching through observation. The sessions are led by member principals, not outside experts or consultants, and often involve university administration and leadership faculty. The New Teacher Induction Program involves principals from participating schools in additional seminars, where feedback from the new teachers is used to fashion year-long orientation programs at the school level. As with superintendents and curriculum directors, commitment to the Partnership at the school level is not taken for granted. Rather, it is thoughtfully attended to and responsively crafted.

At the classroom level, the Partnership acknowledges the importance of teacher engagement. Professional development resources, no matter how rich and varied, are only effective when teachers seek them out and use them. The major setting for capturing teacher interest in Partnership work has been Dine and Discuss evenings; these are gatherings over dinner that bring together like-minded educators for serious conversation and reflection. Sometimes, teachers may discuss an article they have read; other times, they may share work they or their students have created; they may work together to solve a common problem of practice; or they may convene around a common interest, such as mathematics learning or inclusion. In any month, five or six such evenings are held. In February 2000, for instance, there were sessions on scoring rubrics, issues in differentiating instruction, achieving equity for students, the design and review of classroom assessments, current research on instruction, and reviewing state mandates for high school graduation. Well over 150 teachers participated in these evenings, and they brought their insights and learning back to their local schools. In fact, many schools have instituted their own Dine and Discuss sessions, based on the Partnership model. It is important to note that this level of teacher engagement is enabled by the superintendents and principals, who demonstrate their ongoing commitment by assuming the cost of dinner and material preparation for each participant.

Another opportunity for involvement at the classroom level is the production of *in Partnership,* a newsletter that is designed, written, and edited by school-based educators. Published twice a year, each edition is centered on a theme that speaks to a current issue in the region's schools. For instance, issues over the past three years have focused on topics such as the transition from junior high to middle schools; grouping, looping, and blocking options for school organization; rural schools and communities; homework; projects, performances, and portfolios; and the challenge of the state Learning Results. Typically, a K–12 educator assumes responsibility for an issue, solicits articles from other classroom teachers, provides feedback on submissions, assembles the newsletter, and turns the production work over to Partnership staff. The completed newsletter is usually 14 to 17 pages long and is filled with examples of student and teacher work, accessible and relevant text and photographs, and professional updates. *In Partnership* has become an established piece of our school and classroom repertoire.

Finally, school- and classroom-based educators may enroll in institutes and courses that are designed and delivered by Partnership educators and staff. Typically offered during summer, though some are held during the school year, these experiences provide an opportunity for face-to-face interaction about issues and concerns that require dedicated time for study and reflection. In summer 2000, for example, we are offering courses and institutes in: developing a comprehensive assessment system, learner-centered accountability, understanding performance data, collaborative inquiry, coaching for "critical friends" groups, and classroom instructional practice. Some of these offerings earn formal course credit and may be applied to degree programs, while others are connected to district professional development incentives.

Crossing Institutional Boundaries in Response to Needs

It is not enough to have strong footholds within member institutions; it is also essential to link the institutions in common work, responsive to the expressed needs of the field. To this end, the Southern Maine Partnership works hard to connect university, district, school, and classroom. One effort in this regard, the New Teacher Induction Program, has been discussed previously. The major way these connections are made, however, is through grant-funded projects. As a rule, the projects share the following characteristics:

- They are field-based and strive to build local capacity.
- They connect member institutions to each other and to Partnership work.
- They reflect the current iteration of Partnership purpose and vision.
- They develop processes of peer review and strategies to share knowledge.
- They are time-sensitive and build in mechanisms for sustainability beyond the funding period.
- They are co-constructed by school and university members.
- They are subject to frequent review and evaluation.

At this writing, there are seven major funded projects operating within the Partnership. Some of them are connected to other networks, such as the Coalition of Essential Schools, the National Network for Educational Renewal, and the Annenberg Rural Challenge. Others are linked to federally funded projects, such as Technology Challenge and Comprehensive School Research and Development grants (see the Southern Maine Partnership web site at www.usm.maine.edu/smp for descriptions of each of the projects). Below, I describe one of these projects as a way of demonstrating how project work strengthens the Partnership's footing at all membership levels and makes connections among them.

The Electronic Learning Marketplace (ELM) involves all the institutions and role groups in the Partnership. ELM's goal is to provide a "virtual marketplace" for the exchange of ideas, products, and insights through the development of an interactive web site (ELM, 1996). The web site displays teacher-developed assessments and learning activities that are within easy reach of all Partnership members. It invites on-line conversations about assessment work; in effect, it is an electronic professional community for its participants. ELM is governed by an Oversight Committee composed of representatives from higher education, districts, schools, and the community. This committee meets regularly to set benchmarks, monitor progress, and approve changes in operation and structure.

At the university, the College of Applied Sciences and the College of Education and Human Development work together to provide the capacity for web site development and product design. Applied Sciences houses the webmaster and is the center of activity for digitalization and publication of materials. Education and Human Development assists in assessment design and review and conducts staff development. At the district level, the Old Orchard Beach School District is identified as a demonstration site for the integration of technology, assessment, and curriculum development. Additionally, three member districts function as "studios" where products are developed and reviewed before they are published and where professional development activities are generated.

At school and classroom levels, teachers and school teams are involved as assessment developers, reviewers, and users. As developers and reviewers, they have an opportunity to enrich their own practice by participating in collegial conversations that are aimed at refining work before it is published. Using an adaptation of the "tuning protocol" (see McDonald, Chapter 13, this volume), teachers meet face to face in small groups to provide structured feedback and assistance. At this level, ELM is much more than a technology project; it is a professional development initiative that engages educators in collegial review and reflection that leads to improved practice.

ELM not only serves as a vehicle for publishing teacher-made materials; it also provides access to information resources and opportunities for on-line discussion. It includes a searchable data base of the Maine Learning Results; a variety of references relevant to standards-based assessment, teaching, and learning; an information area for parents and community members; and profiles of adult workers outside the field of education and how their work relates to the learning domains of the state standards. It also generates and enables conversation among educators, using electronic media. Teachers can engage in on-line discussion with product developers and can serve as on-line reviewers of assessments and curriculum. As an extension of this work, ELM is now developing an on-line forum for the review and critique of Comprehensive Assessment Systems. District work in progress will be published on the site, and there will be opportunity provided for comment and feedback. In this way, ELM enables districts to respond collaboratively to state policy mandates, relieving them of the burden of working in isolation.

Key to ELM and to other project work is the development and use of tools of inquiry and reflection that guide educator conversation and action. In ELM, the adaptation of the tuning protocol serves as such a tool. It provides a structured format for offering and receiving feedback, which helps teacher-developers refine and improve their work. In addition, ELM has developed a template for reviewing assessments. The template lists quality indicators of good assessments and provides a grid for peer evaluation of work in progress. Tools used by other Partnership projects include

- Structured processes for looking at student and teacher work (see McDonald, Chapter 13, this volume)
- The "vertical slice," a procedure that leads to an analysis of a sampling of what students do in school over the course of several days
- The "descriptive review of the child," a format for looking at one student closely and coming to understand how that student understands and processes the world
- Observational protocols of classroom teaching—approaches for looking at classroom teaching and providing feedback
- "Shadowing" of students for a day, a method for following a student for a day and gaining insights into the school experience from the student perspective
- "Text-based seminars," a blueprint for a conversation about a text that is geared to enlargement of understanding and full participation of members

- School review visits, a week-long investigation of a school's practices performed by a visiting team of educators from other Partnership sites
- "Critical friends" and coaching groups, a mechanism for ensuring an ongoing relationship between a group of teachers in a school and an external "friendly critic" from another Partnership setting

Although project work depends initially on outside funding, the work does not end with the funding. When individuals and institutions value the tools and perspectives that a project embodies, they often draw on local staff development funds to continue and deepen their inquiry and action. In this way, project work insinuates itself into Partnership practice in an ongoing way.

ENSURING INCLUSIVE DECISION MAKING

There is a tension in a school/university partnership about who sets the agenda. Is it done by the university? Or the schools? Or by the director and staff? There is always the danger that if agenda-setting is not distributed among the membership, a partnership will lose its way. What begins as a collaboration can turn into a traditional service provider, depending on one individual or small group of individuals to determine its course. In order to protect against this and to maintain the integrity of collaboration, the Southern Maine Partnership uses multiple sites for agenda-setting.

Previously, I identified the Superintendents' Group as the governing body of the Partnership, which makes decisions about general Partnership direction and policy. Recently, it adopted a set of priorities, or challenges, for the Partnership:

- The development of local Comprehensive Assessment Systems to meet state law
- The construction of connected curricula in line with the Learning Results
- The deepening of teaching practice and expansion of teaching and assessment repertoires
- Leadership development, pre-service and in-service, for administrators and teachers
- Pre-service teacher education and new teacher induction

- Communicating and disseminating information about best practices
- Developing the capacity for organizational change

These policy directions, while critical, do not tell the whole story of Partnership decision making. While superintendents and deans play a pivotal role, they are not the exclusive authors of the agenda. Their perspective is too role-bound to ensure a broad-based platform, their sights being more focused on policy than practice. This is not meant as a critique; it is presented as one of the realities of the position. While the policy perspective of the superintendents and deans is acknowledged and respected, it is complemented by the practice perspective of faculty and building-based leaders.

Previously, I have noted that principals, curriculum leaders, and teachers set the agendas for their particular groups. These decisions are made out of the sight of superintendents and deans, but they impact what the Partnership actually does and how it does it. For instance, Dine and Discuss groups are all self-governing; often they take on a life of their own. The Math Leaders Group, one of the original conveners of Dine and Discuss evenings, provides an example. It met regularly for about five years, lost its momentum and stopped meeting, and then re-emerged as a strong presence. Overseen by a professor of mathematics education at the university, the group has been very active and meets monthly to plan its own staff development. All that occurs within the group is self-designed. Group members communicate regularly through e-mail, study texts together, connect to other mathematics groups and networks, and plan full-day workshops for themselves and others. The Math Leaders Group is clearly in charge of its own agenda, and it is one that focuses on problems of practice rather than issues of policy.

Grant-funded projects also serve as venues for agenda-setting. The ELM Oversight Committee, as indicated earlier, makes decisions that guide the project's objectives and operations. Every project has a similar form of self-governance and review. Decisions about basic operations and tools, the allocation of personnel and resources, and changes in direction are all made at the project level by project participants.

Over a period of three years, it became obvious that the Partnership needed a bridge between the formal, policy-oriented agenda-setting of the superintendents and deans and the informal, practice-centered approaches of the diverse discussion groups and projects. From that need, the Advisory Council was born. It is comprised of 17 members, equally distributed among teachers, principals, superintendents or district administrators, district at-large representatives, parent/community members, and higher education faculty. Meeting four times a year, the Advisory Council is charged with developing strategies for realizing the Partnership's commitment to equitable futures for all students. The Council looks closely at Partnership projects and activities and critically assesses how closely they are connected to desired outcomes. Based on this scrutiny, the Council then makes recommendations for either continuing the work, making alterations, or discontinuation. The council also suggests new avenues to explore, such as grant possibilities and connections to people and resources. It is one more avenue for agenda-setting within an organization that is dense with such possibilities.

CREATING NEW VENUES FOR EDUCATOR DEVELOPMENT

One of the unique characteristics of a school/university partnership is that it connects the university-based credit and certification structures for the education of educators to the less formalized arrangements for professional development and institutional renewal that exist at the school level. At its best, a partnership becomes a new location for pre-service education and continued educator development.

The Southern Maine Partnership has been successful in establishing a new berth for pre-service teacher education. In 1989, the education faculty at the University of Southern Maine voted to terminate its undergraduate teacher education program. This decision was applauded, in fact encouraged, by the superintendents of the Partnership, who had for some time voiced concern about the quality of teachers the university was producing and had written a letter to that effect. The Extended Teacher Education Program (ETEP), a post-baccalaureate certification program, was piloted the next year in a Partnership school under the direction of the Partnership Executive Director. From this beginning, a new and collaborative approach to pre-service education was launched. Based on a full-year internship in a Partnership school and complemented by university courses delivered on-site, ETEP depends on the joint work of university and school-based educators in designing and delivering the preparation of new teachers.

In a recent examination of the ETEP program (Whitford, Ruscoe, & Fickel, 2000), researchers concluded:

> One of the distinctive features of ETEP is that it was conceived from the beginning as a collaboration among public school and university educa-

tors who had already established a history of trust and mutual respect through the Southern Maine Partnership (SMP). . . . repeatedly cited by many respondents as significant to the shaping of school reform, teacher education reform, and the substantial intertwining of the two. (p. 213)

The researchers further noted how ETEP has served to influence university and school practice.

Due to the high degree of collaboration, ETEP functions within and across the variety of organizational structures comprising schools, districts, and the university. A result has been new organizational roles, arrangements, and distributions of responsibility (including time) related to teacher preparation, bringing in new practices as well as new tensions. (p. 213)

ETEP stands as a concrete example of how the Partnership enables member institutions to create new collaborative settings where quality pre-service teacher education can occur.

To be sure, pre-service education is not the only venue for educator development. The continuing education of classroom teachers and the preparation of school leaders also require attention. The Partnership leverages change in these jurisdictions as well. Because it is closely linked to the Department of Professional Development at the university (where I have my faculty appointment and where other faculty are involved in its work), the Partnership influences advanced-degree programs as well. A new degree program for teachers in their first three years is under development, due to the Partnership's New Teacher Induction Program initiative. So, too, a new approach to graduate education in leadership has been influenced by Partnership work. Recently, a group of 10 Partnership districts approached the Educational Leadership Program and asked it to modify its master's degree in administration and to design a new pathway toward principal certification. A two-day retreat that involved school and university faculty; district, school, and higher education administrators; and business and community leaders resulted in the articulation of six goals for the new leadership program:

- To have school systems accept the responsibility for creating, nurturing, developing, and exemplifying leadership
- To ensure that leaders of the future will be committed to high achievement for all students
- To ensure that bountiful leadership exists at every school for the purpose of focusing on the needs of every teacher and student as continuous learners

- To forward the work of high-performing school districts
- To have school systems support and collaborate with each other, business, state-level organizations, universities, and the community at large in creating leadership opportunities
- To promote and support changes in the curriculum of the University of Southern Maine's administrative certification program, including increased site-based work, collaboration with cohort groups, and mentoring.

These goals are being realized in the "Leadership for Tomorrow's Schools" program that admitted its first class last summer. Nominated by their superintendents and supported with release time for graduate course and leadership work, 36 teacher leaders are participating in a collaboratively developed degree and certification program that is significantly different from the one devised solely by university faculty.

SUSTAINING SCHOOL/UNIVERSITY PARTNERSHIPS

A partnership remains viable to the extent that it fulfills its core tasks successfully. Establishing strong bases in both school and university, crossing institutional boundaries to respond to emergent needs, ensuing inclusive decision making, and creating new venues for educator development all contribute to its sustainability.

At root, a school/university partnership is a precarious organization. Bridging two cultures, it remains marginal to each. This marginality, though difficult to manage, is essential for survival. It not only protects against overidentification with one institution; it guarantees that diverse and multiple voices will be heard and valued. Because a partnership is a regional entity, it struggles to maintain a local agenda within a state policy environment. It must respond to state initiatives, of course, but it must also remain true to grassroots interests and priorities. A partnership must also guard against being unduly influenced by external funding agents and national affiliations. Its power derives from its ability to remain connected to local concerns, issues, talents, and capabilities.

A partnership's viability is also tied to the degree to which it can provide multiple points of entry and re-entry for its members. This overview of the Southern Maine Partnership has identified such locales for superintendents, principals, classroom teachers, deans, and university faculty through role-alike groups; Dine and Discuss evenings; occasions for collaborative inquiry and reflection; writing for print and nonprint publication; telecommunications and face-to-face conversation; review of student and teacher work; opportunities to design, deliver, and participate in degree programs for pre-service teacher education, leadership development, and ongoing teacher improvement; involvement in project work; participation in institutes and courses; and engagement in policy groups.

Finally, a partnership's vitality is connected to its utility, to the value it adds to the work of member institutions, and to the contribution it makes to educator and institutional development. This can best be judged by the level of commitment that member institutions maintain, the degree of participation in events and opportunities, and—most important—the extent to which partnership tools, perspectives, and language become embedded in the everyday work of people and institutions. In southern Maine, the establishment of district-level Dine and Discuss evenings, the school-wide and university use of protocols and tools for looking at teacher and student work, and the district and school application of ELM templates for reviewing quality curriculum and assessments have become commonplace. A shared vocabulary for talking about teaching and learning is taking hold within both school and the university, and the need for dedicated time for collegial conversation, review and critique, and reflection is becoming acknowledged as well.

In a sustainable school/university partnership there is no espoused "one best way" to engage educators and institutions in their own development. Nor is there room for territorial concerns about the ownership of ideas and the hierarchy of knowledge. Rather, school/university partnerships create spaces that are responsive, flexible, and inventive. They provide occasions for the reciprocal discovery and distribution of tools, understandings, and information that inform and influence the work of all of its members.

REFERENCES

Electronic Learning Marketplace (ELM). (1996). @ *www.elm.maine.edu*

Lieberman, A., & Grolnick, M. (1996). Networks and reform in American education. *Teachers College Record, 98*(1), 7–45.

Southern Maine Partnership. (1999). *Mission statement.* Gorham: Author.

Webster's New World Dictionary of the American Language. (1974). Cleveland: William Collins and World Publishing Co., Inc.

Whitford, B., Ruscoe, G., & Fickel, L. (2000). Knitting it all together: Collaborative teacher education in southern Maine. In L. Darling-Hammond (Ed.), *Studies in excellence in teacher education. Preparation at the graduate level* (pp. 173–257). Washington, DC: AACTE Publications.

CHAPTER 8

Professional Learning Through Assessment

BEVERLY FALK

As standards-based reforms sweep the country and educators grapple with how to support an increasingly diverse student population to realize their academic and social potentials, there is a growing consensus among educators that professional development for teachers and administrators lies at the center of educational reform and instructional improvement. Over the last decades many reforms have focused on other aspects of schools and schooling: on providing guidance to schools about what students should be taught (content standards), on changing the structures and processes by which schools are held accountable (student performance standards, assessments, rewards, and penalties), or on creating new forms of governance structures that define and uphold accountability (site-based management, vouchers, charter schools). The assumption behind these initiatives is that attention to these aspects of schooling will result in better student learning that will, in turn, be demonstrated by better student performance on tests.

What has been missing from such formulations, however, is attention to the actual teaching practices that produce better student learning. Recently this issue has received more attention because of an emerging body of research pointing to the quality of teaching as a critical influence on student performance. Numerous national studies report that increased professional knowledge on the part of teachers yields higher levels of student achievement (National Commission on Teaching and America's Future, 1996, 1997). It is becoming increasingly clear that, far more than policies and organizational strategies that only provide the backdrop against which educators are able to do their work, teachers' abilities to teach in powerful ways are essential to improved student learning.

This being the case, to ensure that all students have richer learning experiences and are enabled to reach more challenging goals, school systems are faced with an enormous task: developing teachers' capacities to teach so that a range of different learners are able to understand and effectively use new knowledge. Without investing in this kind of teacher learning, standards and standards-based assessment reforms, rather than raising achievement levels for all, could prove to have harmful effects in the long term—particularly for those struggling students who are already least well-served by the educational system.

What kind of professional learning opportunities develop the capacities of teachers to support more ambitious teaching and learning for all students? Over the years we have come to understand the limitations of the short-term teacher "training" model—the one-shot workshop or "expert" lecture—that transmits information and skills to passive recipients (Fosnot, 1989; Giroux, 1988; Lieberman, 1995; Lieberman & McLaughlin, 1992; Little, 1992, 1993; Meier, 1992). Increasingly, these forms of professional development are being replaced by a more long-range, capacity-building approach that offers "meaningful intellectual, social, and emotional engagement with ideas, with materials, and with colleagues both in and outside of teaching" (Little, 1993, p. 10). In this approach, teachers get opportunities to focus on the application of general ideas, to try out new kinds of practices that bring them directly into contact with students and their work, and to collaboratively examine and reflect on their beliefs and their practices (Elmore, 1997; Noble & Smith, 1994; Wilson, 1990).

Working with performance assessment offers teachers just these kinds of opportunities for professional learning. In this chapter I share studies and stories of how teacher involvement with standards and performance-based assessment has enhanced their knowledge and their growth. I give examples of how examining and assessing students' work—with other teachers, students, and sometimes their families—helps teachers understand what their students know and can do as well as how their students process their learning. I describe how working with standards and standards-based assessments stimulates teachers to think about their curricular vision and to consider how different instructional approaches can be used to support the varying strengths, needs, and learning approaches of their students. And finally, I portray how teacher involvement in performance assessment use supports reflection and provides opportunities for collaboration, which, in turn, enhance professionalism and strengthens abilities to engage in meaningful change.

Three different types of assessment initiatives that impact on teacher learning are presented: Teachers assessing student learning by observing, documenting, and collecting student work over time with classroom-based assessment frameworks; teachers scoring student responses to externally administered standards-based performance tests; and teachers examining and validating their own practice by participating in the National Board of Professional Teaching Standards certification process.

TEACHER LEARNING FROM CLASSROOM-BASED ASSESSMENT

For many years, teachers in classrooms across the country have been developing, using, and exploring the power of performance assessments. Processes for observing and recording children's behavior and for collecting and looking at children's work have been used— sometimes individually, sometimes in groups—to learn about children and their learning.

Classroom-based performance assessments are generally used in formative or summative ways: to inquire generally about the processes that go into learning—the learner's ideas, understandings, and approaches; or to evaluate the results of a specific learning experience. In either case, because they are embedded in the curriculum and because they call on students to apply knowledge and skills through real-life–like performances—such as essays, projects, or experiments—performance assessments provide a window into learners' thinking that can be useful to teachers' work.

Performance assessments help teachers learn how to identify and appreciate students' different strengths and approaches to learning. Some also provide teachers with a guide for their teaching, pointing out what strategies and behaviors to look for as students progress in their learning. Both types of performance assessment have been found to stimulate changes in the ways teachers teach. At the same time, such performance assessments provide occasions for colleagues to collaboratively reflect on and inquire about their own work.

A growing number of studies are documenting this relationship between teacher learning and classroom-based performance assessments (Allen, 1998; Darling-Hammond, Ancess, & Falk, 1995; Dorfman, 1997; Falk, 1994, 1998; Falk & Darling-Hammond, 1993; Falk, MacMurdy, & Darling-Hammond, 1995; Falk & Ort, 1999; Kates, 1999). Below I share some of the details that reveal the power and possibilities they offer.

Learning About the Strengths of Diverse Learners

When teachers get into the habit of collecting and reflecting on evidence about their students, they become more able to recognize and appreciate the different ways students learn. These understandings enhance teachers' abilities to provide effective instruction. An elementary-grade dual-language teacher explains:

> Keeping observational records helps me to become aware that each child is learning at her own pace and that each child knows something and is good at something. I now gear my work more to each child, individualizing and giving children the support they need. (Falk, MacMurdy, & Darling-Hammond, 1995, p. 35)

Teachers' appreciation for the strengths of different learners resulting from keeping track of student work also helps to safeguard against any bias that teachers may have about students' capabilities. Recognizing the varying strengths of diverse learners makes it harder to attach labels to children (i.e., José is a troublemaker) or to make all-inclusive judgments about them (i.e., Shanta can't read). These labels and judgments often have the unintended effect of becoming self-fulfilling prophecies—the child for whom adults have low expectations dutifully produces what is expected; the child who is labeled with a particular problem conforms to the image of him held by others. As a result, teachers often inadvertently set limits on the learning opportunities for these students. Although the intent may be to provide appropriate settings for students with special problems, the actual effect is to deny students access to challenging curricula. This, in turn, constrains their abilities to develop as thinkers and limits their chances to achieve the rigorous expectations currently demanded by their school communities.

In addition to safeguarding against bias, observation and documentation of students and their work helps to understand students in the context of their culture and to appreciate student strengths that might otherwise go unnoticed. This recognition subsequently leads to providing better supports for student learning and to making more informed decisions that affect them and their futures.

This was the case for nine-year-old Kendall, a recent emigrant to New York City from Jamaica, who had low scores on standardized reading tests and was receiving extra supports through Title I assistance. Described by his classroom teacher as "non-functioning in literacy" and "unable to read, speak, or write," Kendall was referred for a special education evaluation.

However, Kendall's Resource Room teacher had a very different perspective of him and his oral language expression based on a broad array of evidence that she had collected. In addition to her documented observations of him and the samples of his work that she had saved, she also had notes from an interview that she had conducted with Kendall and his family. These proved to be critical in offering insights into his learning. Her records of the interview with Kendall's family presented information that revealed cultural differences between their home and the school, differences that were responsible for what Kendall's teachers saw as his "lack of spontaneity" in oral language. Kendall's family explained that their culture expected children to be quiet, polite, and obedient in school, to speak only when spoken to, and to do exactly what the teacher asked. When shared with the other teachers in the school, this description of his native country's expectations for appropriate school conduct caused the teachers to question whether Kendall's apparently lagging language development was the result of innate deficits in his abilities or the result of cultural differences.

The Resource Room teacher's own observations of Kendall gave strength to the cultural explanation of Kendall's behavior. Her documentation provided descriptions of him in diverse school contexts that revealed him expressing himself well in many situations and demonstrating considerable interest and ability:

> Kendall continues to be well behaved and very quiet in group situations. Yet he appears to be attentive and interested in all curriculum areas. When called upon, he will respond and read confidently. Otherwise, he will remain quiet and not contribute. He is beginning to initiate comments and questions in the classroom and small group situations. In the playground, however, he is verbal and socializes well. He is noticeably happier in one-to-one situations and when observing and listening. (Falk, MacMurdy, & Darling-Hammond, 1995, 28)

These data filled in many of the gaps that were distorting the total picture of Kendall as a learner. It enabled those responsible for decisions about his future to see the strengths that had been missed by other, conventional assessments, to see that he was making significant progress in his current class, and to avert an unnecessary referral to special education.

Providing a Guide For Teaching

Some classroom-based performance assessments provide a guide to essential aspects of learning simply by virtue of what they ask teachers to observe and record. The *Primary Language/Learning Record* (Barrs et al., 1988), the *Work Sampling System* (Meisels et al., 1993), and the *Early Literacy Profile* (New York State Education Department, 1999), to name just three, are some of the assessments offering descriptions of critical strategies and behaviors that students utilize in their learning and that teachers need to look for as they interact with students. Evidence accumulated through these assessment frameworks can be used to inform instructional decisions. Because teachers are the primary assessors, the feedback about student learning is immediate and context-connected. There is no waiting for months, as after a test administration, to receive students' scores from the test publisher.

Teachers who work with such classroom-based performance assessments report them to have a powerful, positive impact on their teaching. Particularly welcomed are the types of assessments that provide age-appropriate expectations or signposts for the skills and strategies that students need. One primary grade teacher whose use of the *Early Literacy Profile* was studied in depth over the course of a year explains, "An assessment like that gives you an indication of what you can teach toward. It gave me an idea of where the deficits, the holes, in my program are. If you don't have all of the criteria that you need to look for in front of you, then it's easy to leave something out" (Kates, 1999, p. 20).

Changing the Way Teachers Teach

The close-up look at students and their thinking offered through classroom-based performance assessment helps teachers change the way they teach. Many report that using performance assessments has heightened their awareness of both group and individual needs, thus enhancing their abilities to individualize instruction.

> Observing the strategies a child uses and those which he doesn't helped me plan ways to help the child use those strategies he's not using now. I found myself planning with each student's needs in mind. (Falk, MacMurdy, & Darling-Hammond, 1995, 15)

When assessments are embedded in meaningful, purposeful, and real-life experiences, teachers are freed from "teaching to the test" to support a broader vision of learning. They are able to expand the range of their instructional strategies and transform their classrooms to offer opportunities for students to engage in the kinds of behaviors that are more akin to how children learn. Studies of teachers who worked with both the *Primary Language Record* and the *Early Literacy Profile* (Falk &

Darling-Hammond, 1993; Falk, MacMurdy, & Darling-Hammond, 1995; Falk & Ort, 1999) found this to be the case. Among the changes teachers instituted in classrooms as a result of using curriculum-embedded assessments are: providing more opportunities for peer learning and collaboration; providing more choices for students in the learning environment; teaching in more integrated, interdisciplinary ways; utilizing learning contexts that stretch beyond the walls of the school, ensuring that each child has access to materials appropriate for their level of instruction rather than relying on whole class "one-size-fits-all" passages from texts as the primary source for instruction; using classroom libraries as a central aspect of the learning environment; providing regular opportunities for reading aloud; immersing classroom environments in print; and using a range of media as vehicles for students' expression of their learning.

Promoting Teacher Collaboration and Inquiry

Teachers using classroom-based performance assessments are as diverse a group in their thinking and experience as the children they are teaching. Nevertheless, working with this type of assessment supports and challenges a variety of teachers to consider a host of questions and issues that tap into deeply rooted values influencing their teaching. This often leads them to engage in the kind of activities and inquiry that foster professional learning. Some hold dialogue sessions within their schools at lunchtime, preparation periods, or after-school hours. Others participate in out-of-school activities—courses, study groups, and summer institutes—that feature group opportunities for exchanging ideas about teaching and assessment strategies.

The following story from a teacher study group demonstrates the power that reflection can have in shaping and reshaping teachers' beliefs, attitudes, and practices. Denise, a teacher of eight- and nine-year-olds, raised a concern with her colleagues at a study group meeting about a group of boys in her class who read science books and talked together every day during the block of time devoted to the language arts. Although this was a time when the teacher encouraged children to read and write and talk together, she was particularly concerned about one boy in this group who still struggled with fluency in his reading. She was nervous that he was spending too much time talking and not enough time practicing his reading. In relating her concern to her colleagues, she realized that although she openly encouraged the stronger readers to converse, the very same process of chatting with others made her nervous if it was being done by weaker readers. She began to question whether it was fair to hold different standards of behavior for different kinds of students:

> Does that mean that a struggling reader shouldn't talk as much as a competent reader? I thought about the role of practice in learning to read and how I know that practice is very important. But I also thought about the role of choice in learning and how important it is for learner motivation. I thought about the relation between teacher choice and student choice. Classrooms generally are structured around teacher choice. I want to support and encourage student choice but if I decide this boy needs to practice his reading more, and all the while he wants to talk about books, I am taking away his right to make his own choice. And I never do this to competent readers. They get to choose what they want to do because their choices generally coincide with mine. (Falk, MacMurdy, & Darling-Hammond, 1995, p. 42)

The implications of this tension are subtle but powerful; they have to do with issues of standards, autonomy, empowerment, and equity. Denise was torn between her responsibility to have all students achieve high standards and her equally strong commitment to provide all students with equitable learning opportunities.

Denise eventually resolved this tension by structuring a time in her classroom when *all* students were required to engage in quiet, independent reading.

> I played around with ways to make that more appealing. And in fact, after a while, what I did worked! They all did settle into reading independently—to the extent that they were able. They all were willing to engage in doing what readers do—choose a book, sit and give it the attention it requires, trust that something is going to happen that is worthwhile. They all got over the hump of the resistance to reading—everybody would sit or lie on the floor and read. I looked up one day and said, "Wow, everybody's reading!" I know not everybody was reading the way a reading test would measure. But everybody was engaged with a book and this to me is an important measure of reading. (Falk, MacMurdy, & Darling-Hammond, 1995, p. 42)

Denise is quick to point out that if she had not been looking at children in her classroom so closely and if she had not had the opportunity to discuss these issues in her study group, she most likely would not have noticed what these children were doing and would not have contemplated the important issues that were raised by the situation.

> What I came to realize when I was looking at this is that we put so much emphasis on reading and skills development in school we don't nurture other things that need to be nurtured in order for skills to develop. I really want to learn how to do this so that I can help all kinds of learners learn better. (Falk, MacMurdy, & Darling-Hammond, 1995, p. 43)

Through Denise's systematic assessment of her students' learning and through discussions with her colleagues that helped to process this information, Denise came to powerful realizations that influenced her thinking and her practice. Is this not the goal of professional (indeed, any kind of) learning—to help individuals reach the point of questioning, searching, and seeking opportunities to reflect on and change what they do? Weaving performance assessment into the fabric of teaching helps teachers come to this juncture. Because they have experienced powerful learning themselves, they have a better sense of how to bring their students to this juncture as well. Documenting and reflecting on student work helps teachers better support student learning while, at the same time, it also supports teachers to engage in their own knowledge development. They experience firsthand what they come to understand is essential for all to learn well—that each requires a different look and a different pathway to growth.

Meeting the Challenge of Responsive Teaching: Teaching to the Child

Observing students in diverse contexts across the curriculum calls on teachers to take a closer look at themselves, their practices, their students, and their students' learning. In doing so, the details of the learning process are revealed, clarifying the kinds of environments and practices that support different learners to learn in different ways. Rather than "teaching to the test," teachers are supported to "teach to the child."

Assessment processes that document students and their work provide a way for teachers to come to know their students well. They offer a window into children's thinking. They help us to see that children learn not by absorbing information that has been transmitted, but by making connections between new knowledge and the unique understandings and experiences of each individual. Performance assessments demonstrate that children are thinking, capable persons who are filled with impulse, interest, intention, wonder, curiosity, and creativity. They remind us that if we are to support genuine learning, schools need to be thought of as more than mere institutions; they need to be places that offer opportunities to explore, question, experiment, search, problem-pose and problem-solve in ways that connect to each individual.

TEACHER LEARNING FROM SCORING STUDENTS' RESPONSES TO STANDARDS-BASED PERFORMANCE TESTS

Involving teachers in scoring students' responses to large-scale standards-based performance tests offers rich opportunities to enhance teacher learning. Much of the teacher learning resulting from this activity takes place during the orientation process that precedes actual scoring of student work. Scoring orientations are designed to teach potential scorers of standards-based performance tests how to use standards as a reference for evaluating students' responses. The goal of the orientation session is to ensure that scoring will be "reliable," that is, that everyone will develop common understandings of the criteria on which the scoring is based and that everyone will come to share common images of what each level of student performance looks like.

The scoring orientation goes something like this: Teachers, working in small groups, look over each assessment task to discuss the standards that the tasks assess. They then review each task's criteria to discuss what students need to do to accomplish the task. Together they examine sample student responses, referencing each task's rubric (or scoring guide) for descriptions of what the work looks like at different levels of proficiency. Discussing the work, detail by detail, they compare the evidence in each response to the rubric's indicators until they arrive at a consensus for a score. Inevitable differences in opinions and perspectives are mediated by the rubric's clearly articulated criteria for performance and the process's insistence that teachers always justify their evaluation using evidence from the student work. Although viewpoints may initially vary, after going through several sample responses teachers begin to consistently agree on the scores that they assign. Recurring consensus signals completion of the orientation. Only then do teachers move on to begin the actual independent scoring of tasks that is used to assign official exam scores.

Learning how to use a rubric involves learning how to evaluate students' work based on evidence and relative to explicit standards, not based on unsubstantiated feelings or assumptions relative to other students' work. In the course of scoring standards-based performance assessments, teachers learn to apply common criteria and standards to the work of all their students. During this process, content standards, scoring rubrics, and student benchmark papers help teachers to think about their teaching and their students' learning. Content standards specify what the important aspects of a subject area are and provide broad conceptions of the discipline itself. Scoring rubrics make criteria explicit for distinguishing among different levels of performance in student work. The scoring activity itself requires looking for and seeing specific features of student work in terms of these criteria. Actual examples of student work at differing levels of performance provide benchmarks or reference points for how to establish to what degree standards are met.

Studies of teachers who have been involved in using standards and rubrics in scoring sessions such as these suggest that the process positively impacts teacher learning in a number of different ways (Falk & Ort, 1998, 1999; Sheingold, Heller, & Storms, 1997; Thomas et al., 1995). Participating in scoring helps teachers clarify goals and expectations for their teaching as well as for their students' learning, deepens their knowledge of their discipline, reveals important information to them about what their students know and can do, and offers them overall insights that can be useful to teaching. In addition, the highly professional atmosphere of scoring sessions strengthens teachers' sense of professionalism, heightens their understandings about the workings of the system of which they are a part, and reaffirms the central importance of teachers to the evaluation process. Instead of having to rely on outside "experts" to judge the outcomes of students' work, teacher involvement in scoring places assessment back in the domain of teaching, where it can be readily accessed to inform and support learning.

In 1996, I conducted a study with 250 teachers who participated in scoring sessions of the pilot administration of New York State's new statewide standards-based performance assessments. My colleagues and I obtained feedback from teachers who were part of these scoring sessions through observations during scoring, interviews with 30 participants, and an open-ended questionnaire administered to all who took part in the initiative (Falk & Ort, 1998). Below I share some of the findings that resulted from this study.

Clarifying Goals and Expectations for Teaching and Learning

One of the most valuable aspects of scoring standards-based performance assessments is the opportunity that scoring sessions provide for collegial conversations. The discussions that teachers have about standards, assessments, and student work in the context of scoring tests challenge them to learn about state or district expectations for their students and to clarify how their own views differ or agree. At the same time, these discussions present them with opportunities to consider how the standards' expectations might impact on their teaching. Since state standards are, in a sense, political documents, reflecting a consensus opinion of diverse constituents, working with the standards challenges teachers to find a way to balance their individual views about what is important with the perspective of what is valued and valuable in their broader community. One middle school mathematics teacher expressed the views of many when she noted that "The discussion about the scoring rubrics was extremely useful. It was a great way of sharing ideas on what people think is important" (Falk & Ort, 1998, p. 61).

Deepening Teachers' Knowledge of the Disciplines

Scoring student responses to assessment tasks also offers teachers a way to see how the big ideas embodied in standards actually play out in real student work. In addition, the experience helps them to develop shared understandings and a common language about the essentials of their disciplines.

The rubrics' frame for assessing student work guides teachers to use evidence, rather than personal feelings, as the basis for evaluations. One elementary teacher describes how she transformed the way she evaluated student work as a result of participating in standards-based scoring: "I moved away from thinking about work in an A, B, C, or D way, to thinking about the criteria for performance and the evidence that would justify my evaluation" (Falk & Ort, 1998, p. 62).

Learning About Students and Their Work

Looking at student work in relation to standards helps teachers gain understanding about the strategies and approaches students bring to their learning. Of course, the ability to do this is contingent upon having worthy assessment tasks—tasks designed to be as contextualized as possible, to ask students to show and explain their work, and to allow a wide range of students to be able to demonstrate their abilities. When the tasks possess these characteristics, the process of scoring student responses offers teachers a window into *what* their students know and can do as well as *how* their students actually do it.

Teachers who have been involved in scoring student work point to assessments that are "authentic" and performance-based as being most helpful for gaining insights into students' learning. Teachers surveyed in New York State overwhelmingly supported the areas of the new state tests that called for students to explain their thinking and to demonstrate their work. One middle school mathematics teacher said, "When students are expected to explain or support their answers, you begin to learn more about what they understand" (Falk & Ort, 1998, p. 62). A high school English teacher concurred and added, "I began to look more in-depth for what the students *could* do, rather than only focusing on what they *couldn't* do" (Falk & Ort, 1998, p. 62). The deeper look at young people's thinking offered through performance tasks helps teachers to gain a deeper respect for formerly unnoticed students' strengths and to appreciate the variety of ways students solve problems and express their ideas.

Teachers' visions of possibilities for "good work" also expand as a result of scoring. "Looking at student responses to the assessment tasks reinforced the idea that good work can look very different and can take on many forms," noted an elementary teacher who administered and scored a math/science/technology task (Falk & Ort, 1998, p. 62). Teachers' perspectives on expectations for student performance are also broadened because they look at student work from different locales and from a variety of racial, socioeconomic, and linguistic backgrounds. "I learned so much from seeing the work of students other than my own," said one high school English teacher. Another of her colleagues added, "The most valuable part of the scoring session was learning about the differences and similarities of the populations of different school districts" (Falk & Ort, 1998, p. 62).

Other benefits of scoring noted by teachers are attributed to the nature of the assessment tasks used. Some teachers point to the clear and public articulation of expectations in tasks as helping them to help students achieve. "When the expectations are very clear, it seems students will meet them. I learned that all students can achieve" (Falk & Ort, 1998, p. 62).

Other teachers point to tasks that offer students multiple ways to demonstrate their knowledge, skills, and understandings about many dimensions and kinds of learning as being most informative and useful. Because these tests provide opportunities for a wide range of students to reach toward higher standards, they also allow a wide range of students to actually demonstrate higher standards. "I learned that low-achieving students can experience success as well as express an element of critical thought that I never believed possible," reported one high school English teacher (Falk & Ort, 1998, p. 62).

With well-designed standards-based performance assessments, a broad range of students are offered a variety of ways to demonstrate their proficiencies. This is an aspect of testing that many consider essential for a test to be fair. In addition, fairness involves providing all students with equal opportunities to experience challenging learning. An elementary teacher raised this issue in her comments:

> This assessment allows many entry points for kids who are at all levels. Hopefully, this will encourage middle and high schools to begin detracking and allowing all children access to the same curriculum and standards. (Falk & Ort, 1998, p. 62)

Developing Insights to Support Teaching

The process of scoring students' work strengthens teachers' understandings of what students should know and be able to do in ways that help teachers to develop more cohesive programs of instruction. Some teachers attribute this to the conversations that take place during and before scoring. As one teacher remarked:

> The discussions that took place during the scoring session made me more aware of expectations for good teaching and learning. They were a catalyst for my planning and for better teaching. (Falk & Ort, 1998, p. 62)

Many teachers say that participation in scoring motivates them to focus on needed changes in their practice. One teacher's comments reflect this view:

> I think I'm going to be teaching a little differently now: group work activities; making sure students understand the concepts of what they're doing; not looking just for the wrong or right answer. That's very important and so is how students are arriving at their answer. (Falk & Ort, 1998, p. 62)

Other teachers credit the process of looking at student work in relation to standards as helping them become more aware of aspects of their discipline and practice that they feel are in need of strengthening. "Scoring student work for this exam has encouraged me to take a closer look at the way I teach math," said an elementary teacher. At the same time, some teachers find that standards-based work validates and supports what they are already doing. Said an elementary-grade teacher, "It confirms and supports the way I teach and makes me realize that I need to keep asking kids for details—getting them to find the specific evidence from their reading" (Falk & Ort, 1998, p. 62).

The benefits of standards-based performance assessments that teachers experience while scoring student work often inspires them to institute changes in their own classroom-based assessment practices.

They do this not just to better prepare their students for tests but also to improve the teaching and learning that go on in their classrooms. "I plan to give kids rubrics detailing what makes 'quality' work," said one elementary teacher. "I will provide more opportunities for revision, self-analysis, and evaluation," said another. A middle school teacher vowed to "make the open-ended questions I ask clear enough to get the information I want to get from the students. I will also make grading criteria very clear, very related to the question, and available to students ahead of time." A high school mathematics teacher who recognized the value of student explanations said, "I will do more testing requiring justifications—help students to become more comfortable explaining their understandings" (Falk & Ort, 1998, p. 62).

Strengthening Teachers' Sense of Professionalism

Teachers' discussions about students' work in relation to standards in contexts such as scoring conferences offer them opportunities to collaborate, to learn from each other, and to validate their knowledge as competent professionals. The comments of those who took part in the scoring sessions for the state tests that I studied demonstrate teachers' appreciation of this: "Meeting with dedicated, concerned teachers was most valuable to me," noted one high school teacher. "I learned from their positive attitudes, from discussing concerns about my students and about future directions for my discipline" (Falk & Ort, 1998, p. 62).

Looking together at student work in relation to standards also provides teachers with time and a way to learn about new practices and educational processes. "I don't think you can underestimate the need that folks have for getting together and having quality time to reflect on all of the changes that are happening in our schools," said one high school social studies teacher (Falk & Ort, 1998, p. 63). The discussing, debating, and sharing of ideas that take place during scoring processes about what is important and how it is demonstrated provide a structure for teachers to engage in the dialogue and inquiry that are recognized essentials of professional growth. As one high school teacher reported: "Scoring sessions provide valuable professional dialogue. It is a great way to do teacher in-service" (Falk & Ort, 1998, p. 63).

Facilitating Change

Group processes for assessing student work galvanize teachers' support for change. They showcase proposed directions for change in teaching and assessment in ways that directly connect to students and their work. When the standards are well developed and the assessments are performance-based, scoring student responses to these assessments gets at the core of what teaching and learning is about. Such involvement heightens the probability that teachers—who are, after all, the key players in enacting any change—will come to understand and embrace the change (Elmore, 1996). Lauren Resnick (1995) emphasizes this fact in her writings about teachers' work with standards:

> Standards documents, even elegant ones with benchmarks and commentary, can affect achievement only if the standards come to be held as personal goals by teachers and students . . . That will happen only if a concerted effort is made to engage teachers and students in a massive and continuing conversation about what students should learn, what kinds of work they should do, and how well they should be expected to do it. (p. 113)

Involving teachers in scoring assessments thus sends an important message. It signals that teachers can be active participants in shaping the direction of school change. It acknowledges the critical role teachers play in education reform. And it puts teachers in their rightful place: At center stage in the school improvement process.

USING STANDARDS-BASED PERFORMANCE ASSESSMENT TO REFLECT ON AND STRENGTHEN TEACHERS' WORK

As the use of standards and performance-based assessments for students has spread, a parallel development has been taking place for teachers. Through the National Board for Professional Teaching Standards certification process, a process that recognizes accomplished teaching, teachers are offered opportunities to reflect on and learn about their practice. National Board for Professional Teaching Standards certification is a process of documenting teaching practice in relation to rigorous standards that reflect excellence in teaching. It involves developing a professional portfolio and taking a written examination that demonstrates how teachers use standards in their everyday work. The portfolio and the examination are evaluated by peers knowledgeable about how to assess work in relation to standards.

Standards Developed by Teachers to Represent the Best of Teaching

The portfolio and the examination consist of a set of tasks designed to embody the National Board standards for one of 30 certification areas, structured around student developmental levels and subject(s) taught. Developed by a committee of teachers, teacher educators, developmental experts, and leaders in the disciplinary fields, the standards represent consensus about an overall vision of excellence in teaching as well as consensus in each certification field about the critical aspects of teaching that distinguish the practice of accomplished teachers. In contrast to the endless lists of facts or esoterica often found in other standards documents, these standards speak to the essentials of great teaching—what a teacher should know and be able to do—in ways that resonate profoundly with those who are closest to classroom practice. My colleague Lorraine Scorsone, one of the first teachers in the early 1990s to become National Board certified, explains:

> When I read [the standards] I literally got goose bumps! I felt so proud to be a teacher! For the first time in my life I read a document that described the moment by moment life of a teacher. It described everything from the littlest nuance to the larger philosophic underpinnings of teaching. For me, [the standards] were tremendously validating because in [them] I saw all my years of study and schooling put in practice. It was as if the collective wisdom of all teachers were articulated and demystified for all interested people. (personal communication, 1999)

Tasks that Call on Teachers to Synthesize, Apply, and Demonstrate Knowledge

In much the same way that high-quality standards-based performance assessments call on students to demonstrate in real-life situations what they know and can do, the National Board portfolio and examination tasks ask teachers to show what they do to support students' learning in the daily context of their classroom. Developing the portfolio entails a good deal of reflection on teaching practices as well as a close look at students' work. Through written narratives, videotapes, and analyses of children's work, candidates are asked to think about, demonstrate, and reflect on their knowledge of children, child development, subject matters, and teaching. They also must show how they use assessment to inform their teaching, how they respond to the varying needs of the different students in their class, and how they establish family, community, and professional partnerships. Below is an example of an entry for the portfolio required for the Early Childhood/Generalist certificate:

Introduction to Your Classroom Community—Teachers are asked to show how they structure their time, establish rules and routines, and organize space and materials in ways that promote children's social development, mutual respect and emerging independence. Teachers submit a written commentary and an accompanying videotape that highlights their interaction with children. (National Board of Professional Teaching Standards, 1999)

Tasks that Model Features of Good Teaching

By asking candidates to demonstrate their knowledge and skills in real-life experiences, the National Board assessment tasks distinguish themselves as a learning challenge. However, a close look at the design of the portfolio entries reveals other qualities that are responsible for making this assessment such a powerful learning experience. The portfolio is notable for its clarity of explanation, its elaboration of details, and its advance notice of requirements for success. Each task is introduced with an explanation of the purposes for the task and the standards the task is designed to assess. A detailed description of the nature of the task and of what the candidate needs to do to complete it are provided. Criteria and guiding questions for each part of the task are presented. Recommendations for how to proceed through the task are offered as well. A description of how the response will be scored is also included.

The National Board tasks are opportunities for teachers to demonstrate their competencies in multiple ways. Application of knowledge, evaluation, analysis, and reflection are both called for as well as promoted by the very nature of the tasks. Teachers who go through the certification process must take a hard look at their teaching practices and become very specific about describing as well as documenting them. Evidence is required to back up all that the candidate has to say. Every step of the process is purposeful and carefully crafted to stimulate reflection, to go deeper into developing and then demonstrating understandings of what is entailed in teaching and learning. No facts can be memorized, no "right answers" produced, to achieve a passing score that entitles one to National Board certification. No "perfect" portfolio is required, either. Only thoughtful reflection on how the standards for accomplished teaching are either present, or not present, in carefully documented work of both the teacher and her students can demonstrate that a teacher has the knowledge, skills, and reflectiveness to identify her practice as meeting the standards.

Offering Insights into Teaching Practice

Some years ago I attended a conference where I heard one of the National Board's pioneer candidates make a presentation. She told the audience that "outside of the birth of my children, this has been the most powerful learning experience of my life." Other teachers who have gone through the process have similar things to say. A survey of 16 New York City teachers who went through the National Board certification process in 1999 found that all of them thought their experience enhanced their professional development. Some of these teachers noted that "the experience forced me to think more deeply about my practice" and "caused me to focus and be more aware of my teaching practices and the standards that make for 'good teaching.'" Others pointed to how going through the process caused them to gain deeper insights about teaching: "This process has thrust me into the role of an inquisitive observer, wanting to learn what is understood by the student." Almost every candidate expressed a desire to continue the process for another year if they did not achieve a passing score the first time. They attributed their commitment to the value of the process itself: of the changes in their teaching as they conscientiously tried to ensure the incorporation of the standards in their practice; of the systematic reflection that has now become an automatic habit of mind; and of the increased learning they're observing in their classrooms.

A New Form of Professional Accountability

Because it systematically documents the best of what we do every day and who we are as educators, the National Board certification process is not only authentic but meaningful. The high expectations of the standards serve as a signpost that can be used to hold ourselves accountable. They make the elements of quality teaching explicit, bringing them out of the private realm of individual teachers' artistry or intuition and instead making them part of a conversation that can deepen our collective understandings about quality teaching, validate our expertise, and improve both our and our students' learning. The standards and the assessment process around them help to define, empower, and improve our profession. As my colleague Lorraine has said,

> I believe holding ourselves accountable and having high expectations can only improve our field and how we're viewed. Sometimes politicians, the press, and the general public at large seem to police schools without adequate knowledge of the complexi-

ties of our profession. Too often we are told what and how to teach by people who have never set foot in the classroom. The standards not only give voice to excellence, they allow teachers to determine and define and inform exemplary teaching.

Empowering Teachers Through Professional Community

Participating in the work that has grown up around National Board standards and assessments not only gives voice to teachers but also helps to break down the isolation that has been a trademark of our profession. National Board work offers teachers a chance to become part of a broader educational community. In standards development work, in mentoring groups that have sprung up around the country to support candidates' journeys through the certification process, and in the portfolio and examination scoring sessions conducted almost entirely by teachers, teachers are able to share ideas and have collegial exchanges. These experiences offer opportunities to access a larger professional vision that stimulates personal growth. The comments of one Boston teacher who just completed a scoring session of portfolio items seem to express these sentiments well: "I'm absolutely exhausted—but can't wait to get back to my classroom. I just wish the other teachers in my building could have had the same experience: imagine how powerful that would be" (Kelly, 1998, p. 2).

PROFESSIONAL LEARNING *IS* THE JOB

In "Professional Development Is the Job," Anthony Alvarado (1998) enumerates ways that educators can create change in order to support students' learning. Children's abilities to learn depend in large part on teachers' abilities to teach. "We will have to find ways of getting deeply into the specifics of how to help students master subject matter. . . and we will have to create contexts that support changes in thinking and pedagogy on the part of teachers" (p. 18).

A focus on how to better support teacher learning is critical to efforts aimed at improving student learning. Schools' abilities to develop students depend on the existence of teachers who are knowledgeable about the critical elements of learning and can employ the strategies that are needed to connect these elements with the understandings of diverse learners. Standards-based and performance-based assessments help teachers to develop this knowledge and these skills. By clarifying goals and purposes, by making expectations explicit, by requiring knowledge to be applied in real-life contexts, and by providing many different ways to demonstrate abilities and skills, standards-based and performance-based assessments lay the groundwork for better teaching. While they do not ensure that teachers will make the necessary connections with the understandings of their students that result in genuine learning, they certainly point teaching in that direction.

Standards-based and performance-based assessments, in their variety of contexts and formats, support teacher learning in several ways. By virtue of what they ask teachers to assess about their students or about themselves, they provide a guide to essential aspects of the learning process. In addition, this kind of assessment leads teachers to engage in evidence-based work—to collect and rely on authentic student or teacher work to reflect on and inform their instructional decisions. By asking teachers to examine their own practice or the work of their students in relation to standards, teachers increase their knowledge of individual students, become better informed about their students' capacities, and receive guidance about what they need to do next to support students' forward development.

I predict that continued use of high-quality standards and performance assessments over time will help teachers become better informed about teaching and learning. As we become more expert about teaching, due in part to what we learn from using standards-based and performance-based assessments, we can expect to witness continued improvement and progress on the part of students. Not only will our overall pedagogical capacity be enhanced, but control of assessment will be brought back into our hands, away from the "outside experts" and commercial testing companies that presently dominate the assessment process.

Well-developed standards-based and performance-based assessments initiate a dynamic process—an "upward-spiraling double helix" of standards and performance that has the potential to transform the culture of teaching (Kelly, 1998, p. 3). As this transformation takes place across the continuum of teaching—from pre-service teacher preparation programs through the careers of experienced teachers—a new vision of teaching will take root in the hearts and minds of teachers by the millions. This vision will be about a seamless connection between assessment, context, teaching, and learning. Through the linkage of evaluation and practice, teachers and students will develop the capacity to monitor and take responsibility for their own learning. If the expectations are appropriate, the evaluations are fair, and the environment is maintained to be risk-free, then teachers and children will feel comfortable and confident. Success will be demystified, attainable, and doable through a variety of pathways. Effort will be the primary requirement. This is what genuine accountability should be about—a learning experience for all who are involved.

REFERENCES

Allen, D. (1998). *Assessing student learning: From grading to understanding.* New York: Teachers College Press.

Alvarado, A. (1998, Winter). Professional development *is* the job. *American Educator, 22*(4), 18–23.

Barrs, M., Ellis, S., Hester, H., & Thomas, A. (1988). *The Primary Language Record.* London: ILEA/Centre for Language in Primary Education.

Cohen, D. K., McLaughlin, M. W. & Talbert, J. E. (1993). *Teaching for understanding: Challenges for policy and practice.* San Francisco: Jossey-Bass.

Darling-Hammond, L., Ancess, J., & Falk, B. (1995). *Authentic assessment in action.* New York: Teachers College Press.

Dorfman, A. (1997, March). *Teachers' understanding of performance assessment.* Paper presented at the annual meeting of the American Educational Research Association, Chicago.

Elmore, R. (1996). Getting to scale with good educational practice. *Harvard Educational Review, 66*(1), 1–26.

Elmore, R. (1997). *Investing in teacher learning: Staff development and instructional improvement in Community School District #2, New York City.* New York: National Commission on Teaching and America's Future.

Falk, B. (1994). *The Bronx New School: Weaving assessment into the fabric of teaching and learning.* New York: National Center for Restructuring Education, Schools, and Teaching (NCREST), Teachers College, Columbia University.

Falk, B. (1995, April). *Authentic assessment as a catalyst for learning: An inquiry model of professional development.* Paper presented at the annual meeting of the American Educational Research Association, San Francisco.

Falk, B. (1998). Testing the way children learn: Principles for valid literacy assessments. *Language Arts, 76*(1), 57–66.

Falk, B., & Darling-Hammond, L. (1993). *The Primary Language Record at P.S. 261: How assessment transforms teaching and learning.* NCREST, Teachers College, Columbia University.

Falk, B., MacMurdy, S., & Darling-Hammond, L. (1995). *Taking a different look: How the Primary Language Record supports teaching for diverse learners.* New York: NCREST, Teachers College, Columbia University.

Falk, B., & Ort, S. (1998, September). Sitting down to score: Teacher learning through assessment. *Phi Delta Kappan, 80*(1), 59–64.

Falk, B., & Ort, S. (1999). *Technical report on the Early Literacy Profile.* New York: NCREST, Teachers College, Columbia University.

Fosnot, C. T. (1989). *Enquiring teachers, enquiring learners.* New York: Teachers College Press.

Giroux, H. A. (1988). *Teachers as intellectuals: Toward a critical pedagogy of learning*. Granby, MA.: Bergin and Garvey.

Kates, L. (1999). *Performance assessment and two teachers' learning: A model of possibility*. Unpublished paper. New York: Teachers College, Columbia University.

Kelly, J. (1998, March). A place called accomplished teaching. *Teacher to Teacher, 9*, 3.

Lieberman, A. (1995). Practices that support teacher development: Transforming conceptions of professional learning. *Phi Delta Kappan, 76*(8), 591–596.

Lieberman, A., & McLaughlin, M. W. (1992). Networks for educational change: Powerful and problematic. *Phi Delta Kappan, 73*(9), 673–677.

Little, J. W. (1992). Teacher development and educational policy. In M. Fullan & A. Hargreaves (Eds.), *Teacher development and educational change* (pp. 170–193). London: Falmer Press.

Little, J. W. (1993). *Teachers' professional development in a climate of educational reform*. New York: NCREST, Teachers College, Columbia University.

Meier, D. (1992). Reinventing teaching. *Teachers College Record, 93*(4), 594–609.

Meisels, S., Liaw, F., Dorfman, A., & Fails, R. (1993, April). *The Work Sampling System: Reliability and validity of a performance assessment for young children*. Paper presented at the annual meeting of the American Educational Research Association, Atlanta.

National Board for Professional Teaching Standards. (1999). *Early childhood/ generalist assessment and scoring kit*. San Antonio, TX: The Psychological Corporation.

National Commission on Teaching and America's Future. (1996). *What matters most: Teaching for America's future*. New York: Author.

National Commission on Teaching and America's Future. (1997). *Doing what matters most: Investing in quality teaching*. New York: Author.

New York State Education Department. (1999). *The Early Literacy Profile: An assessment instrument*. Albany: New York State Education Department.

Noble, J. A., & Smith, M. L. (1994). *Old and new beliefs about measurement-driven reform: "The more things change, the more they remain the same"* (CSE Technical Report 373). Los Angeles: National Center for Research on Evaluation, Standards, and Student Testing.

Resnick, L. (1995). Standards for education. In D. Ravitch (Ed.), *Debating the future of American standards*. Washington, D.C.: The Brookings Institution.

Sheingold, K., Heller, J. I., & Storms, B. A. (1997, April). *On the mutual influence of teachers' professional development and assessment quality in curricular reform*. Paper presented at the annual meeting of the American Educational Research Association, Chicago.

Thomas, W., Storms, B., Sheingold, K., Heller, J., Paulukonis, S., Nunez, A., & Wing, J. (1995). *California Learning Assessment System portfolio assessment research and development project: Final report*. Princeton, NJ: Center for Performance Assessment, Educational Testing Service.

Wilson, S. M. (1990). A conflict of interests: The case of Mark Black. *Educational Evaluation and Policy Analysis, 12*(3), 293–310.

CHAPTER 9

Lessons from an Inquiring School: Forms of Inquiry and Conditions for Teacher Learning

LAURA STOKES

Everybody is asking themselves, "Is what I am doing helping, or not helping? Am I doing it because it's easy for me, or because it's good for the kids? . . . What can we do to change our practices? Are we really going where we want to go? Are our practices really reflecting what our goals are?"

—Teacher describing the professional community at Will Rogers Learning Community school

The image of teacher-as-researcher has become a familiar one. The rise in visibility of the teacher-research movement (Cochran-Smith & Lytle, 1993, 1999; Hollingsworth & Sockett, 1994; Noffke & Stevenson, 1995) and the lasting appeal of Schön's notion of the "reflective practitioner"(1983, 1991) have helped practitioners and researchers alike to imagine teachers not only as consumers of others' knowledge but also as *creators* of knowledge about teaching and learning. Similarly, the notion that a school faculty can (even must) work together as a professional community of practice and of inquiry has become a fundamental principle of progressive education reform (Barth, 1990; Darling-Hammond, 1993; Elmore, Peterson, & McCarthy, 1996; Fullan, 1993; Holly, 1991; Lieberman, 1995, 1996; Newmann and Associates, 1996). Many prominent school reform networks—including the Coalition of Essential Schools, Accelerated Schools, the Southern Maine Partnership, the Philadelphia Schools Collaborative, and the Bay Area School Reform Collaborative—try to foster a professional culture of inquiry as an integral condition of and contributor to a high-quality environment for teaching and learning.

While these ideas are present in the discourse of reform, the fact remains that most teachers experience precious little support in their workplaces for critically inquiring into their practices. "Professional culture of inquiry"remains less a reality than a phantasmagoric ideal. With the exception of a modest number of studies, the action of inquiry as teachers in schools really experience it remains hidden inside a black box (see Goldsberry et al., 1995; Wagner, 1997, 1998; Watkins, 1995). The absence of grounded portrayals can perpetuate unrealistic notions, including the common (mis)conception that inquiry in reform context is as straightforward as moving teachers rapidly through a cycle of data collection that will point to clear directions for change.

In this chapter I portray the multiple forms of teacher inquiry that arose over five years' time in one elementary school, Will Rogers Learning Community. Each form of inquiry conditioned teacher learning in a different way—sometimes enabling and sometimes constraining teachers' collective or individual abilities to gain knowledge in relation to questions they were interested in. Furthermore, the different forms of inquiry were heavily intertwined with the moral values, norms, and beliefs that teachers held in relation to the problems they were inquiring into and the goals they held out for students. The variations in inquiry form were important to teachers' ability to examine teaching strategies and also to probe into dilemmas associated with equity and race. My hope is that the experiences of Rogers school can contribute to a more complex and realistic appreciation of the promises and the challenges of sustaining an inquiring school culture.

WILL ROGERS LEARNING COMMUNITY

Will Rogers Learning Community is in the Santa Monica-Malibu Unified School District, an urban district adjacent to Los Angeles serving roughly 12,000 students. A 50-year-old neighborhood school of 700-plus students, Rogers sits in a community that combines rent-controlled apartments housing a relatively stable population of people in poverty, upscale beachside shops and homes, and commercial strips lined with fast-food outlets and graffiti-embellished storefronts. The students at Rogers reflect the considerable socioeconomic and language diversity of the south side of Santa Monica: 61% of the students are of ethnic minority backgrounds (primarily Latino, and also African American and Asian); 31% percent are Limited English Proficient; 12% have disabilities; and nearly 50% qualify for a free or reduced lunch. The teaching staff at Rogers is ethnically diverse. White and Latina teachers comprise the larger groups, with small numbers of African-American and Asian teachers. Rogers has had a pattern of relatively low teacher and administrator turnover. The principal during this period was an energetic, respected, and knowledgeable leader.

The staff of Rogers school embraced the image of teacher learning and professional culture that Judith Warren Little characterizes succinctly as the "systematic, sustained, and collective study of student work—coupled with a collective effort to figure out the roots of student work in the practices and choices of teaching" (in press, p. 3). Rogers participated in two multi-year grant-funded reform projects that supported inquiry-based learning and change. One was a state-funded school restructuring project that included creation of the California Center for School Restructuring (CCSR), intended to support the 144 participating schools. Working from the notion that "the missing link in the restructuring equation is a robust 'culture of inquiry'" (Szabo, 1996, p. 76), the CCSR built explicit practitioner inquiry processes into the restructuring work. School teams were to specify "critical questions" and analyze student work to ascertain the extent to which "ALL students are habitually experiencing" (or not) positive outcomes (CCSR, 1996). The other project was a district-initiated reform initiative funded by a grant from the Los Angeles Annenberg Metropolitan Project (LAAMP). A core activity included voluntary inquiry groups in school sites that met in structured, biweekly dialogue sessions, with the help of a critical friend from outside the school. District leaders believed this process of inquiry would enable administrators and teachers to focus on the values and beliefs that underlay instructional practices. Both reform projects espoused a strong social justice agenda focusing on equitable student outcomes, and both saw practitioner inquiry as a kind of teacher learning that could lead to those outcomes.

Over five years' time—and with tremendous effort and persistence amid conflict—the Rogers staff's stance toward learning and professional practice evolved to the extent that systematic, critical self-study had become habitual.[1]

INQUIRY FORM AND CONDITIONS FOR TEACHER LEARNING

The different forms of inquiry arose from different kinds of questions and conditioned teacher learning quite differently.

Inquiry Form 1: Whole-School Assessment of Learning Outcomes

In the first form of inquiry that developed at Rogers, which I identify as *whole-school assessment of learning outcomes,* all teachers participated in development of performance benchmarks, created and administered assessments, scored them, and examined the results. Teachers worked in grade-level groups to evaluate student work and talk about it. Also, a staff member created a data base of all scores, making results available to everyone in the school. The entire staff spent a full week of pupil-free days each February discussing these results. The school developed this form of inquiry with support of the state restructuring project—and it was only after three years of trial and error that they developed the normative commitment, emotional resilience, and technical skill to jointly examine and discuss learning outcomes across different ethnic backgrounds. This form eventually became refined as one in which the whole staff carried out cross-sectional and longitudinal comparisons of student learning outcomes through their own school assessments, publicly reported and discussed data, and collectively deliberated on their implications.

Teacher Learning That This Form Enabled. This form of inquiry produced a comprehensive portrait of student performance in reading and writing. Because the whole school was involved in generating the data, the teachers developed truly *common* knowledge about student learning. Over time, the staff learned a sequence of specific lessons from these data. First, in 1994–95, they saw that students were not reading as well as teachers had assumed based on intuitive judgement. Later, in 1996–97, they saw that across the board, students were demonstrating improvement in reading and writing as a result of the changes they were making in the program. However, when they disaggregated scores by racial groups, they found a persistent pattern of what they called "inequitable achievement."[2] The staff inferred that they were getting better at teaching reading, on average, but they were not remedying the problem of differential achievement. At this point, their collective focus shifted from pedagogy to equity, and they began to inquire into their strategies and expectations for students of different racial backgrounds.

Lessons learned from this form of inquiry provided important motivation for change. This motivation stemmed from the school staff's collective belief that they—not the students, not the families, not society—were responsible for the variation in student outcomes. Note that in a school where the staff does not accept this responsibility, such data may not generate motivation to change. The Rogers' staff's technical capacity for inquiry was tightly intertwined with their beliefs.

Learning That This Form Did Not Enable. Even when teachers inferred that new teaching approaches might be called for, this form of inquiry—these data, the norms of public exposure, and the process of whole-school deliberation on a predetermined schedule—did not create conditions supporting teachers' experimentation with new approaches. Also, the one-dimensional portrait of student learning did not provide in-depth understanding about the learning conditions of particular groups of students. This form thus created broad-brush knowledge and motivation, but little support for specific actions of change.

Inquiry Form 2: Small-Group Action Research Projects

In the second form of inquiry, which I identify as *small-group action research projects,* grade-level teams developed focused research questions quasi-independently from other groups. Teams then developed their own approaches to pursuing those questions—their own mini-experiments and reflective processes—and prepared reports for their colleagues. This form arose as a descendant of the whole-school assessments when discussions of outcome data prompted new questions. These were joint inquiries but at a small-group level, and they were focused more on change in programs and practices than on creation of outcome data. Like the first form of inquiry, this second one demanded school-wide participation and had expectation of public reporting.

Learning That This Form Enabled. Teachers' ability to use this form of inquiry for learning and change depended on the degree to which individuals in the small groups shared beliefs and norms about teaching, learning, and students. It also depended upon the degree to which the inquiry tools that groups used were well-suited not only to the questions they wanted to answer, but also to some of their underlying beliefs.

For those groups where teachers began with a threshold level of shared beliefs, this form created conditions in which groups could carry out focused studies of student learning and experiment with new practices in a context of ongoing, supportive critical reflection. This form permitted subgroups to attend to different interests and responsibilities. For example, one group experimented jointly with a new series of lessons to move students toward a grade-level writing standard, another tried out new behaviors toward a group of disengaged students, and a third compared outcomes for English Language Learners across different school programs. The common knowledge the groups had gained from the whole-school assessments created a context for their narrower studies.

Learning That This Form Did Not Enable. Precisely because this form was data-driven and came with a schedule for public reporting, however, these action research groups did not create a context in which teachers could work through deep-seated differences in ideologies of teaching. For example, when one group wanted to conduct a survey of students' subjective experiences of school, the process of creating the survey items brought to the surface such profound differences of teacher belief that this form of inquiry did not help them learn together. In fact, it was the school's (and thus this group's) inquiry into the problem of racial inequity that brought the limitations of this form into sharp relief. Individual group members discovered that they held dramatically different beliefs about whether students at Rogers experienced racial discrimination and, more generally, about whether one's race affected one's experience of school at all. In response to pressure to carry out the study on a schedule, the teachers in this group experienced their divergences of belief as conflict that was obstructive rather than as opportunity for reflection that could be illuminating. Furthermore, individuals in this group differed in the extent to which they gave validity to what they called "student voice," in this case students' self-reports as reflected in a survey. While some teachers felt that students' reports of differential treatment according to their race was "a victim response" that signaled "manipulation" of oversensitive teachers, others felt that "if students are *feeling* it, it's a problem." The student survey was not an effective instrument of inquiry for this group because a survey demands some fundamental belief in self-report.

This group finally managed to conduct a joint student survey, but only because they had publicly committed to do so. The persistent differences of belief among group members meant that individuals drew different conclusions—that is, generated different knowledge—from the same set of evidence: "We all interpreted the [survey] data completely differently . . . We didn't anticipate what kinds of issues would come up in the survey. It was a really emotional thing. We're all at different levels of experience dealing with these issues." The experience of framing their differences as arguments frayed their relationships, impeded individual inclination to change (because they only became more polarized), impeded their collective ability to learn, and, ultimately, limited the group's contribution to the school staff's collective store of knowledge.

Inquiry Form 3: Individual Reflection with
Small-Group Support

In the third form of inquiry, which I identify as *individual reflection with small-group support*, teachers voluntarily met twice a month in support groups for the purpose of critically reflecting on their own practices, with an emphasis on exploring the values and beliefs that underlay them. The school created this form of inquiry with the support of the district's reform project. Over time, this form became increasingly important and increasingly differentiated from the other two. This occurred as the school staff became more aware that deliberation about outcome data—however locally situated—did not necessarily foster change. They became more persuaded that the problem of inequitable achievement might be rooted in beliefs about students more than in teaching technique per se. They thus grew more acutely aware that change strongly implicated individual practice in a way that was primarily personal. As one teacher said,

> Unlike with other topics, when you're talking about race, you're talking about people. If you talk to me about my racial practices in the classroom, you're talking about *me*—you're talking about my parents, you're talking about how I was raised, and my experiences as a person, and there's no way to separate that.

With regularly scheduled meetings that were gently facilitated by an external critical friend, this form of inquiry permitted a very fluid reflective discourse in which teachers probed any problems of interest to them, with or without systematic data. They did so in a context of collegiality, but with group privacy and with *no* expectation of public reporting. Whereas the other forms emphasized production of public knowledge about student learning, this form emphasized generation of self-knowledge. Teachers made the distinction this way:

> The other forms are product-driven, there's work that needs to be done, whereas this can be more self-generative, more reflection, it can be very non-product-oriented. So it puts a piece in that has been missing. [In the other groups] you can't discuss what you're feeling because there's no time. If you do, you don't get your work done. In this group people are willing to deal with problems.

It was this more intimate feel that enabled teachers to "say things you wouldn't say" in other settings.

The critical friend role made an important contribution to teachers' ability to explore difficult issues because the supportive outsider could shoulder some responsibility for upholding the norms of conversation. The critical friend reinforced the legitimacy and value of what the teachers were doing, and was also a conduit of information—of books and articles—about the problems at hand. They treated readings less as a knowledge resource and more as prompt and permission for personal reflection. Some white teachers began to talk about the meanings of their whiteness, and teachers of various backgrounds began to say things to people of other races that, for all their lives, they had only said to people of their own race.

Learning That This Form Enabled. The norms and processes of this third form gave more legitimacy to the idea that changing practice was a complex, long-term effort involving both technical and moral clarity and change. Individuals could create a fit between what they wanted to learn and how they might go about changing. This form fostered reflective experimentation with new behaviors and ideas in a setting that valued individuality and multiplicity of perspective, and that also granted teachers an individual pace of learning and change.

One teacher, for example, discovered in her small-group action research project that she lent out reading books from her personal library to children whose parents she judged to be reliable, and did not lend her books to children whose parents might not make sure they were returned. She was unwittingly limiting the education of the most disadvantaged children. She was emotionally devastated by this realization because she feared this one example might be the tip of the iceberg in her practice. It was only in this more individualistic and more fluid form of personal inquiry, though, that she took the time and had the support to continue looking systematically at her teaching behaviors and at the beliefs underlying them to the extent that she could make deep-seated changes.

In this reflective, self-paced form of inquiry, the legitimate subjects of inquiry were the content of teachers' beliefs and the nature of their personal histories. Here, and *only* here, was conflict a legitimate avenue to greater understanding. It was this form of inquiry, not the others, that enabled Rogers teachers to begin, eventually, to approach the problem of inequitable achievement not as a technical problem awaiting a single solution, but rather as a dilemma that could be approached from any of a number of morally based actions.

Learning That This Form Did Not Enable. It would be a mistake to infer, however, that this form enabled all teachers to find clear resolution about the most difficult, ingrained problems. It was never so simple. As one teacher suggests, questioning one's deep beliefs about race took a real toll on individuals and on the staff as a whole:

> In this inquiry group we are struggling with race on a deeper level. But it's very painful, and you can't see the end, it could go on forever . . . If it's too hurtful, and too painful, who's going to want to do it? . . . It's like, how does that help you continue to go on and do good work?

For teachers who were personally prepared to identify and challenge deeply held beliefs, this form served as a setting where they could undergo a truly transformative experience if they sustained their emotional energy for it. For teachers who were not prepared to question whether their personal beliefs were consistent with the espoused goals of equity, this form did not provide for that kind of experience. And for all teachers, this personal reflection brought about considerable anguish. This inquiry form, in other words, created learning conditions that they felt were necessary to asking the hardest questions and addressing the most difficult problems, but those conditions were not a panacea.

Beyond these limitations, teachers also found varying degrees of success in linking personal inquiry to change at the level of the school. On the one hand, this form of inquiry gave teachers a chance to approach school-level decision making more thoughtfully when whole-school issues found their way into these groups: "We're more prepared to look at different sides." On the other hand, when individuals created radical change proposals within these groups, they sometimes found it difficult to extend those proposals to the level of whole-school consideration. Some teachers thus remained deeply frustrated that whole-school deliberation could remain at least somewhat immune to personal insights about racial inequities.

LESSONS FROM AN INQUIRING SCHOOL

In their fifth year, the Rogers staff began to see the goal they had been striving for in race-based patterns of achievement: finally, all student groups were showing greater growth in literacy *and* students of color were closing the gap. This case shows the promise of a professional community's investment in critical self-study and experimentation. Those benefits came with some costs, however, and a school staff would want to pursue the promise of inquiry with sufficient appreciation of the challenges that lie down the road. In this section I explore some insights about practitioner inquiry, learning, and change that stem from the Rogers case.

Developing Both Normative and Technical Capacities for Inquiry

It is commonly understood that the practice of inquiry requires technical mastery of tools and processes for self-study. What is less obvious—and more complicated—is that practitioner inquiry is first a normative process. A professional culture of inquiry develops both normative and technical capacities for inquiry.

Normative Capacity. A school's normative capacity for inquiry is the staff's collective embrace and enactment of values that support self-study as an important kind of learning and process of change. At Rogers, two values in particular created a normative context supporting inquiry practice. One was *critical will*, by which I mean genuine willingness to call practice into question not only at the level of procedure but also at the level of core beliefs and principles. The principal and teachers were tempted many times to call a halt to self-study because of the heavy demands it made on their individual and collective emotions. Over the five years they developed the resilience to sustain critical reflection. The foundation of this critical will and the key contributor to their resilience was the moral imperative to redress inequity. Many members of the Rogers staff felt this imperative internally and espoused it publicly and repeatedly, and the whole school received support for it from two external reform projects.

The second value was *collectivity of effort* to learn and change from self-study. The principal and many of the teachers struggled quite consciously to sustain a spirit of collective responsibility for student learning throughout the five years. At times, this struggle meant they had to slow down the pace of overall change so as not to alienate individuals or subgroups. Working to prevent splintering and to galvanize effort toward common goals consumed tremendous energy; however, enough teachers shared a vision of themselves as a collective entity that this was the prevailing stance.

Teachers' experience of inquiry within their workplace and as part of a whole-school change effort differs in important ways from teachers' experiences of inquiry in a teacher network (such as the National

Writing Project) independent of their school. For better or worse, existing workplace relationships and routines create a powerful context for teacher learning. Norms supporting teacher inquiry are nontraditional in schools (Little, 1982, 1990), and there are many cases in the literature in which individual teachers, subgroups, and whole faculties struggled unsuccessfully to infuse those norms into the professional community of their workplace (Goldsberry et al., 1995; Miller & Martens, 1990; Wagner, 1998). At Rogers, on the other hand, the professional community embraced critical inquiry as a collective effort.

Technical Capacity. A school community's technical capacity for inquiry includes the structures, processes, knowledge, and activities by which the school staff does the actual work of inquiring into their practice. At Rogers, several technical elements eventually bundled together in such a way that over five years, three distinct forms of inquiry evolved. Those forms of inquiry differed in the intended *purpose* for the particular inquiry activity; in the *processes and instruments* used to gather and examine evidence; and in the *norms of behavior* (confidentiality, collectivity, etc.). Teachers' particular learning purposes (the questions they asked, the units of change they focused on) gave shape to the inquiry forms; reciprocally, the features of inquiry forms (norms, tools, processes) created conditions that served specific learning functions. Table 9.1 summarizes key features of the different forms.

The Importance of Relatedness *and* Differentiation of Inquiry Form

The overarching goal at Rogers was to redress the pattern in which students of color had less access to academic success and advantages than white students. This mission helped create coherence among the different inquiry activities that evolved. Every year, the school staff worked through a deliberative, often weeks-long process to develop "essential questions" about their practices as a school and their effects on students. These questions created a focus and purpose for learning and school reform that all teachers were aware of and to which many were genuinely committed. Thus, while teachers participated in a variety of inquiry (and other learning) opportunities simultaneously, the focus of the essential questions lent coherence to the efforts.

However important it was that a shared sense of mission underlay multiple inquiry activities, it was the differences between the various forms of inquiry that helped the staff begin to get at what they really wanted to understand and change—the pattern of racial inequity in

Table 9.1. Evolved System of Differentiated Inquiry Forms at Rogers School

Inquiry Form	Purpose	Unit(s) of Analysis	Types of Evidence	Norms	Structures	Processes/Tools
Whole-School Assessment of Learning Outcomes	Summative: • Assess/ portray school effectiveness	Whole school	Quantitative (test scores) Uniform over time	Public—grade-level team and whole school All participate	• Cycle of: - pre-service days, - semi-monthly mtgs of grade-level groups - mid-year institute - spring reflection • Computerized database	• Essential questions • School-spec'd, group-developed instruments (assessments, rubrics) • Data collection and analysis procedures • Protocol discussion format OR analyst's report
Small-Group Action Research Projects	Formative: • Build deeper causal understanding • Support group-level or program-specific change • Motivate individual learning	School programs Subgroups of teachers Individual teachers	Multiple forms, mostly qualitative	Public (with discretion for privacy)—grade-level team and whole school All participate	• Cycle of: - pre-service days, - semi-monthly mtgs of grade-level groups - mid-year institute - spring reflection	• Essential questions • Any instruments, multiple kinds of evidence • Protocol discourse format
Indiv'l Reflection with Group Support	Exploratory: • Foster individual learning and change	Individual teachers	Story and anecdote	Private— confidential within small group Voluntary	• Semi-monthly small-group meetings all year • External critical friend	• Free exploration, reflection • "Hard" questions • Any relevant resources

152

learning outcomes. Furthermore, the variation in forms addressed one of most vexing tensions in any approach to change: the relationship and interplay between the individual and the collective. The system of differentiated inquiry forms that arose at Rogers created conditions for teacher learning and change that are consistent with Little and McLaughlin's powerful notion of "collective autonomy" (1993), in which a balance is struck between interests of individuals and the collective judgement and authority of the group. Rogers teachers could focus on different units of analysis and change (e.g., the whole school, their-grade level group, a specific school program, their own classroom, their personal beliefs) and they could gain knowledge and skills related to different problems and questions (e.g., strategies for teaching reading, contours of student achievement, beliefs about race and equity). The complexity of this system of inquiry was vitally important in the context of a school restructuring effort because that approach to reform demands that teachers become knowledgeable change agents both inside and beyond their classrooms.

The Challenges of Inquiry-Based Learning and Change

It is important to remember that it took the Rogers staff three years (and the support of a state reform project) to learn how to generate data that painted a sufficiently clear and credible picture of student learning outcomes. And it took five years (and the support of an additional district reform project) to develop the complex system of multiple inquiry forms that enabled Rogers staff to address the problem of equity to the extent that they began to see real improvement in those student outcomes. An appreciation of the challenges they faced along the way may help practitioners delve into critical self-study with open eyes.

Inquiry Generates Powerful Learning—But Also Guilt and Conflict. Once the Rogers staff mastered inquiry processes well enough to generate knowledge they trusted, the teachers afforded that knowledge greater credibility than they afforded other sources of knowledge. They learned more and better lessons from inquiry than they did from their personal intuitive judgement and external information such as standardized test scores. Inquiry-generated knowledge felt more "real"— more believable, immediate, and inescapable—and powerful because it was simultaneously more valid, more in-common, more specific to their students, and more imbued with moral weight than knowledge from other sources.

Inquiry-generated insights did not come without a price, however. The teachers' sense of their moral purpose as educators was concrete, immediate, and present in their relationships with their students. Thus, when they generated knowledge about student learning and about their own (and their colleagues') treatment of students, they often felt guilt, anger, and anxiety. Furthermore, what teachers observed rarely produced clear implications for change and never produced simple ones. Learning from inquiry sometimes motivated and guided change, but just as often it caused paralysis, resistance, and open conflict.[3] As one teacher put it, "We've had a lot of ah-ha's and some of them come with tears. And you won't understand the whole process unless you're here when we're fighting."

The Challenge to Voice Difference and Sustain Professional Community. The fact that Rogers teachers chose to inquire deeply into the meanings of racial experience as part of their study of inequitable achievement brings into especially sharp relief the importance of raising hard issues and the potential for those issues to fracture the community. Many teachers at Rogers made an effort to voice differences of beliefs and assumption stemming from their personal experiences of being schooled, from their reasons for becoming schoolteachers, and from the hopes they held out for children. With teachers of color leading the way, ever-increasing numbers of the Rogers staff (including the principal) made conscious efforts to speak out against racism and inequity of all kinds. They did so out of awareness that not to give voice to these ideals signaled implicit support of an educational system that produced (and tolerated) inequity. At the same time, however, Rogers teachers were aware that the dialogue they groped toward—whether public or private—*always* had the potential to fracture the relational bonds they valued and that they believed were necessary to their goals.

The likelihood that school faculties who critically examine their own practices will encounter the problem of racial inequity in student experiences and outcomes extends a challenge to practitioners and school reform enthusiasts alike. It is difficult enough to learn how to ask hard questions about one's work, but it may be even more difficult to sustain a discourse about the implications of what one learns.

The Uncertain Relationship Between Inquiry and Change. Even if inquiry into practice seems to be a powerful—even necessary—kind of teacher learning, it is still the case that teacher learning relates to school improvement in complex, probably uncontrollable ways. Even when the professional staff shares important norms and values, schools are political organizations in which competing interests and knowledge sources vie for power. Also, the realities of teaching and school keeping are such that there are very few problems awaiting simple answers.[4] At Rogers, any inquiry activity generated evidence that individuals and subgroups could use to support any of a number of actions that could be deemed reasonable and yet that sometimes opposed one another. In one particularly heated year-long discussion, teachers used student outcome data to argue convincingly both for and against reconstituting the school's "house" system of grouping students. In reality, data do not provide answers about intractable social problems, including those in schools; rather, they give fuel to a meaning-making process in an organizational context characterized by ambiguity and conflict. That is the normal role of social science within a democratic society (Levin, 1975). It was precisely because of this uncertainty about the implications of "hard" data that teachers needed more reflective and experimental forms of inquiry to explore many avenues of change. And it was precisely because positive change involves so many dimensions of practice—belief, moral values, technical and pedagogical knowledge—that teachers needed these diverse opportunities for experimentation and reflection over time.

Inquiring with Eyes Wide Open

Practitioner inquiry is a more complex process than many reformers want it to be, one that makes very strong and intertwined normative and technical demands. The Rogers staff's effort to preserve new norms and practices against the continual threat of factionalism and individualism serves as a reminder that norms of collective inquiry run against the grain of prevailing school culture. On the other hand, their sustained effort to critically examine student outcomes, teaching practice, and the beliefs underlying practice did, in fact, enable them to learn and change in ways they had not been able to before. They began to break a pattern of inequitable outcomes that had persisted throughout the school's history.

The lesson from this case is not that the particular system of inquiry forms that evolved at Rogers should be "implemented." In fact, the Rogers principal issues the following admonition to any observer of their case: "You can't learn from this story if you interpret it as a planned model." Rather, the lesson is that school practitioners—and the reformers and researchers who support them—are more likely to develop capacity for inquiry-based learning if they have their eyes wide open to the complex realities of inquiry-in-practice.

NOTES

1. This chapter does not discuss the process of cultural evolution in which these forms arose and developed. For the full-length case study see Stokes, 1999.

2. Throughout the paper, all quotes attributed to school staff are taken from audiotaped interviews or field observation notes between March 1995 and June 1998.

3. See Hargreaves, 1994, for an analysis of the role emotion—especially guilt—and conflict plays in teachers' work. See Achinstein (1998) for an analysis of the role of conflict in teacher community.

4. Larry Cuban's distinction between problems (which have technical solutions) and dilemmas (which have no solutions, but can be addressed reasonably from a range of values position) rings very true to the Rogers experience (Cuban, 1992).

REFERENCES

Achinstein, B. (1998). *The ties that bind: Conflict within teacher professional communities*. Unpublished doctoral dissertation. Stanford, CA: Stanford University.

Barth, R. (1990). *Improving schools from within*. San Francisco: Jossey-Bass.

California Center for School Restructuring. (1996). *The SB 1274 Support Network: Joint work for 1996–97*. Foster City, CA: San Mateo County Office of Education; Author.

Cochran-Smith, M., & Lytle, S. L. (1993). *Inside/outside: Teacher research and knowledge*. New York: Teachers College Press.

Cochran-Smith, M., & Lytle, S. L. (1999). Relationships of knowledge and practice: Teacher learning in communities. *Review of Research in Education*, (Vol. 24; pp. 249–305). Washington, DC: American Educational Research Association.

Cuban, L. (1992). Managing dilemmas while building professional communities. *Educational Researcher, 21*(1), 4–11.

Darling-Hammond, L. (1993). Reframing the school reform agenda: Developing capacity for school transformation. *Phi Delta Kappan, 74*(10), 752–761.

Elmore, R. F., Peterson, P., & McCarthy, S. J. (1996). *Restructuring in the classroom: Teaching, learning, and school organization*. San Francisco: Jossey-Bass.

Fullan, M. (1993). *Change forces: Probing the depths of educational reform*. London: Falmer Press.

Goldsberry, L., Holt, A., Johnson, K., MacDonald, G., Poliquin, R., & Potter, L. (1995). The evolution of a restructuring school: The New Suncook case. In A. Lieberman, (Ed.), *The work of restructuring schools: Building from the ground up* (pp. 136–156). New York: Teachers College Press.

Hargreaves, A. (1994). *Changing teachers, changing times: Teachers' work and culture in the postmodern age.* New York: Teachers College Press.

Hollingsworth, S., & Sockett, H. (Eds.). (1994). *Teacher research and educational reform.* Chicago: University of Chicago Press; National Society for the Study of Education.

Holly, P. (1991). Action research: The missing link in the creation of schools as centers of inquiry. In A. Lieberman, & L. Miller, (Eds.), *Staff development for education in the 90s: New demands, new realities, new perspectives* (pp. 133–157). New York: Teachers College Press.

Levin, H. M. (1975). Education, life chances, and the courts: The role of social science evidence. *Law and Contemporary Problems, 39*(2), 217–240.

Lieberman, A. (Ed.). (1995). *The work of restructuring schools: Building from the ground up.* New York: Teachers College Press.

Lieberman, A. (1996). Practices that support teacher development: Transforming conceptions of professional learning. In M. McLaughlin, & I. Oberman, (Eds.), *Teacher learning: New policies, new practices.* New York: Teachers College Press.

Little, J. W. (1982). Norms of collegiality and experimentation: Workplace conditions of school success. *American Educational Research Journal, 19*(3), 325–340.

Little, J. W. (1990). The persistence of privacy: Autonomy and initiative in teachers' professional relations. *Teachers College Record, 91*(4), 509–526.

Little, J. W. (in press). Organizing schools for teacher learning. In L. Darling-Hammond & G. Sykes (Eds.), *Teaching as the learning profession: Handbook of teaching and policy.* San Francisco: Jossey-Bass.

Little, J. W., & McLaughlin, M. W. (Eds.). (1993). *Teachers' work: Individuals, colleagues, and contexts.* New York: Teachers College Press.

Miller, J. L., & Martens, M. L. (1990, Fall). Hierarchy and imposition in collaborative inquiry: Teacher-researchers' reflections on recurrent dilemmas. *Educational Foundations,* 41–59.

Newmann, F., & Associates. (1996). *Authentic achievement: Restructuring schools for intellectual quality.* San Francisco: Jossey-Bass.

Noffke, S., & Stevenson, R. (Eds.). (1995). *Educational action research: Becoming practically critical.* New York: Teachers College Press.

Schön, D. (1983). *The reflective practitioner.* New York: Basic Books.

Schön, D. (Ed.). (1991). *The reflective turn: Case studies in and on educational practice.* New York: Teachers College Press.

Stokes, L. (1999). *Becoming an inquiring school.* Unpublished doctoral dissertation. Stanford, CA: Stanford University.

Szabo, M. (1996). Rethinking restructuring: Building habits of effective inquiry. In M. McLaughlin, & I. Oberman, (Eds.), *Teacher learning: New policies, new practices* (pp. 73–91). New York: Teachers College Press.

Wagner, J. (1997). Discourse innovations in a restructuring school: Alternative perspectives on linking research and practice. *The Elementary School Journal, 97*(3), 271–292.

Wagner, J. (1998). The pragmatics of practitioner research: Linking new knowledge with power in an urban elementary school. Under review: *The Elementary School Journal*.

Watkins, J. M. (1995, April). *Growing a culture of inquiry: Collaborative action research in systemic change*. Paper presented at the annual meeting of the American Educational Research Association, New Orleans.

CHAPTER 10

The Narrative as an *Experience Text:* Writing Themselves Back In

ANNA RICHERT ERSHLER

President Abraham Lincoln was a well-known storyteller. In one of his stories he tells of a journey through the rainy backlands of Illinois. "When I was a young lawyer," Lincoln began,

> and Illinois was little settled, I, with other lawyers, used to ride the circuit. Once a long spell of pouring rain flooded the whole country. Ahead of us was Fox River, larger than all the rest and we could not help saying to each other, "If these small streams give us so much trouble, how shall we get over Fox River?" Darkness fell before we had reached that stream, and we all stopped at a log tavern, had our horses put up, and resolved to pass the night. Here we were right glad to fall in with the Methodist Presiding Elder of the circuit, who rode it in all weather, knew all its ways, and could tell us all about Fox River. So we all gathered around him, and asked him if he knew about the crossing of Fox River. "I have crossed it often, and understand it well. But I have one fixed rule with regard to Fox River: I never cross it till I reach it" (Sandburg, 1959, pp. 19–20).

I think a lot about how to prepare new teachers to cross the Fox Rivers of their early school placements. Like Lincoln and his colleagues, teachers—especially novice teachers—wonder how they will fjord the next raging river. They imagine how things will be. They anticipate what they and others (students, parents, administrators) will say, want, and do. But until they are at that river, the truth is that they cannot cross it. Nor can someone tell them how. Once they have crossed it, however, they will be better prepared to cross the next one. That is, if they can learn from the experience.

This chapter is about that process—learning from experience. It describes a narrative methodology I designed to facilitate that learning. The underlying premises of the methodology are that teachers can learn from their school experiences if they have the opportunity to do so, and that experience is the most powerful of all contexts for teacher learning. While it is impossible to cross Fox River before one gets there, it is also probably true that if you have crossed the river once, and thought about how you accomplished that feat, crossing it the next time will be easier. Our Methodist Elder above says he understands Fox River well. Our teacher learning challenge here is to arrive at that place of understanding.

There is a corollary to my argument that experience is a powerful context for learning. It is that learning and experience are not one and the same. Nor does learning necessarily follow from experience. In order to learn from experience, one must think about it and make sense of it. Given the press of demands facing teachers every minute of every day, productive learning from experience is difficult, in fact. In the following pages, I will discuss one strategy for linking teacher experience and learning. I will draw on my current experience working with novice teachers in urban settings who, like the curcuit lawyers Lincoln describes, cannot quite imagine how they will ever get across their own Fox Rivers.

LEARNING FROM EXPERIENCE AND THE NOVICE TEACHER

The puzzles of teaching abound for all teachers: "Should I use this book, or that?" "Would Nika do better with one math partner or another?" "Should I start the project on Friday, or would Monday be a better day to begin?" No one experiences those puzzles more profoundly than novice teachers. The novices with whom I work tell me that in facing the myriad of dilemmas of their everyday practice, they have trouble knowing where to begin to make sense of their work. Yet they must begin, for it is in these puzzles of practice that the promise for teacher learning is held. Dewey pointed out decades ago that reflection typically begins when teachers face puzzling circumstances and make the choice to probe those puzzles (Dewey, 1933). The probing process leads to new understandings and changed practice; at least, that is the hope.

To render this particular hope a reality, one might begin by confronting the obstacles novices face to systematically examining their practice. A place to begin is the teacher's ability to focus. It is well documented that the teaching world of novice practitioners is so fraught with complexity and immediacy that it is difficult for them to focus their attention. In his work on teacher expertise, David Berliner (1988) reveals that focus is one of the characteristics that distinguishes novice teachers from their more expert colleagues.

The reasons for this are many. One is the structure of school, which does little to help novice teachers become productively focused in their work. The number of students they serve, the number of interruptions they face, and the number of noninstructional matters they have to attend to every day all contribute to the confusion many of them feel. Amy, a novice high school English teacher, wrote about this confusion in a narrative account of one morning in her classroom. She explained:

> The first bell rings and about a third of my class trickles in on time. I deliver my daily mantra to write down the homework into their study planners as I take roll. Is there any point to filling out the attendance sheet? So many of these absent students will turn out to be tardy. I stand and begin to explain the homework. The phone rings. As I approach the phone, two more students arrive, laughing and seeming oblivious to being in class now. I talk to an anxious mother who works downstairs, checking to see if her daughter is in class. I tell her "No. . . . She's started to skip more and more of her classes, and why doesn't she call either before or after class?" She knows I'm teaching. I return to the chalkboard to continue explaining the homework, and notice how jumpy and unfocused the students are. I tell them I need their attention and start speaking; I'm interrupted. I immediately stop and wait.

Nowhere in this cacophony of sounds and demands is it obvious to Amy which of these many factors is most important. Nor would this determination be easy for any of us, novice or experienced alike. But unlike those of us on the outside of this experience, Amy must act. She knows this. In fact, she feels an urgency to act. Well over half of her students have minimal reading and writing skills; more than half of them are failing her course. In the midst of the confusion she describes here, she must determine what the demands mean, whether or not they are "reasonable," where, if at all, they fit into her plans for the day and the week. Or she must act without having that clarity. All the while, she knows full well that the next 10 minutes will be no less confusing.

Action is only the first reason for which Amy needs focus. Learning from that action is part of her teaching work as well. Focus is needed both for action and for learning from action in teaching. While improved practice—or changed action—is the necessary outcome of teacher learning, the first step in getting there is to stop the action so that learning can occur.

"CAPTURING" EXPERIENCE TO FOCUS AND LEARN

There are many ways to "stop the action" in teaching in order to create what I have come to call *experience texts* of classroom life. Experience texts are representations of classroom experience that provide teachers the opportunity to focus their attention and examine that slice of practice captured by the text. Through the systematic examination of the representation, the teacher is able to learn from and about her work. I am using the term "text" here in a broad way with the idea that it can take many forms, and in so doing, offer many different opportunities for the teacher's contemplation of practice. For example, I would consider all of the different forms of student work to be experience texts.[1] Student papers and tests can stop the action of teaching long enough to capture some of what students know and are able to do at any given moment. By examining these texts carefully, a teacher can re-create the events that led to the student's journey to produce that work, and reexamine the opportunities for learning that were created in the classroom that contributed to make doing that work possible. The learning opportunities for teachers who view student work in this way are rich and many. They can see how the student is making sense of the course materials by reading what they write, for example. Or they can see into the student's world by considering the illustrations he or she uses. By reviewing the procedures employed by students, teachers can see where stumbling blocks occur in mathematical reasoning, and so forth.

A classroom video, which captures classroom events including what the teacher and students do as they engage with the classroom work at hand, might be a more obvious example of an experience text. In viewing a video, teachers can see and hear what they said and did (often much to their chagrin) and also observe the actions and reactions of the students who were engaged with them doing the work. The power of a classroom video comes in its potential to capture classroom action in a way more traditional written textual materials cannot. Classroom nuances—which require being seen at the same time as being heard—for example, are possible to view in a video production. Movement in the room, exchanges that happen on the side, and facial expressions that indicate engagement, boredom, joy, or grief are all possible to capture in a video representation of classroom life. Even if a video is less than skillfully produced, it offers an opportunity to view (and review) classroom happenings. In that process of view and review lies the opportunity to learn.

While videos hold tremendous potential as learning texts for some teachers, they are also experienced by many teachers as extremely intimidating. Novice teachers are especially vulnerable when viewing a video representation of their work. So much happens all at once in a classroom. Given that the video captures so much of the action of classroom life, the challenge of focus is re-created by the video representation. The feelings of fear and being overwhelmed that many novices experience when they begin to teach are potentially recreated in the video viewing as well. It is easy to understand why this might be so: there for the record—and in clear view—are all the mistakes the novice teacher believes he made: his voice is "too gruff," his attention "too split," his answers "not clear." For these reasons, video representations as experience texts might be better used with more veteran and confident teachers.

NARRATIVES AS EXPERIENCE TEXTS

One form of experience text that I have found extraordinarily powerful as a learning tool for novice teachers is the stories they tell, both written and verbal. Building on the human capacity for storytelling, a narrative approach to novice teacher learning begins with the lives of teachers, and builds learning opportunities based on what they know best—life in the classroom, including their own. To tell their stories, novices necessarily name and reflect upon their experiences. This process of naming clearly is important to how novice teachers learn from their work. In part, this is because the process requires that they actively think about what they have done as they prepare to articulate it for others.

This thoughtful examination of their practice that precedes the teachers telling their stories provides the opportunity for teacher learners to come to know their experiences in new ways. It requires that they place themselves *in* the experience, which is key to the learning opportunity this narrative methodology provides. When Maxine Greene (1991) talks of teacher storytelling, she recounts Proust's argument that experience has little value unless it is fused with stories—a position that makes good sense when one considers how telling the story of an experience makes one aware of the significance of that experience so that it warrants that the story be told. The everyday happenings that easily can slip by become fodder for consideration: the child's black eye, the parent's surprise visit, the blue paint that spilled on the red rug. Telling the story to an audience that actively listens interrupts the dailiness and celebrates the details. "Seeing my experience as something important . . . was amazing," one teacher wrote. This feeling was corroborated by another who explained: "I just get caught up in the day-to-day that I rarely get the opportunity to stop and recognize the dilemmas I deal with each day and how important they are to my experience as a teacher."

Novice teachers who are invited to construct narrative accounts of their classroom events—and to share them with others—are welcomed into a culture of teaching that acknowledges teaching experience as a context for learning. The learning context created by such an invitation also recognizes teachers as the authors of their classroom lives—ironically, an authorship that is seldom acknowledged by a profession whose formal text pays only scant attention to the voices of those who do the work (Chapter 11, this volume; Hargreaves, 1996).

In addition to highlighting teacher authorship, a narrative methodology suggests audience. The readers of the narratives (who are colleagues in this model) reflect back to the teacher writer/learners what they read in the text; in this way, those colleagues become part of the learning event. The teacher sees herself as centrally part of the experience as her colleagues query her about it. Going public in this manner creates the conditions for establishing a teacher learning community in which teachers do their work and study it with others at the same time (Lieberman & Miller, 1999; Lampert, 1999).

THE TEACHER'S PLACE *IN* THE TEXT AND OUT

I have worked over several years with novice teachers in one such teacher learning community and have noticed a phenomenon that helps us understand why the narrative methodology might be so powerful as a learning context for novice teachers. The phenomenon has to do with where the novices see themselves in the work of teaching, and what the process offers for building the teachers' sense of agency in their work. It appears in reading their narratives that the uncertain world of teaching—which is rigid and hierarchical on the one hand, and changing and chaotic on the other—causes many novices to remove themselves early on in their teaching careers from the center of the text of their teaching practice to a place more on the outskirts. Why is this so? How does it occur?

A look at the narrative accounts themselves helps make this marginalization process clear. They describe policies that place teachers outside decision making for their own classrooms, and their disempowered choice to acquiesce rather than to fight. They describe administrators who dictate curriculum and the teachers' seeming lack of confidence to defend what they teach. They describe parents who push for their own agenda and leave little room for the teacher's view of what ought to occur.

Wendy is a K–1 teacher in an urban school. Her narrative, "Missed Opportunity," provides a rich example. In it she describes a circumstance where an administrator's unexpected visit to her classroom corresponded with an unmistakable collapse in confidence about the curriculum she had in place for her students. Her story itself reveals Wendy's fear and consequent reluctance to speak. Rather than explain to her administrator the purpose of her children's work, she chose to remain silent even when opportunities for an explanation arose. Her narrative begins with an enthusiastic and confident voice:

> It was late morning, and the children were engaged in making ocean animals. I was circulating the room. Some children were spread on the floor, working in pairs, drawing sharks, octopuses, and giant squid on large white butcher paper. Others were spread out at the tables, surrounded by colorful paper, yarn and colored sequins. There was a group of children using black paper, white chalk, and pipe cleaners to make x-ray fish, sharks, and stingrays. You could hear the excitement of young voices across the room.

When her vice principal unexpectedly appeared, Wendy's confidence began to slip away:

> When the children were about half way through their drawings, I looked up and saw Sharon, our vice principal, standing in the doorway. I invited her in, and I explained that we are beginning a unit on ocean animals that emerged from the children's interests, and now we are busy creating our ocean animals. I sensed my eagerness to let her know what was happening, and I sensed my self-doubt. I feel apprehensive around these particular creative opportunities, but only when administrators cast their shadows as they are taking place.

In the "shadow" of her administrator's presence, Wendy began her retreat into self doubt. She says, "[S]lowly, my spirits were let down in the midst of the whirlwind that was taking place." Wendy's choice of the passive voice in this account is instructive. When she says "my spirits were let down," we can ask ourselves, as I did when I read this narrative the first time, "By whom?" and "Why?" Was it Sharon's interrogation of Wendy's students, which began soon after she entered the room, that caused Wendy's self-doubt to appear? Was it something else that Sharon did or said? Or was it Wendy's internalized judgment about her own competence and the effectiveness of her work?

The school world of high stakes, high accountability, and low efficacy places novice teachers at great risk for holding onto what they believe, and for feeling confident about what they know. As they question what they believe and know, novices also question what they do. If the high stakes and low efficacy were not accompanied by such high accountability, schools would be wonderful learning contexts for teachers. As it is, however, these conditions couple to silence teachers and, for many of them, shut down their ability to learn from their work. Rebecca explains at the end of her narrative:

> Learning as a process is an idea that is painfully neglected in my own growth as a teacher . . . In order to survive we must often pretend we know exactly what we are doing. And when asked to make improvements, we are simply expected to incorporate new techniques . . . This is a burden under which I feel buried, voiceless, unable even to think straight. I don't know how long I will last as a teacher if I am supposed to function as though I have nothing to learn.

Under that cloud of being "voiceless" and "buried," the teacher's presence in her work is obscured. Wendy's narrative provides some clues as to how the process of sliding into the margins of the text of classroom life—or the paralysis attached to losing one's voice—occurs. Her account reveals the way judgment casts its glow in schools, and the way the burden of needing to "do it right" renders novice teachers voiceless. In her narrative Wendy describes her students Homer and Marubi eagerly sharing with Sharon (their classroom visitor) that they were "making very large octopuses with twelve to twenty legs and giant eyes." Sharon's response to the students was far less enthusiastic. Or so it seemed to Wendy. Nor was it directed toward the students. Rather, it was directed toward Wendy. Wendy describes in the narrative: "I stood nearby waiting for Sharon's reply. She looked over at me and said with a smile, 'I thought octopuses had only eight legs.'"

Wendy interpreted Sharon's comment as an assessment not of the children's work, but of her teaching. This becomes increasingly significant as we learn later in Wendy's narrative about her subsequent retreat into silence. Perhaps, had Sharon directed her comment to the students rather than to Wendy, she would have communicated to Wendy a partnership in the teaching of the children in Wendy's room. Importantly, a comment directed toward the students might have also indicated a concern for Wendy's professional learning, since it would have offered Wendy a chance to hear her students respond to an authentic question from a visitor. With the rhetorical question directed at Wendy, however—and with no accompanying invitation to describe the context or the goals for the octopus work—Sharon's visit underscored Wendy's vulnerability, silenced her, and caused her to step out from rather than into the text of her teaching.

It wasn't until she wrote her narrative that Wendy was able to step boldly back into this story and recapture her voice. Notably, between Sharon's visit and before writing the narrative, Wendy had several opportunities to talk with Sharon about what she was teaching and why. Her narrative reveals that she was unable to do so. Instead of seizing those opportunities to speak, she continued to revel in self-doubt, questioning her teaching decisions, her students' learning, her classroom processes. She lamented that Sharon had not come on another day when "she would have witnessed much neater and quieter activities, the kind which administrators like." When Sharon did appear on the subsequent day looking for a computer to borrow, Wendy labored in agony trying to find a way to speak. At that point she was still unable to do so. She explained in the narrative, "I so much wanted to tell her and show her what we were doing . . . about the connections the children were making about the writing and research they were doing." However, after Sharon's 15 minutes of computer time in Wendy's room, when she got up to leave, instead Wendy "wished her a good weekend," passing up again "the opportunity to tell her about the children's work." It appears that the circumstances surrounding Sharon's visit so intimidated Wendy that she was unable to garner enough confidence to speak. Writing her narrative gave Wendy an additional chance.

NARRATIVES AND NOVICE KNOWING:
THE METHODOLOGY AT WORK

The narrative methodology I have described here begins with the teachers writing narrative accounts of different events or instances of teaching practice. These narratives are then distributed to the others in the learning group for reading and review.[2] The narrative texts themselves are short—typically two or three pages long—and are focused on one event each. The instructions for the narrative writing direct the novices to write a story of practice that contains enough detail so as to recreate as closely as possible the event as the teacher remembers it happening. The goal is to provide a vicarious experience of the event for the reader. The only criterion about the experience itself is that it must be true.

I find it is in their truth that these stories come alive in gloriously rich ways. We see "lanky Jamar" with his "Cleveland baseball cap" and his "toothy grin" coming into class several minutes late. We ponder Tyrone's fascination with "Power Rangers, swords, and monsters" and lament that neither he nor his teacher can connect those interests to the schoolwork at hand. We are alerted to the fact that in spite of "Mrs. Johnson's blond hair, neatly ironed but well worn clothes," she struggles to hide fear behind "her Jackie O. sunglasses that covered her black and blue swollen right eye." Typically these narratives reflect the beginning teacher's imagination, with every detail being as important as the next. In this richness, they provide both the teacher-author and the audience access to the teacher's world.

It is the richness of these stories and the details they contain that remind us over and over that the details of classroom life matter, as do the lives about which they are written, and the stories they are constructed to tell. The novice teacher's capacity to focus is enhanced by looking at the details that make up the rapid events of their lives in school. In attending to the details of her challenging work, a teacher can hold onto the humanity that brought her to the profession in the first place. One teacher explained:

> The writing of the narrative seems to give me an opportunity to consider a brief moment of what I am seeing in the classroom in depth, and draw implications. There are so many moments in school every day that are worthy of narratives. To examine one occasion allows me to feel human about it because I can acknowledge that these moments matter. (Robin, 1/2000)

To see that the moments matter is a learning outcome of the work of narratives. In the process—when the rush of school gets slowed down for a moment—the teacher can focus her attention and come to better understand what matters most. For some, part of what matters is themselves, or their own learning and professional growth. An example is Dana, a Latina teacher, whose narrative "How Much Should We Know" reveals the layers of knowing that the novice accesses as she writes and shares her account. An overriding concern of Dana's—and a perspective she brings to the narrative work and to our conversations throughout the year—is the high dropout rate of the Latino students at her school. In her narrative, she describes one such student, Eduardo, whose home situation presents many challenges both to the student himself and to the teachers who teach him. The provoking circumstance about which Dana wrote her story concerned Eduardo's mother, who uses school as a lever to punish Eduardo when she is angry with him.

The narrative begins in September with the first day of school. Eduardo is notably absent. His friends tell Dana they think he's in jail. The administration tells her that he has dropped out. When Eduardo appears several days later looking "upset and noticeably shaken," Dana reports feeling shaken as well. She probes to find out where he has been, why he was late to register, and whether there was something wrong in his life. It isn't until three weeks later (when Eduardo is hanging around in Dana's room) that he explains to her that he missed the beginning of school because his mother kept him home; she was angry with him for wanting to stay with his aunt and uncle, who lived closer to the school. "The more I learn about my students," Dana writes, "the harder it is for me to remain neutral."

When our narrative group discussed Dana's story, we covered such topics as the relationship between school and home, parents, teacher identity, teacher expectations, span of influence, and the success rates of Latino students in our Bay Area schools. In reflecting on the narrative process several months after having experienced the exchange, Dana explained:

> Writing my narrative allowed me the opportunity to simply tell the story of one of my students who tends to often be on my mind. I've talked about his situation before with colleagues, but in writing about him, I discovered a new dimension in thinking about him. It created a clearer more lucid picture that not only told his story, but *allowed me to tell mine* (emphasis mine). I don't know what else in education allows for this type of process. (Dana, 1/2000)

WRITING THEMSELVES INTO THE TEXT

Dana's comment suggests that the narrative process affords teachers the opportunity to see themselves in the stories they tell. This is one of the intriguing outcomes of this narrative work. Perhaps in the world of urban education, where the Eduardo-like life circumstances are so extraordinarily challenging (and so common at the same time), the lives of the teachers who negotiate this rocky terrain get obscured or even lost. It strikes me that learning opportunities that connect teachers with themselves—with what they think, what they believe, what they know, what they care about, why they are there—highlight the lives of teachers so that they can see themselves in the work. Connecting with oneself in teaching must be a central part of any teacher learning plan. If the being of the novice teacher is lost in the confusing and uncertain circumstances of her everyday life, she can easily slip out of the profession, and no one will know why. Among those things we want teachers to learn to see, therefore, is *themselves* as agents in the workings of school. About this unanticipated outcome of the narrative exchange, another teacher wrote: "Seeing and being seen is a most powerful thing. I want it for my students—I must try it for myself."

CONCLUDING THOUGHTS

Doing for ourselves as teacher learners what we would do for our students is a good place to bring this chapter to a close. Current research on learning theory has offered some important and relevant new frames for thinking about how children learn, and about how the adults who teach them learn as well. Putnam and Borko (2000) write about those frames and suggest that in working in professional development contexts we consider that learning is *situated*, it is *social*, and it is *distributed*. The narrative methodology described in this chapter attends to all three.

In terms of being situated, the teacher learning described here—like the teacher learning described throughout this book—is situated in practice. In this type of narrative methodology, the situational nature of the learning opportunitiy for teachers has several distinct features that are critically important to the work. These features concern how the situated learning opportunity is defined, and by whom. By design, the definition of practice, and what parts of it in particular will be the learning text, are defined by the teacher her- or himself. In authoring the experience text, the teachers write themselves into the situation they describe, either literally or as the observer/author who defines what matters most. Writing themselves into the text is critically important to the learning opportunity the narrative methodology affords novice teachers. It seems that all too often, novices' experience is written *out* of the teaching text by the plethora of programs and policies that neither ask what they think nor seem to care how they feel. By carving out a piece of the action for themselves and others to review, the teachers seem to gain some ownership of the work. In the process, they either strengthen or, in many instances, establish their voice. This carving-out process is intriguing indeed. One teacher explained:

> Narratives give me a set of walls or boundaries, regarding time and content, to draw in relation to my teaching. Boundaries are necessary so we have a place to start, a guide for direction, and something to topple over if necessary. . . . Narratives demand I tell *some* story, which, in turn requires me to come up with the content—a content that is necessarily relevant as it is about me and is worthy of dissection. (Matt, 1/2000)

The boundaries Matt talks of here refer to the boundaries he places around the piece of practice that becomes the focus of his narrative account. Setting those boundaries around some aspect of his work is an important step in the learning process for him, and for his colleague novice teachers as well. As we consider how without-boundaries novices feel in their classrooms, we begin to see the challenge of creating meaningful learning opportunities that are situated on the one hand, and accomplishable on the other. Professional development methodologies designed for new teachers need to find ways to carefully define what part of the challenging "situation" will be the focus of the learning. The task of constructing these types of narratives assigns this important part of the learning process to the novices themselves.

The social and distributed nature of learning are also part of the narrative methodology. From the start, when the teacher-authors write their narratives, they do so with the assumed audience of their novice teacher colleagues. Many of them speak about the anticipated conversation that will occur when their stories are shared, thus suggesting that the conversation begins in their heads even before it begins in reality. However, when the discussion does begin in real life, the teacher-author holds a position of expertise because she speaks with the "authority of her own experience" (Richert, 1992). Others in the exchange hold different kinds and amounts of expertise as well. The high school teachers know more when high school texts are discussed, for example, just as teachers who are parents do when parents are part of the story being told. The dimensions of expertise (even among a group of novice teachers) are many—gender, grade level, subject matter, ethnicity, and/or age—thus making conversations about the narrative texts extraordinarily rich and provocative. The healthy construction of knowledge that occurs in these narrative exchange conversations relies on the multiple and varied voices that come to the table.

We can close by remembering the Methodist Elder who sat at the table with Abraham Lincoln in the story with which this chapter began. He brought to that conversation the expertise of a knowing traveler. His insight about crossing Fox River—that one can't do it until you reach it—was instructive in that it reminded the other travelers that the river always changes and that the conditions that exist one day may not be the same the next. Like Fox River, schools change all the time as well; the circumstances that teachers face one day are often different the day after. We can alert novice teachers to this uncertainty; in fact, we would be remiss to do otherwise. In addition, we can encourage beginning teachers to confront the ever-changing elements of practice and to study them carefully. So while the message is that there is no "right" way to cross Fox River, I propose that there is a lot to learn from everyone's experience of the crossing. I believe we must commit to that agenda of learning in teaching; the narrative methodology I describe here is one means of doing so. In honoring and supporting teacher learning, we are honoring and supporting our teachers, their students, and the complex work of school.

NOTES

1. Currently I am working on a project in which I am developing this notion of "experience text," and have begun to build a framework that takes into account various forms these texts can take and what opportunities they offer for learning and under what conditions. For example, in this chapter I argue that narratives are particularly powerful as a focus text for novice teacher learning. Elsewhere I have discussed the use of narratives with veteran teachers. In those settings the format and procedures are different; the outcomes are different as well. Similarly, when student work is used as an experience text around which teacher learning is organized, the processes and procedures diverge from when these texts are used for student assessment purposes alone.

2. The data I'm drawing on for this chapter come from a group of full-time novice teachers who are currently enrolled in a class I teach entitled "Inquiry into the Teaching Process: Practice into Theory." Over the course of the academic year, each teacher writes two narratives to share with the class. As much class time is spent discussing the teacher narratives as is spent discussing other forms of written texts—the research literature in particular. Although these data are drawn primarily from that group, I have used this methodol-

ogy with several other groups of novices, always with the same results—a greater clarity and focus in their thinking, a stronger sense of professional identity, a clearer understanding of the role and importance of learning in teaching, and an enhanced sense of their own place in their teaching (with the attached growing sense of the value of their voice). It is that uniformity of response that compels my writing this piece.

REFERENCES

Berliner, D. (1988). *The development of expertise in pedagogy.* Lecture presented at the annual meeting of the Association of Colleges for Teacher Education, New Orleans.

Codell, E. R. (1999). *Educating Esme: Diary of a teacher's first Year.* Chapel Hill, NC: Algonquin Books.

Dewey, J. (1933). *How we think* (rev. ed.). Lexington, MA: Heath Publishing.

Greene, M. (1991). The question of personal reality. In A. Lieberman, & L. Miller, (Eds), *Staff development in the 90s: New demands, new realities, new perspectives.* (pp. 3–14). New York: Teachers College Press.

Hargreaves, A. (1996, January-February). Revisiting voice. *Educational Researcher, 25*(1), 12–19.

Lampert, M. (1999). Knowing teaching from the inside out: Implications of inquiry in practice for teacher education. In G. A. Griffin, (Ed.), *The education of teachers: Ninety-eighth yearbook of the National Society for the Study of Education* (pp. 167–184). Chicago: University of Chicago Press.

Lieberman, A., & Miller, L. (1999). *Teachers transforming their world and their work.* New York: Teachers College Press.

Putnam, R., & Borko, H. (2000). What do new views of knowledge and thinking have to say about research on teacher learning? *Educational Researcher, 29*:(1), 4–16.

Richert, A. E. (1992). Voice and power in teaching and learning to teach. In L. Valli, (Ed.), *Reflective teacher education: cases and critiques* (pp. 187–197). Albany: SUNY Press.

Sandburg, C. (1959). *Abraham Lincoln: The prairie years and the war years* in three volumes. New York: Dell Publishing.

CHAPTER 11

When Teachers Write: Of Networks and Learning

ANN LIEBERMAN
DIANE WOOD

The history of professional development for teachers is a landscape littered with failed approaches. While the names have changed over the years—from "in-service education" to "staff development" to "professional development"—the assumptions, forms, and substance have remained virtually the same. Most professional development approaches position teachers as passive consumers of prepackaged knowledge or, at best, compliant participants whose role has been to absorb information from the research and reform communities—whether or not it is useful or appropriate (Little, 1993). Needless to say, this "professional development" of teachers fails fairly consistently. Although the need for high-quality professional development is very clear, particularly given shifting demographics and rapid technological changes, there is little knowledge about how, or if, teachers are learning and implementing the new ideas and skills offered them through the in-service experiences afforded them by their schools and districts.

School districts frequently organize professional development opportunities without regard to the perceived needs of their teachers or the daily classroom dilemmas they face. Too often, experts hired to provide these opportunities know little about the teachers they are supposed to be "developing" and the culture of their schools. Differences among teachers in terms of experience, age, or context are invariably glossed over or ignored. Presented as a series of workshops, this sort of professional development rarely provides sufficient follow-up and support for meaningful and lasting improvements. Teachers are "in-serviced," as if teaching were merely a set of technical skills to be memorized and applied uniformly in all times and places. In the face of these traditional approaches to professional development, it is not surprising that improvements in schools have been minimal and that teachers have grown weary of efforts to "develop" them and improve their classroom practice.

Over several decades, the National Writing Project (NWP) has developed a provocative alternative approach to the professional development of teachers. Rather than conceptualizing teaching as a set of techniques, the NWP builds on the notion that teaching demands a continuous cycle of learning, trial, and evaluation. Rather than providing preset answers to generic problems, the NWP asks teachers to articulate their own dilemmas and pursue means to resolve them. While providing a context rich with resources for gaining "outside" knowledge, the NWP especially encourages professional collaboration to inquire into the considerable "inside" knowledge that teachers have accrued from years of classroom practice. To accomplish these tasks, the NWP established regional and national networks of teachers who, in the process of working on their own local problems, transcend the barriers of school walls by reaching out to other teachers—to give and receive ideas, support, and critique.

This networking approach to professional development, involving teachers as primary actors in their own development, is becoming increasingly significant. Unlike professional development strategies that have a "one size fits all" orientation, educational reform networks provide opportunities for teachers to commit themselves, in small and large ways, to topics that are of intrinsic interest to them and that arise naturally out of their work. In addition to formal learning (lectures, workshops, etc.), participants build collegial learning communities where they have opportunities to develop stronger voices to represent their perspectives, while learning to exercise leadership among their peers. Participating in learning communities built around shared understandings, where peers learn to give and receive critical support, helps teachers to enrich their classroom practices while providing the intellectual and emotional support necessary for personal and enduring growth (Lieberman & McLaughlin, 1992; McLaughlin & Talbert, 1993; Putnam & Borko, 2000; Wenger, 1998).

A 1993 study of 16 educational reform networks identified some central characteristics that, regardless of their differences of origin or purpose, were shared by all 16 networks. These included

- Agendas more challenging than prescriptive
- Learning more indirect than direct

- Formats more collaborative than individualistic
- Work more integrated than fragmented
- Leadership more facilitative than directive
- Thinking that encouraged multiple rather than unitary perspectives
- Values that were both context-specific and generalized
- Structures that were more movement-like than organization-like (Lieberman & Grolnick, 1996).

These characteristics created improvement opportunities for teacher growth that suggest a marked contrast to traditional organizational models. While many of the teachers studied stated that their experiences in these networks had been "transforming," there was little information about how this transformation happens, the activities that bring it about, and the structures that support it.

As educational networks become a larger and more influential part of the reform landscape, it is becoming increasingly important to understand the nature of the "work" of networks, the specific activities that are created for their members, and the principles of teacher development that emanate from them. Getting "inside" the National Writing Project, arguably the most successful teacher network in history, has helped us to understand the subtle links between teachers' learning in a community of peers and their sense of efficacy and confidence.[1]

"THE HEART OF THE WRITING PROJECT": THE FIVE WEEK INSTITUTE

> What I learned at the Writing Project was that I needed to create the environment [in my class] that I had experienced as an adult. There was shared work, making it public, getting it critiqued. I laughed, I cried and I wrote. I made myself vulnerable (but I had support). I wanted to do the same for my kids.

These words were spoken by a fifth-year teacher who attended the five-week Invitational Institute of the Writing Project (NWP) at the University of California at Los Angeles (UCLA). These institutes, held regionally across the nation, provide the first set of experiences for teachers new to the Writing Project. This particular teacher was one of 20 selected to participate in the UCLA summer institute. Many NWP teachers describe the institutes as the "heart of the Writing Project." The set of experiences that takes place during these few weeks galvanizes community and inspires a sustained commitment to ongoing professional learning and collaboration. Central to the entire enterprise is the notion that "the best teacher of teachers is another teacher"(UCLA Writing Project, 1998, p. 1).

The Core Activities

During the first day of the institute, the directors introduce and model a variety of activities that represent the core work for the participants during the five weeks. By the second day participants are involved in these activities, on the way to becoming the primary actors in their own development. Facilitators use several strategies to accomplish this, among them the "author's chair," small writing groups, and teaching demonstrations.

The Author's Chair. The author's chair is a forum for teachers to voice their ideas and experiences through writing. Volunteers take the "chair," bringing an unfinished poem, the beginning of a story, a piece prompted by other activities (e.g., write about the strangest person you have ever known), or any written work that they are willing to share with others. They read their contribution and receive feedback from the audience. In the following weeks, as they return to read their revised work, the audience eagerly awaits the new installments that reflect the deeper insights and changing character of the participants' contributions.

This interaction between author and "audience" establishes the basis for a constructively critical community. The audience may praise the work unconditionally, ask for clarifications or explanations, explore possibilities, or make other constructive comments. As the teacher-writers learn to share their thoughts and feelings with each other in story, poem, or narrative, it helps them to recognize the connections between personal and professional learning. They see how writing and teaching are infused with personal meaning and cultural assumptions that may need to be clarified to reach an audience of peers—or students. Just as important, they learn to "hear" criticism as an opportunity for reflection and growth, not as a threat. As teachers witness and participate in the processes surrounding the author's chair—writing, sharing, reflecting, revising—they come to realize that this is not only an experience for the participant as writer, but also a model for teaching and working with students.

Writing Groups. Another core activity involves working in writing groups. Four or five teachers form a group that meets for a few hours two or more days a week. They share their own writing with the group, give and receive feedback, and revise and rewrite as time allows. (At UCLA a professional writing coach also participates.) Encouraging potential writers to write and bolstering the confidence of writers to share their writing requires both an understanding of and participation in the various stages of the writing process. The institute demonstrates, for instance, pre-writing activities such as generating topics through discussion and brainstorming, organizing writing by clustering ideas, and developing a plan through mapping or outlining. As first drafts are completed, teachers bring them to their writing groups for suggestions and critique. Teacher-writers then reflect on what they've heard from their peers and undertake further revision and editing before the final product is shared. Many teachers spoke of the "luxury" of having concentrated time to write, the importance of recapturing the subjective meaning and passion of writing, and the satisfaction of sharing their thoughts and feelings with an interested and sympathetic audience.

> The best a-ha for me was being in a writing group and having a chance to write—getting good sensitive criticism. I had forgotten what it was like to write. My life had developed so many other stresses that I realized I had not written myself in years.

Something the participants learn clearly is that the arduous experience of writing takes on greater meaning when the author writes about something that s/he cares about deeply. Having the time to write and the support of their writing groups, teachers become students in some most important ways. As learners, teachers *get* feedback on their work so that they can continue to improve. As teachers, they learn to *give* feedback; having become more connected to themselves as writers, they become more connected to their students.

> It reminds you that people's writing is personal, and that when I critiqued people's writing, student writing, that I need to be sensitive and not just tear it apart, or not just say it's good when it isn't. When I changed schools [after the Invitational], I realized that I had to teach writing. I had always given assignments, but I hadn't explicitly taught writing as a process, breaking it down in all its parts.

Teaching Demonstrations. Another core activity provides individual teachers with the opportunity to teach a class of their peers. Such model lessons tend to include the goals teachers hold for their students, what materials and resources they use, and, if appropriate, the subject matter standard their lesson helps to reach. In the process of teaching these lessons, the teacher learns from constructive feedback—and from reflection and practice—what it means to be a good "presenter." Such characteristics as being well organized and well prepared, knowing the subject and communicating its importance, and the impact it has on students are considered and discussed. In "going public" with their work, teachers make their implicit understandings explicit, both to their audience and, most importantly, to themselves. The resultant learning goes beyond the subject of the lesson itself to the heart of a process that teaches what it means to be part of a community of colleagues who take one another's work seriously—seriously enough to provide constructive criticism as well as encouragement. Teachers teach each other how good ideas can become even better and how it is possible to tailor powerful practices to specific contexts and learners.

Some teachers can only muster the courage to present if they choose a favorite lesson to teach, one that they have refined over the years. Once they've gone public and put themselves on the line with their peers, however, the responses they receive build mutual trust, and the safety they feel in that context vastly extends subsequent risk-taking. Perhaps the reason for the development of such trust lies in the norms that the institute establishes. Receiving feedback from fellow teachers is simply seen as a basic part of the process. At UCLA, feedback is given in the form of a letter to the presenter. (At other sites, giving feedback may take other forms.) The UCLA participants are encouraged to use a PQS format (praise, question, suggest) and to consider how a lesson might be adapted for use in their own classes.

As these teaching demonstrations unfold, both the audience and the presenter play several roles, just as they do when participating in the author's chair. The presenter teaches, but also learns from being critiqued by an audience of peers. The audience learns how to play the role of "friendly critic" and, by inference, how to receive and make use of constructive criticism. Very important to teachers, these demonstrations succeed in modeling teaching practices that they can actually transport to their own classrooms. Collectively, their most important learning is that teachers' knowledge, crafted by teachers for use in their own classrooms, is legitimate and worthy of respect as knowledge to be shared, improved, built upon, and used in other contexts. Reversing the folklore that says, in effect, "teachers steal lessons from one another," teachers are proud that *their* lessons are judged to be worth using by other teachers (Cochran-Smith & Lytle, 1993).

Ancillary Activities

In addition to participating in model lessons, the author's chair, and writing groups, teachers are also involved in other activities. These include mini-lessons on particular subjects such as vocabulary words, using similes, "quick writes" (five minute thought-pieces on a particular insight or idea), and so forth. Teacher consultants offer workshops on a variety of topics:[2] assessing student writing, using a variety of multicultural stories as prompts for reading and writing, making use of rubrics to score student work, and so on. Sometimes groups of teachers who teach the same grade come together to react to particular issues or lessons. From time to time directors raise important issues, suggest articles and books to read, or make available materials that they have found useful. Subjects may range from state standards to reading and teaching multicultural literature, from writing in bilingual classrooms to performance-based assessment and standardized tests, or other issues that they consider of interest to the participants. In the course of the institute, teachers are introduced to many resources that will be made available to them over time to serve as ongoing opportunities for professional growth. The activities are rich and varied, but it is the overall environment that teachers respond to and are most affected by.

> The Invitational was a magical time. We did all the lessons as if we were students. It became part of the fiber of the day. We practiced. We experienced. We thought about it. We wrote letters saying how we would use the ideas. Every time I wrote a letter I was modifying lessons in my classroom. It was a time to be reflective on myself as a person, as a teacher.

Through these various activities, the Institute takes on a set of daily rhythms of its own, punctuated by subtle changes in tone, format, and pace. Participants move from sharing the deep emotional experiences of writing that is often personal and revealing, to serious intellectual discussions about the role of the state in determining standards. The changing activities—from author's chair to model lessons, from a 10-minute mini-lesson to a two-hour writer's group—develop a rhythm and pace that involve participants emotionally, intellectually, and practically.

Even the voluntary role of keeping the log of each day's activities plays a role in enriching the environment. Every morning a "logger" reports on the highlights of the previous day. As the teachers get more comfortable, the log expands to include pictures and other odds and

ends from the day's activities, as well as humorous descriptions and
more intimate details about the nature of their group and its idiosyn-
cracies. The logs help to document the learning experiences of the
participants, building community by raising awareness of the shared
philosophy that underlies and enriches their daily activities.

> The ideas of the writing project had become a part of me. In fact
> it was less about "implementing" a specific lesson, but more
> about what kind of philosophy I had about students as writers
> and myself as a teacher.

PRINCIPLES FOR GROWTH AND DEVELOPMENT:
THE WRITING PROJECT WAY

The philosophy, variety, and pace of the activities during the five-
week institute has, many teachers say, a transforming effect on their
teaching. Inherent in all the activities are underlying principles that
empower teachers to build on their knowledge by finding their strengths
and supporting them. Connecting learning, community, and efficacy,
the NWP provides teachers with a variety of opportunities not only to
shape ideas for use in their own contexts, but to take leadership in and
become members of a larger professional community.

Teachers learn by teaching other teachers. Teachers who come to
the NWP are expected to teach other teachers. This principle is at the
heart of the NWP approach, reversing assumptions of the deficit mode
of professional development. Instead of teachers assuming that they must
learn only from experts, they learn that they have knowledge that is
valuable and can be shared and built upon by other teachers. The assumption here is that *teachers' knowledge* is the starting place for learning, not "outsider knowledge." As teachers teach each other, they become
more aware of the complexities of context and the variety of activities
that are possible. In the process, teachers openly and unashamedly talk
about their successes and their failures. As they become more open to
learning from each other, they begin to inquire more broadly into articles, books, and people that deal with problems that they are confronting.

*Teachers learn from making their work public and having it dis-
cussed and critiqued by a group of peers.* Teachers come to understand
that learning from one another involves having the courage to go public
with their own teaching practices. They find that their peers can help

them: to clarify the purposes of a lesson or strategy; to articulate their objectives; to perceive how student interest and needs are linked; to relate these interests and needs to the kinds of teaching strategies they use; to talk about student responses to these strategies; and to discuss their means of assessing what students learn. Although teachers appear uneasy at the beginning of the five weeks, the evident respect for teachers' knowledge enables them to develop the self-confidence to ask questions of their own practice as well as of their peers'.

Teachers learn that in facing one's peers they must be well prepared, clear in their instructions, and engaging in their presentation. But while going public with their work is always difficult, it is easier to do it knowing that the presenter one day will be in the audience the next day.

Learning to write and learning to teach have a great deal in common. Taking the author's chair makes self-evident that writing as a process is implicitly and explicitly connected to the process of teaching. To learn to write better, one must write, go public, be critiqued, and revise. To learn to teach better, one must teach, go public, be critiqued, and revise. They are both social acts, although much of the work must be done alone. In the NWP the writer's isolation from his/her audience and the teacher's isolation in a classroom are alleviated by their interaction with peers. The individual is recognized and supported by the group of which s/he is a part.

The problems of writing are worked on: going public, being critiqued, revising, clarifying meanings, improving dialogue, refining character, and so on. The problems of teaching are worked on: going public, being critiqued, revising lessons, teaching technical skills, awareness of context and community, providing different points of entry to the conversation, and constantly asking questions of one's practice. Teachers develop new understandings for evaluating their own work. This self-critique involves questions such as: Did this have the impact I intended? Did I teach the necessary skills so that students could work together in a group? Did I provide good feedback—the kind that helps students clarify their thoughts (not to show that I have power)? Am I continually inquiring into what I am doing? Is there any research on the questions I have? What can I learn from my peers? Excited and stimulated by participating in a community of teachers, they are reminded of why they wanted to become teachers in the first place. As one participant said: "Finally I was able to go to a summer institute, and I remember walking in and it was like dying and going to heaven. Five weeks being with people who really care about writing and teaching."

Teaching and writing both require craft and skills that have to be learned and mastered. They both have to be *about* something, and the good practitioner has to find the best ways to illuminate that something. The broader the repertoire, the more craft confidence, and the greater the knowledge of the subject, the better the chance of being successful in reaching one's audience—in writing or teaching (Grossman, 1990). The level of artistry will vary with the talent and insights of the practitioners, but without craft and content knowledge it will have little chance to emerge.

Real learning for teachers is both timely and contingent. Mondays come every week, and teachers must be prepared to face them with skill and confidence. However, teachers are often confronted with new situations that require new ways of thinking and acting (Little, 1993). The Invitational's many ideas, lessons, and strategies, embedded in the process of teachers teaching each other, combine useful specific knowledge with gaining the self-confidence to face new challenges as they arise.

There are strong value commitments in the NWP, but methods and means to get there are nonideological. Although teachers have different views about such issues as core curriculum, phonics, or whole language, no one is criticized for their viewpoint when they present. Feedback is non-ideological and non-judgmental. (The acceptance of a wide variety of views on teaching allows the NWP to appeal to a broad range of teachers.) Nevertheless, while the differences are respected, the commitments and values are implicit in the forms and practices of the institute. For example, it is axiomatic that writers are more involved when they have a choice of subjects to write about; that writing helps learners to think and express themselves more clearly; that making writing public attaches people more strongly to the community; and that writing as a social process benefits both the individual—personally and professionally—and the community.

Teaching is accepted as messy, uncertain, and unfinished. As teachers continue to work with each other, they make public the fact that teaching is a messy process that is filled with uncertainty. While teachers acknowledge this privately and learn to make do on their own, the context of the NWP encourages them to question their practice publicly, and to seek and share solutions with others. "Habits of mind" developed at NYP include a deeper understanding of how to make sense of the environment. These newly learned habits of mind become part of the community's norms, turning problems into possibilities for rethinking and reworking teaching practice. And these habits remain with teachers when they return to their complex environments. In the words of two participants:

> When school started after the institute, I started thinking what can I do to solve some of these problems and to be helpful and supportive of my colleagues. It was like the institute was sitting there waiting to come out and I started looking at problems in a whole new way.

> The Writing Project is like an "angel on my shoulder."

Over the years teachers learn to reluctantly accept the "endemic uncertainties" in teaching that create "conservatism, privatism and individualism" (Lortie, 1975). The NWP gives them the support, courage, and opportunity to change these attitudes by becoming part of a community that is both collaborative and inviting, and that encourages participation in their own learning by both teachers and students. Being part of such a community provides an alternative to the usual isolation, alienation, and privatism that plague many teachers in their schools—an alternative that turns teachers toward asking questions, taking risks, and trying new strategies, and away from turning inward and blaming the students for their lack of success.

Teachers learn by taking different roles and seeing the world through different perspectives. Shifting roles provide multiple opportunities to experience the "lived lives" of teachers and learners—emotionally as well as intellectually. Personal and professional learning are naturally connected. Teachers learn objective facts and subjective truths: from specific suggestions for improving a lesson, to how it feels to have your work critiqued by others or being one of the critics. Instead of prescriptive strategies devoid of context, teachers learn to adapt new ideas to fit their own teaching context. They become active and interactive, developers rather than developed, passionate instead of passive.

> It opened me up. I understood who I am as a teacher. It opened pathways for me. I took back so many little things (like giving writing prompts, having writing folders, taking the author's chair) but there were big things too.

Teachers get used to new ways of working: struggling with difficult problems and contexts, expecting and receiving supportive and critical comments, and being with fellow teachers who are committed personally and professionally to improving their teaching and learning as a lifelong commitment. Teaching others, quite naturally, becomes an important way of learning (McNiff, 1993), since it encourages teachers to examine their own practice constructively and critically (Cochran-Smith & Lytle, 1999). In the process of teaching their peers, some teachers find that they not only develop good strategies for use in their own classrooms, but that engaging adults is stimulating and challenging.

Teachers take leadership learning back home. Excited by their experiences in the NWP, some teachers take a leading role in creating a similar environment for their peers at their home school. As one teacher new to the NWP reported:

> I left the Writing Project so excited and energized that I asked my coordinator if I could give an in-service during August. I did the whole thing. We had snacks. We focussed on poetry. We charted everything so teachers would know their work was taken seriously. People came up with amazing stuff. They asked if we could start a writing group.[3]

Directors encourage teachers in the NWP to become "teacher consultants," teaching peers in their home schools and districts, at subsequent Invitationals, or in many of the numerous other offerings of the NWP that take place during the summer and at different times during the year.[4] Those who become consultants do more than teach "model lessons" to other teachers. They seek to create environments similar to the NWP Institute that encourage respect for teachers and teacher knowledge.

> I never thought of myself as a leader. I had never had an opportunity to present. This led to my thinking differently of what I might do as a professional and expanded my thinking in many ways. The WP is a significant part of my professional life.

Networks provide powerful contexts for teacher learning, community, and enhancement of teachers' confidence and self-esteem. It is of great importance to understand the organization of the NWP as a network. Teachers who come together virtually as strangers become colleagues, sharing the struggle to know more and to be more effective as teachers. The central idea—placing teachers and teaching practices at the center of the experience—is so powerful, and so absent from most teachers lives, that it becomes a transforming experience for many teachers. They become part of a local community at their particular site, and through this association part of a national community, the National Writing Project.[5] As in other successful networks, there are many opportunities for teachers to keep their connection to the NWP. Some become teacher consultants; others come to conferences, summer seminars, or Saturday workshops on particular topics during the year. By taking advantage of the variety of offerings run by the NWP, participants remain connected to this loosely organized but supportive community.

> I've been back to visit a couple of times. When the Director needs me to do something, I try to respond. I went to the Fall Conference. I've been on e-mail, the list serve. I wrote an article for the WP newsletter. I work with WP teachers at my school. That keeps me connected.

The NWP has been in existence as a network for 25 years with its primary focus on writing and literacy, even as it has expanded its work into other related areas. For example, at both UCLA and Oklahoma sites, the NWP was running other types of workshops, using many of the tools of the NWP, but, most importantly, putting teacher practice at the center.

Over the years, the NWP has increased its presence in both urban and rural areas while, consistent with its ideals, continuing to revise and refine its work. Sensitive to the lives and work of teachers, it has created a form of professional development that is centered on practice and rooted in respect for teachers' knowledge.

NOTES

1. The data reported here are from a two-year study entitled *Teacher Development in a Network Context: The National Writing Project*, sponsored by the National Partnership for Excellence and Accountability in Teaching (NPEAT), 1997–99. The first purpose of the study was to find out how the Writing Project facilitates technical learning in the context of a professional community. The second was to find out what teachers take back to their classroom. Third, we sought to understand the link between learning in the network, practices in the classroom, and its impact on student learning. This chapter presents data that deal with our first purpose.

2. Teacher consultants are those teachers who have been in the WP previously and provide staff development, to their own school, district, or the Writing Project. Some of them become leaders at the site, some develop new areas of learning for the WP, and some go on to take leadership in other programs, sites, or at the national level.

3. This teacher was brand-new to the WP. She was in a school where new state legislation called for learning English in one year, along with learning to read and know elementary mathematics.

4. At UCLA there were extended workshops on "Assessing Students' Reading and Writing Ability," National Board Certification, Teaching Writing to English Language Learners, and Leading Socratic Seminars. In addition, there was a three-week Writing Institute for Students held in a nearby school.

5. There are currently 165 sites of the Writing Project in the United States.

REFERENCES

Cochran-Smith, M., & Lytle, S. L. (1993). *Inside/outside: Teacher research and knowledge*. New York: Teachers College Press.

Cochran-Smith, M., & Lytle, S. L. (1999). Relationships of knowledge and practice: Teacher learning in communities. A. Iran-Nejad & C. D. Pearson (Ed.), *Review of Research in Education*. Volume 24. Washington, DC: American Educational Research Association.

Grossman, P. (1990). *The making of a teacher*. New York: Teachers College Press.

Lieberman, A., & Grolnick, M. (1996). Networks and reform in American education. *Teachers College Record, 98*(1), 7–45.

Lieberman, A., & McLaughlin, M. (1992). Networks for educational change: Powerful and problematic. *Phi Delta Kappan, 73*(9), 673–677.

Little, J. W. (1993). Professional development in a climate of educational reform. *Educational Evaluation and Policy Analysis, 15*(2), 129–151.

Lortie, D. (1975). *Schoolteacher*. Chicago: University of Chicago Press.

McLaughlin, M. W., & Talbert J. (1993). *Contexts that matter for teaching and learning*. Stanford, CA: Context Center for Teaching and Learning in Secondary Schools.

McNiff, J. (1993). *Teaching as learning: An action research approach*. New York: Routledge.

Putnam, R. T., & Borko, H. (2000). What do new views of knowledge and thinking have to say about research on teacher learning? *Educational Researcher, 29*(1).

UCLA Writing Project. (1998). *1998 Programs for Classroom Teachers and Administrators*. Los Angeles: Center X UCLA Graduate School of Education and Information Studies.

Wenger, E. (1998). *Communities of practice: Learning, meaning, identity*. Cambridge, UK: Cambridge University Press.

CHAPTER 12

Teacher Research and Professional Development: Purposeful Planning or Serendipity

SARAH WARSHAUER FREEDMAN

I've been working with teacher research networks for almost 10 years now, but only recently have I begun to think seriously about the relationship between teacher research and professional development. I first became involved in teacher research almost 20 years ago when I came to Berkeley as a new assistant professor in the School of Education. Since I was the first faculty member hired in the area of writing research, Jim Gray, then director of the Bay Area and National Writing Projects, asked me to teach a summer course on teacher research. I had no sense of what teacher research was and could find little guidance in the literature, but I didn't want to turn him down. So I organized a class in university-based research methods. In the five weeks allotted, there was not enough time for the teachers to learn much about research or even to get much of a start on a research project. The course bore little relationship to what we call teacher research these days, and certainly did not offer much of a professional development opportunity for the participating teachers.

In retrospect, I should never have agreed to teach something I knew so little about. I buried the memory as quickly as I could, considering the course a relative failure. It was not part of my regular teaching job in the School of Education; it was not part of my research agenda; and it was not part of the teachers' normal jobs. It had no institutional home. At the end of that summer, I was convinced that the interest in teacher research was destined to fade away.

How wrong I was! Over the next decade, I watched a movement take shape (Elliott, 1991; Goswami & Stillman, 1987; Lytle & Cochran-Smith, 1989; Mohr & Maclean, 1987; Schön, 1983; Stenhouse, 1985). By 1991, with Liz Simons, who had been a leader in many of the Writing project's professional development projects, I started another teacher research effort. This time it was connected to a relatively well-funded research project. Our goals were to involve teachers in the knowledge generation process, something I had been doing for a decade in increasingly more collaborative arrangements in my research projects on the teaching and learning of written language (Freedman, 1994; Freedman, with Sperling, & Greenleaf, 1987). Teacher research was a natural next step in this collaborative research program (Freedman, Simons, Kalnin, Casareno, and The M-CLASS teams, 1999). For 10 years now, I have been involved with three different teacher research networks, one of which included the institutionalization of teacher research–based Master of Arts (MA) to Berkeley's secondary English teacher credential program.

Given my experience in the early 1980s, I came to these three teacher research networks with a number of reservations. Why would teachers take time from already packed days to do research? What rewards would be significant enough to keep them interested? What would be the rewards for me and my university-based colleagues? How would we manage the time commitment? I knew from the start that even with a relatively well-funded grant, the compensation would be inadequate for the time all of us would need to contribute. I also worried about the danger of using teachers to achieve my ends rather than theirs. Finally, what would happen at the end of the project?

Although I cannot answer all of these questions, I have begun analyzing the teachers' talk and writing in these networks to try to understand the teacher research process and what motivates the participating teachers. I have found that teacher learning is at the heart of all of the networks, whether I planned it that way or not, and that the opportunities to learn seem to be central to sustaining the teachers' interest. In this chapter I will explore what and how the teachers learned.

THEORETICAL POSITIONING

Cochran-Smith and Lytle's (Cochran-Smith & Lytle, 1999; Cochran-Smith & Lytle, Chapter 4, this volume) useful and important theoretical framework, which characterizes competing conceptions of professional development, offers a helpful way to frame the teacher learning in the three Berkeley-based networks. In addition, my close look at this learning may also help elaborate on and further define the professional development categories that Cochran-Smith and Lytle have proposed.

Since Cochran-Smith and Lytle describe their theory fully in their 1999 chapter in *Review of Research in Education* as well as in Chapter 4 in this volume, I will only summarize relevant parts here. The first conception of professional development that they propose, knowledge-*for*-practice, is common in the profession. In this approach, university-based researchers provide knowledge and theory, which teachers are then supposed to use to improve their practice. This approach is antithetical to what happens inside teacher research groups, where the focus is on teachers generating knowledge for themselves.

Cochran-Smith and Lytle label their second professional development category knowledge-*in*-practice. In this approach the assumption is that expert teachers come to professional development activities with tacit practical knowledge that underlies their everyday decision making in the classroom. Professional development consists of helping them reflect on this tacit knowledge and thereby learn to make it conscious and available for examination. This approach is consistent with what happens inside many teacher research groups, including those in the Berkeley networks.

Cochran-Smith and Lytle's third and final category, knowledge-*of*-practice, describes teachers who study their schools and classrooms in ways that lead them to look critically at and interrogate both their own learning and the research of others. These teachers ultimately aim to "theorize and construct their work and to connect it to larger social, cultural, and political issues" (1999, p. 250). This type of professional development contrasts with knowledge-*in*-practice in that teacher knowledge is grounded in more than the teachers' reflections on the choices they make in their classrooms and carries with it a critical and political force. Like knowledge-*in*-practice, this kind of professional development is consistent with the goals for teacher growth in many teacher research groups and is also consistent with what occurred in the Berkeley networks.

Cochran-Smith and Lytle's distinctions between knowledge-*in*-practice and knowledge-*of*-practice are clear on the surface. However, I found that both categories applied to how teachers learned in the Berkeley networks, even though the categories are meant to be distinct. I will use specific instances of teacher learning, which I analyze in the rest of this chapter, to consider how one might begin to elaborate these categories and perhaps connect them.

THE NETWORKS AND THEIR PURPOSES

Before discussing the types of teacher learning in the three Berkeley-based networks, I will provide background on the structure and goals of each network and the university participants' changing intent with respect to professional development. In the first network, Simons and I set out to work with classroom teachers to better understand what we and many teachers thought was one of the most complex and important issues of our time: literacy learning in urban multicultural settings. With funding from the U.S. Department of Education's Office of Educational Research and Improvement (OERI) through the National Center for the Study of Writing and Literacy, in 1992 we recruited 24 teachers who were ideologically committed to and experienced in offering high-level instruction to inner-city students in complex teaching-learning environments. The teachers were a multi-ethnic group who taught English and social studies—six each from Boston, Chicago, New Orleans, and the San Francisco Bay Area. The network was called M-CLASS, Multicultural Collaborative for Literacy and Secondary Schools, and included the teachers, university-based site coordinators in each locale, and a Berkeley-based team led by me and Simons, with Alex Casareno playing a major role in the early phases of the project and Julie Kalnin in the later phases. The goal of the M-CLASS network was to complete a collaborative research project that would generate and synthesize knowledge from the academy and knowledge from teacher researchers (reported in Freedman et al., 1999b). The teachers in this network were chosen because they were known for their expertise in the classroom. The university facilitators saw them more as collaborators in making contributions than as in need of professional development. And many of them began with the same idea. Ultimately, it was as much professional development as the opportunity to contribute to knowledge that kept these teachers involved and that led to an increased professional development focus within the subsequent networks.

The second network was an extension of the first. Three experienced teacher researchers from the San Francisco site of the original network (Verda Delp, Deborah Juarez, and Ann Lew), two university-based colleagues who had collaborated with me on the original M-CLASS project (Liz Simons and Julie Kalnin), and I designed the M-CLASS Site Based Network (SBN). We received funding from the Spencer Foundation's Practitioner Communication and Mentoring Program and the University of California Office of the President. Delp, Juarez, and Lew each invited two other teachers from their schools to participate. The nine teachers in the SBN taught in three schools in three San Francisco Bay Area school districts (Berkeley, Oakland, and San Francisco). This network's goal included action at these school sites and, secondarily, contributions to knowledge by the teacher researchers (see Freedman & M-CLASS/SBN team, 2000; Kalnin, 2000). Although the main goals were not focused on professional development, the university and teacher facilitators were attentive to the professional development possibilities for the teachers who were new to teacher research and the leadership development potential for the more experienced teachers.

The third network was explicitly a professional development network. I designed a teacher research seminar as the final course in the newly designed Multicultural Urban Secondary English (MUSE) Credential and M.A. program. I taught this seminar for 12 first-year teachers who had received their credential in the Berkeley program the year before. For their final M.A. projects and as the paper for the teacher research seminar, the new teachers were to conduct teacher research projects related to their teaching. As the course instructor, my goal was to use teacher research to teach new teachers to study their practice in ways that would help them solve problems throughout their careers (see Freedman, 1999).

On the surface, the first two networks fall quite neatly into Cochran-Smith and Lytle's "knowledge-in-practice" category. The teachers in the original M-CLASS network were recruited because of their expertise in literacy learning in urban multicultural classrooms. We at the university thought that by reflecting on their practice, a multiethnic group of English and social studies teachers with experience, interest, and special competence in urban teaching in multicultural settings would be especially well positioned to add to our understandings of literacy and learning in the classroom. In the SBN, we also worked with a multiethnic group of teachers whom we thought would offer especially interesting contributions. However, we also had a critical political agenda that involved bringing teachers together to act as key agents in the school change process, and we did not work just with teachers whom we thought had special expertise. Teachers in the third network could fall into either category, depending on the political force of their work.

SOME EXAMPLES OF PROFESSIONAL DEVELOPMENT

In my research, I found that teacher learning in these three networks often was visible when teachers used talk and writing to grapple with teaching and research problems; to get support for taking teaching and research risks; and to figure out the motivations behind their students' actions and how their students learned (Freedman, in press).

The different teachers in the networks I studied did not all use talk and writing in the same ways. Rather, some focused on problems; of these, some seemed to benefit from airing their problems, while others gave advice and listened. Some talked about and received support from other group members for experimentation and risk-taking. Some discussed their students and got help in understanding the motivations behind their students' actions and the details of their learning processes. In these teacher research networks, talk or writing on any one of these topics provided space for the teachers to shift their stance toward their work and to renew their commitment to their profession and ultimately to their students and their students' learning. During their talk and related writing, the teachers elaborated and often changed their notions about their teaching and their students' learning (see also Kalnin, 2000). They all reported rarely finding space for this kind of talk and writing in their everyday teaching lives, including in other professional development activities.

I now turn to examples of each type of talk and writing. General points come from an analysis across all three networks, but the main examples come from the original M-CLASS network, in which professional development was not purposeful but rather serendipitous, emerging in spite of, not because of, the way this network was organized.

DISCUSSING PROBLEMS OF PRACTICE

During teacher research meetings across all the networks, the teachers talked freely about problems that were extrinsic to their teaching and their classrooms—institutional or societal problems that affected their schools and their students' abilities to learn—such as safety in the school, administrative incompetence, violence in the neighborhoods, poverty, gang activity, and the like. But they varied in their comfort levels in talking about and ultimately conducting research on and writing about intrinsic problems—such as their ability to control the class, difficulties teaching certain types of students, and their failures in getting students interested in grappling with difficult curricular material. The new teachers in the MUSE group felt somewhat freer to discuss varied kinds of problems. As first-year teachers, they fully expected to have problems and seemed generally used to coming to the university to get advice from faculty and from one another. However, like their more experienced counterparts, some talked more openly about problems during group discussions than others.

Readings often provided a sense of distance that created a comfort zone for this talk. Members of the original M-CLASS network read and discussed Lisa Delpit's "The Silenced Dialogue" (1988), which evoked many complex emotions about race. In Boston, Nancy O'Malley responded by describing a dilemma she faced when interacting with her Asian students:

> I think a lot about this [how members from different racial groups interact] in the writing workshop class especially, the creative writing class that I'm doing research on . . . The students who want the authoritative figure and want to listen most to me as the teacher are the Asian students who, in fact, need the verbal and oral skills the most. Because most of them are coming into a new language after only two and three years. And so there's some great dichotomy in the class where they're the ones who need it [oral practice] most, and yet they're the most unwilling because their culture says to them, "It's not so important to listen to Eileen's piece of writing." They want to know what the answer is, and we have this constant tension. (M-CLASS, Boston site meeting, October 31, 1992)

O'Malley then claims, "It's gotten better. They have listened to each other . . . but it's . . . a constant struggle." After voicing a problem, the teachers often used this strategy of diminishing the significance or difficulty of the problem, saying something like O'Malley's "it's gotten better." This is perhaps a face-saving gesture, but in O'Malley's case it also was a move that seemed preparatory to taking the bigger risk of ruminating about her role in the problem: "I have to watch myself, too. In encouraging everyone to listen and all, I don't want to be too much of just the orchestrator. So it's a balancing act."

Junia Yearwood, a Black immigrant from the Virgin Islands, provides an alternate interpretation of the Asian students' lack of participation, identifying with them and then looking from their points of view:

> You kept saying it's a cultural thing, and that's true. But it's also that the Asian kids want access to the keys of knowledge, which for them is the mechanics of language, of your language, and that's why they're impatient. . . . I'm not Asian, and that's how I felt when I came to school here in America. I came to college with specific [O'Malley: Yeah, sure.] reasons and the reasons was to get access to this great wealth of

knowledge that I just knew was in these gates. [O'Malley: Mmhmm] And when American kids took up half the period talking and arguing, I was livid. [O'Malley: Sure.] I did not want that because to me, and I heard Asians say the same exact thing, it is not that they are culturally programmed to do this; it's just that they're focused. They know what they want, and they think that they're being cheated of it.

In this transcript O'Malley's words are placed in brackets because they function as backchannels, the soft and unobtrusive language a listener uses to show that she is attending to what the speaker is saying and also to signal that she wants the speaker to continue talking and that she does not want to take a turn of her own. Given the fact that O'Malley only offers backchannels, it is unclear how she feels about Yearwood's analysis of the students' behavior. She neither agrees nor disagrees with her comments. She does not solicit help from the group and participates only minimally in the discussion. Following Yearwood's alternate analysis of the problem, another one of the teachers, Eileen Shakespear, tries to move the talk toward a solution, suggesting increasing the rigor of class discussion. O'Malley does not respond to Shakespear's suggestion, either.

As time went on, O'Malley used her research to continue to learn about her varied students' interactional styles. She tells how she used the research opportunity to find ways to create a classroom community that included the participation of all of her students. She established ways for students to participate that ensured that they all would take a turn sharing their writing, eliciting response from the rest of the class, and providing response to others. O'Malley discovered how to teach her students to attend carefully to their classmates, to notice what made professional writing and one another's writing strong and effective, and then to articulate their observations during the class discussion and apply those observations to their own writing. After analyzing O'Malley's process, Kalnin (1999) writes that ultimately O'Malley found that she taught her students "interpersonal skills—ways of listening and responding—and analytical skills—ways of interpreting and expressing experiences" (p. 210).

O'Malley writes about Eric, an immigrant from Vietnam. She is pleased not only with his oral participation but with the results for his writing. Eric wrote about his father's struggle to carry him from Vietnam to an Indonesian refugee camp. O'Malley commented on the power of his words and their impact on his fellow students when he took his turn sharing his writing:

> Nothing that we could have read about Vietnamese struggle during the war could have been more vivid than that firsthand account, told by the infant who was saved, now a writer telling his own father's story. (Boston site meeting, October 31, 1992)

Eric himself stated in an interview: "When I write, I feel like I am in a holy world—a world of my own. I feel powerful because anything I want I can just write it down. It's in my head" (Kalnin, 1999, p. 207). His strong feelings about writing likely sustained him during the class discussion of his and the other students' work. O'Malley concluded that through her research with Eric and other students, "[I] recovered my own sense of worth as a teacher, privileged enough to witness great beauty and fortunate enough sometimes to help make it happen" (Kalnin, 1999, p. 205).

TAKING RISKS

In all three of these networks the university facilitators set risk-taking as a goal for the teachers as researchers but not necessarily as teachers. Our idea was to create a community where the teachers would receive support for taking risks in their thinking about their research and in their writing. However, for the teachers in the first two networks taking research-related risks often implied taking risks in the classroom. In the MUSE program, the new teachers did not talk about taking risks in the same ways that the more experienced teachers did. They did not yet have safe classroom routines from which it would feel risky to deviate. Instead, they discussed the importance of the group providing a safe haven for them as new teachers, since everything they did felt risky.

In the first two networks, the risk-taking was associated with reconceptualizing well-established teaching routines. The teacher researchers sometimes used the group for support in taking risks and then in dealing with the consequences. In Chicago, Griselle Diaz-Gemmati changed her stance as a teacher as a result of the risks she took with her research, her writing, her curricular decisions, and her interactions with her students. Her talk during the group meetings revealed her perceptions of these intertwined risks and the ways group members supported her efforts. From the start, her research topic—what's involved in explicitly raising issues of race, ethnicity, and social class in her classroom—felt risky to her.

She was nervous about the political tone of her research topic and her new curriculum. She was concerned that introducing sensitive curricular issues for her research would push her students to grow up too fast. She was shocked by their adult-like worries "about inequality in society, gender issues, racial issues, [and] ethnic issues." What seemed shocking to Diaz-Gemmati seemed normal to Landau-McFarland, "But they're [Diaz-Gemmati's students] a microcosm of society." When Diaz-Gemmati retorted, "You never think that these kids worry about stuff like that," Landau-McFarland again reassured Diaz-Gemmati that her students were behaving normally: "Sure they do. It affects them every day." A few turns later I reinforced Landau-McFarland's point:

> I think bottom line for Griselle is that these kids live in a really complex world that they have to navigate in, and they're not oblivious to it. Even though they're little, it affects them. And they are going to cope in various ways, but if everything is pushed under the table at school where they have people who can guide them and who can help them through it, if those people don't do that, then I think they're [the students] missing something.

In the course of the discussion, Diaz-Gemmati began to feel more comfortable about her new curriculum, but she still voiced lingering qualms because one of her students asked her, "Why are you bringing all this crap into the room?"

Group members were surprised that Diaz-Gemmati's student wanted to see only what one of the teachers called an "Alice in Wonderland" view of the world. I asked Landau-McFarland how she would deal with such a student, hoping she would suggest strategies that Diaz-Gemmati might find helpful. She replied that she thought students should explicitly be told:

> It's something that has to be learned, and this is what we're working on, and this is the way the world is. You may not have experienced it yet, but it will come your way. If it doesn't come your way, you're very fortunate, but you need to be aware that it's there.

She also notes that because of these tensions many students end up "killing each other, literally."

An extended discussion ensued among the other teachers about what they consider a mistaken sense that school should be "antiseptic," a place where the difficult and potentially explosive issues are avoided. Like O'Malley, Diaz-Gemmati remained uncomfortable. She

was not immediately convinced about the wisdom of raising potentially explosive topics.

But this conversation, and the many others like it across the year,
provided Diaz-Gemmati with the support she needed to pursue explicit
discussions of race in her classroom, to ultimately study and write about
them, and to grow as a teacher (see Diaz-Gemmati, 1999). She concludes
her chapter for *Inside City Schools* with the following admission:

> I would be lying to myself if I pretended to be the teacher I was before I
> had initiated this project. If anything, this research has taught me that
> hard talk on candid issues can take place within the safety of classroom
> walls. I know that a society that is free of prejudice is many, many years
> away, but it's something I hope to keep striving for—even if it's only in
> the microcosm of life that comprises my classroom. (p. 76)

Across all three networks, the university facilitators worked with
the teachers to create "safe" and nonjudgmental research groups where
we all would be comfortable taking risks as researchers and writers and
talking about our risk-taking. For the more experienced teachers, this
risk-taking in the research arena and the support in the group setting
fed into risk-taking in the classroom. For the new teachers, it made the
whole act of teaching, which was generally a risky business, more
manageable.

UNDERSTANDING STUDENTS

Many teachers focused on learning about their students' lives, with
a goal of better understanding their students' behavior and their ways
of learning. Of these, many were especially interested in the teaching-
learning interactions between their students and themselves. Much of
the time the need to understand students emerged because of a need
to solve a problem related to helping a particular student, as was the
case with O'Malley and with the example I will present in this section.
Still, understanding students was also a large concern for these teachers on its own, independent of problems with particular students.

The teachers in all three networks began with knowledge of the
importance of "listening" to their students and "hearing" what they
say. However, they learned from the multiethnic group of teachers and
university facilitators in their teacher research groups and from the
multiethnic students in their classrooms that it is not always easy to
"hear" in multiethnic classrooms. For this reason, many focused their
research on figuring out how to listen better, especially across cultural,

class, ethnic, gender, and generational divides. They learned about their students both through their teacher research and through their conversations with others in their research groups.

For these teachers a major reason to listen to students was to figure out how to help them become more engaged in the academic enterprise and thereby reap its benefits. In New Orleans, Karen Alford, who is White, was beginning to open her eyes to signs of resistance from many of her Black students. She studied and wrote about her experiences with several of them as part of her teacher research project (see Alford, 1999). Here I will tell the story of one of these students, Tracey, whose resistance was not subtle. Tracey openly voiced a negative attitude toward Whites and also refused to write or do other schoolwork in Alford's class.

Alford opened a conversation about Tracey with her colleagues by reading a vignette she wrote about the time when Tracey told the whole class that she didn't like White people, not even her teacher "Ms. Karen." Alford explained her conflicts about handling the incident:

> She's entitled to a feeling. Still if a White child had said, "I do not like Black people," in my class, I would at least have a private conversation with that person. Somehow that remark would sound so hateful. But now I wonder how some of my White students might feel about Tracey's comment. It separates her from half of the students. (New Orleans local meeting, December 22, 1992)

Soon thereafter Tracey was suspended for other reasons, providing Alford with an opportunity to discuss Tracey's behavior with a social worker. The social worker concluded that Tracey "has a real problem with authority." However, Alford told the group that she was not comfortable with this analysis. She saw the problem as more complex and offered an alternate analysis to suggest that the issue was more specifically race-based:

> The only teacher she likes is Bernie, our P.E. coach who's Black. But to me, Bernie has been angrier at Tracey than any of us have. He's much stricter with the kids than I am. She likes him because he's African American, and she doesn't like us because we're White.

Cindy Roy, the site coordinator, also disagreed with the social worker's analysis, but she suggested a more general psychological explanation:

I have to admit, social workers always kind of choke me up when they say, "These children have problems with authority." Children have problems in that their lives are out of control, and they don't [Alford: Yeah.] have any way to take it back and control.

Alford had mentioned earlier that Tracey's home life was difficult. Roy hypothesized that when life feels out of control at home, Tracey may see school as "a place where she feels some control over what she can do" and that her behavior may be a way of exercising that control. Roy also reminds the group that adolescence is a time when students normally think "how much power can I get from a parent, from a school, from my friends." Others concur with Roy's analysis, offering many backchannels of agreement while she speaks.

Alford then offers yet another possible psychological explanation, that Tracey may be trying to protect herself from rejection:

If somebody likes her and supports her, she starts putting up [Roy: Barriers?] this outright thing, "I do not like White people, and not even Ms. Karen" thing. Seemed to be like she was trying to get me to say, "Well then, I don't like you either." [Roy: Hmm.] [Herring: Uh huh. Uh huh.] And I'm not going to fall for that.

Alford tells the rest of the group that the social worker recommended that she "stop caring," basically that she protect herself emotionally and in effect not try to solve the problem with Tracey. Alford's fellow teacher researchers, several of them Black, respond with shock and outrage:

Herring: You can't stop it. You can't stop caring.
Galley: What? The social worker told you?
Alford: "You aren't gonna change her." She said, "You aren't gonna change things for her."
Galley: Is that right? Jesus Christ.
Valenti: I don't think she meant stop caring about, did she use those words?
Alford: She said, "Stop taking a personal—" Caring wasn't the word. She said, "You get personally involved with your students. Don't get so personally involved with them."
Williams Smith: Involved.
Galley: You can't help it.

Alford: To me that means stop caring, but—

Galley: You can't help it.

Herring: How can a teacher not become personally affected with—

Williams Smith: Involved.

Herring: Especially if you carry those problems around, you've weighted down.

Alford: I've been with Tracey since she was in fourth grade because I was the teacher's aide in her class. So I mean it's not like somebody I could just go off and do what you want to do.

Roy: Ah, right, it's not like some child who's new.

Sarah Herring and Reginald Galley are adamant in their disagreement, repeatedly saying "you can't" think the way the social worker does; from their points of view, teachers inevitably become personally involved if they care, and caring is necessary for good teaching. Meanwhile, Elena Valenti tries to see the social worker's point of view, saying she couldn't have meant what Galley and Herring say she meant, "to stop caring." Alford, however, agrees with Galley and Herring's interpretation.

In the end, all the teachers of color, led by Galley and Herring, make a touching attempt to reassure Alford that all will end well, that Tracey really likes her even though she says the opposite:

Galley: She really doesn't dislike you.

Sarah H: When they [unclear word here] how to get the attention that they want.

Roy: Uh huh.

Galley: She really likes you.

Herring: She probably does. From all those years, she probably does.

Galley: But she really doesn't—

Herring: But she doesn't know how to express it at first.

Galley: —know how to say it to you or express it you in terms of your way. . . . But she really doesn't dislike you. She likes you. . . . Because if she disliked you, she wouldn't have anything to say to you.

Alford: Mmhmm.

Herring: Mmhmm. And you would know it.

Valenti: That's true.

Sarah H: She'd be really hostile. She would be hostile.

Valenti: She wouldn't have anything to say.

Galley: Nothing at all.

Valenti: She just would ig—I mean that's what you do with people you don't like.

Herring: Yeah. Right. You just, avoid them.

Valenti: You just do anything with them.

Galley: She goes out of her way to talk to you, so she likes you. She's just trying to—she's having some real difficulty with you being the person that you are, and just happen to be White. She would love for you to be Black, but you're not, and she doesn't know how to deal with that.

Herring: She just has to find a way to connect.

Alford: Yeah.

Galley: Because she's been taught that—has some idea that all White people are bad, so she figures you have to be bad, but you're not. You don't fit the mold. You're good, but you're also White, and that's creating some real—

Valenti: Yeah, conflict.

Alford: Uh huh.

Galley: —conflict in her mind.

Herring: Yes. I think that's true.

Galley: If you've been with her since the fourth grade,

Sarah H: I'm telling you. I'm telling you (unclear: it's so?).

Galley: She loves you. I mean, my goodness.

Williams Smith: Yeah.

Herring: That's almost your child. [Laughter].

As the conversation unfolds, Galley and Herring strengthen their claims about Tracey's feelings for Alford. Galley moves from "she really doesn't dislike you" to "she likes you" to "she loves you." Herring, meanwhile, begins with "she probably does [like you]," and moves to argue along with Galley and Valenti that Tracey would ignore Alford if she really disliked her, and then concludes that Tracey is "almost your child." Their explanations for Tracey's behavior move from she wants "attention," to she likes you but she "doesn't know how to express it," to if she really disliked you, "she wouldn't have anything to say to you," to she's conflicted because you're White and good.

Meanwhile, throughout this conversation Alford remains concerned about more than Tracey's affect. Her goal is to get Tracey to do her schoolwork. She explains that calling Tracey's parents, "that's not gonna bother Tracey." She further concludes, "I can't make her sit down and write. When she writes, she's a very good writer." The others try to help Alford find a way to involve Tracey in the work of the class. Sarah Herring recalls how she handled one of her difficult students. She told this student "to get a diary, make sure it has a lock and key. That's your personal partner there that you can talk to at any time you want to." She then suggests that Alford try this technique with Tracey: "So maybe you could suggest that she [Tracey] get a diary." Alford builds on Herring's idea with an even better one: "Maybe I could give her one." Herring adds optimistically, "Then maybe, she would feel personalized to you, and you could have a dialogue that way. And you could probably help her because I know it really helped this young lady."

Elena Valenti offers a suggestion from her classroom experience: "Those personal notes from the teacher usually bring them out a little bit." Others agree that any personal contacts make a difference. As Herring says, "She may be looking for that attention, and she's saying that to you because sometimes they are rebellious."

Alford thought that once she got Tracey to participate in the history curriculum she was developing for her teacher research it might provide her with a way to help Tracey consider the effects of her behavior on others and reconsider her actions. In this curriculum, students write about history in ways that teach them to take the perspectives of others:

> I think that some of this writing, the kind of writing and learning in the learning logs, would help her put things in perspective. If you put yourself into other people's stories, you see different points of view. It seems like that would help Tracey. Adolescents are so wrapped up in their lives. Everything is important and immediate. Maybe part of the reason we study history is to slow down a little.

Through her research Alford developed a strong and productive working relationship with many of her Black students. Although Alford intended to get a diary for Tracey, she never did. Still, as Alford and Tracey continued to work together and as they both practiced seeing from others' points of view, their relationship developed in positive ways, and Tracey began to do her work, albeit somewhat reluctantly at first. The next year, when she was in ninth grade at another school, Tracey returned to visit Alford and to thank her for helping her with her writing.

Alford concludes that the process of watching students, which she worked on as she became a teacher researcher, became critical to her teaching:

Doing this research project too. We had to be, so observant of
our kids and so noticing them and noticing who they really
were as learners that it helped me I think this year be a better
teacher. (New Orleans local meeting, April 4, 1993)

CONCLUSIONS

The professional development process in these teacher research
networks was slow and complex. It required that teachers spend time
reflecting on and analyzing their work, and it depended on structured
time for them to interact with peers and others who had something to
contribute, as well as time to collect and analyze data and think and
write on their own. There were a number of ways in which the research
process seemed to contribute to the teachers' growth.

First, the teachers decided what they want to learn about. They
were not told what to learn. They decided based on the issues they faced
in their classrooms and their schools. They could choose to avoid the
difficult issues. In fact, many of the highly experienced teachers entered these teacher research networks with the idea that they would
take the opportunity to write about what they did well, to tell other
teachers about curriculum they had developed and found successful
over the years, and to share their expertise. But most quickly learned
that the idea behind research is to look critically, not merely to share
successes. It is through this process of critique, analysis, and self-
challenge that the teachers found ways to learn and grow, regardless
of where they began (see also Kalnin, 2000). This learning is consistent with what Cochran-Smith and Lytle describe for knowledge-
of-practice.

However, different teachers took different routes to learning, depending on what was comfortable for them. Not only did they focus
their attention during group meetings and oftentimes their research
on different topics, but they often took different developmental paths.
What and how they learned seemed to depend on their initial interests and comfort levels. It was common that the process of becoming
a teacher researcher led the teachers to grow in confidence and prepared them to take a more consciously political stance. Still, some teachers gained as individuals from the process but did not see themselves
as part of anything larger professionally, while others became politi-
cized as part of the research process or used the process to deepen and
develop longstanding political commitments. Whereas Cochran-Smith
and Lytle define the inquiry stance in knowledge-*of*-practice as funda-

mentally political, in M-CLASS the politics often seemed to emerge from the work, and seemed to emerge for some more than for others. Within the same network, then, some teachers followed more of a knowledge-*of*-practice route while others followed more of a knowledge-*in*-practice route.

Consistent with Cochran-Smith and Lytle's knowledge-*of*-practice, I found that building a supportive community where teachers can work together to analyze their classroom life seemed essential to the process. Although the data here do not support Cochran-Smith and Lytle's claim that the inquiry community is "the central context within which teacher learning occurs" (1999, p. 282), it does support a modification of this claim, that the research community is integral to the research process. For a number of the teachers in the three networks in this project, the independent research process itself seemed equally central. Nevertheless, the research community, if not the central context for every teacher, was central for many and necessary for the rest.

Another aspect of the research process that seemed critical to teacher growth was the fact that it gave teachers permission to focus narrowly and deeply, something that seemed luxurious in a work world filled with so many competing demands. Although not all chose to focus narrowly and some even resisted (see Kalnin, 2000), those who did often were hesitant at first. They feared that it was unfair to focus on one student more than another; they did not want to show favoritism. As teachers, they were responsible for the whole curriculum, not just part of it; they had to cope with large chunks every day. However, most teachers felt relieved once they began to focus, and they quickly saw how they could turn what they were learning about a student or a slice of school or classroom life into something that would have greater benefit and wider implications for them as teachers and for their students generally. Focusing narrowly was especially valuable for the new teachers. JoAnna Buechart in the MUSE program explains:

> It was very relaxing to just be like, okay, I can just look at one thing and not feel like, "Okay, well, how am I in classroom management? How am I in this, how am I in that?" . . . It was very nice too because that's what you don't have time as a teacher to be thoughtful, you know. (JoAnna Buechart, MUSE exit interview, May 5, 1993)

Finally, teachers in all three networks worked on a research product for an audience beyond their local group—either a paper or a report or a workshop for other teachers. This research process and the pressure to produce a product took the group talk to increasingly higher levels; the group talk and its rigor then cycled back into the research and according to the teachers into their teaching.

Mary Ellen Bayardo in the M-CLASS Site Based Network prepared her workshop about her research with the hope of sharing the power of the discovery process with other teachers. She explains her goals:

> My goal is that these teachers leave saying, "Hey, maybe if I did a teacher research process, perhaps I would look at my teaching and the lessons and my students in a different way. It could give me a whole new perspective. And you know, maybe I will take a few risks as a teacher. Maybe I won't just let students sit wherever they want, and you have African-Americans here, Asians here, Latinos here. Maybe it's my responsibility as an educator to create a state where they can all come together." So . . . that's my goal . . . in an hour and a half . . . (Site Based Network meeting, March 20, 1999)

Bayardo hopes that other teachers will become teacher researchers and get "a whole new perspective," one that will lead them to change their stance. Bayardo thinks that then teachers might, among other things, begin to "look at . . . students in a different way" and "take a few risks," two of the three ways the teacher researchers in these three projects changed. These changes might lead the teachers to enter the larger political arena, but they might also lead to small but significant personal accomplishments. It is all of these accomplishments, be they large or small, that seem to be central to what teacher research is.

Acknowledgment. Preparation of this chapter was supported in part by grants from the U.S. Department of Education, Office of Educational Research and Improvement; the Spencer Foundation; and the University of California Office of the President. It was written while I was a fellow at the Center for Advanced Study in the Behavioral Sciences, where I was supported by grants from the Spencer Foundation and the William and Flora Hewlett Foundation.

REFERENCES

Alford, K. (1999). "Yes, girl, you understand": History logs and the building of multicultural empathy. In S. W. Freedman, E. R. Simons, J. Kalnin,

A. Casareno, & The M-CLASS teams (Eds.), *Inside city schools: Investigating literacy and learning in multicultural classrooms* (pp. 126–141). New York: Teachers College Press.

Cochran-Smith, M., & Lytle, S. L. (1999). Relationships of knowledge and practice: Teacher learning in communities. In A. Iran-Nejad & P. D. Pearson (Eds.), *Review of research in education, Vol. 24*. Washington, DC: American Educational Research Association.

Diaz-Gemmati, G. (1999). "And justice for all": Using writing and literature to confront racism. In S. W. Freedman, E. R. Simons, J. Kalnin, A. Casareno, & The M-CLASS teams (Eds.), *Inside city schools: Investigating literacy and learning in multicultural classrooms* (pp. 57–76). New York: Teachers College Press.

Delpit, L. (1988). The silenced dialogue: Power and pedagogy in educating other people's children. *Harvard Educational Review, 58*, 280–298.

Elliott, J. (1991). *Action research for educational change*. Milton Keynes, England: Open University Press.

Freedman, S. W. (1994). *Exchanging writing, exchanging cultures: Lessons in school reform from the United States and Great Britain*. Cambridge, MA and Urbana, IL: Harvard University Press and National Council of Teachers of English.

Freedman, S. W. (Ed.). (1999). *Beginning teachers do research*. Berkeley: University of California, School of Education.

Freedman, S. W. (in press). Teacher research, professional growth, and school reform. In G. Hillocks (Ed.), *The English Teacher as curriculum*.

Freedman, S. W., & M-CLASS/SBN team. (2000). *M-CLASS Site Based Network*. Final Report to the Spencer Foundation, University of California at Berkeley.

Freedman, S. W., Simons, E. R., Kalnin, J., Casareno, A., & The M-CLASS teams (Eds.). (1999). *Inside city schools: Investigating literacy and learning in multicultural classrooms*. New York: Teachers College Press.

Freedman, S. W., with Sperling, M., & Greenleaf, C. (1987). *Response to student writing* (Research Report 23). Urbana, IL: National Council of Teachers of English.

Goswami, D., & Stillman, P. (Eds.). (1987). *Reclaiming the classroom: Teacher research as an agency for change*. Portsmouth, NH: Boynton/Cook Publishers.

Kalnin, J. (1999). What teacher researchers say about creating communities of achievement: Empowerment in and beyond the classroom. In S. W. Freedman, E. R. Simons, J. S. Kalnin, A. Casareno, & The M-CLASS Teams (Eds.), *Inside city schools: Investigating literacy in multicultural classrooms*. New York: Teachers College Press.

Kalnin, J. (2000). *Teachers learning: A collaborative research network in action*. Unpublished Ph.D. dissertaton, University of California, Berkeley.

Lytle, S. L., & Cochran-Smith, M. (1989). Teacher research: Toward clarifying the concept. *The Quarterly of the National Writing Project and the Center for Study of Writing, 11*(2), 1–3, 22–27.

Mohr, M., & MacLean, M. (1987). *Working together: A guide for teacherresearchers*. Urbana, IL: National Council of Teachers of English.
Schön, D. (1983). *The reflective practitioner: How professionals think in action*. New York: Basic Books.
Stenhouse, L. (1985). What counts as research. In J. Rudduck & D. Hopkins (Eds.), *Research as a basis for teaching: Readings from the work of Lawrence Stenhouse*. Portsmouth, NH: Heinemann Books Ltd.

CHAPTER 13

Students' Work and Teachers' Learning

JOSEPH P. MCDONALD

Like other chapters in the book, this chapter has an argument to make. In fact, it has two arguments to make. The first concerns the value of using student work in professional development activities, and the second concerns the value of doing so in bridging ideological divides. However, the chapter will not be entirely argument. As I write it, I am mindful of Jerome Bruner's (1990) warning that arguments are often insufficiently convincing. He recommends complementing them with stories, which, he says, have the power to bridge the writer's and the reader's different senses of the truth. That is because stories are so clearly shaped by the storyteller's perspective, and thus remind the reader implicitly that other perspectives are possible. In the field of education, now so full of polarized arguments, it seems especially sensible to follow Bruner's advice.

The chapter begins with argument number one, and concludes with argument number two. Between the arguments comes the story, along with an analysis of it. Also between arguments is a kind of map to the existing traditions of teacher learning from student work. The ideological tensions I seek to resolve with argument number two arise from differences among these traditions.

ARGUMENT: WHAT TEACHING AND LEARNING REALLY ARE

It should be commonplace that teachers take cues for their own learning from their students' work. It should be commonplace that schools, under extraordinary pressure today to raise standards of achievement for all their students, search the students' work for signs of what to do. The fact that these practices are far from commonplace derives from a widespread confusion about what teaching really is. It is commonly thought that teaching involves the transmission of knowledge to students, knowledge defined by curriculum. In this view, teachers transmit knowledge more or less successfully, depending on their own skills and also on their students' capacities and receptivity. This is what teachers look like they do. This is also what many teachers say they do. And it is what many policymakers, school and district leaders, and even parents expect them to do.

Consequently, there is widespread public interest today in what the official curriculum covers or does not cover—evolution? phonics? the multiplication tables? There is also much public interest in standardized test scores. From the perspective of a transmission view of teaching and learning, the most important question to ask about schools is whether they teach what they should, while the most important question to ask about students is how much of it they learn. The first question seems to demand an answer in lists of content covered, while the second seems to demand an answer in percentiles. To offer the students' actual work instead—with the schools' assignments implicit—seems an evasion. To explore the work seems a distraction.

What teachers really do, however, is more complicated than the transmission view of teaching and learning suggests. Conditioned by their own experience and by their interpretation of the curriculum, teachers want their students to achieve certain kinds of understandings. They may say that they want them to know certain things, but they mean something deeper and subtly different than the words convey. This is true, by the way, whether the "things" are how to reason about fractions or how to apply an algorithm to add them. To encourage the development of their students' understandings in the right direction, teachers create relationships with the students anchored in explorations of particular material. It is not just the scope and sequence of the explorations, but also the quality of the relationships that determine how much understanding the students reach.

Teachers estimate their effectiveness in reaching the aims they set by attending to their students' performances. This is how students reveal their new understandings or their lingering misunderstandings (Gardner, 1999; Perkins, 1992; Wiske, 1998). Performances of understanding are therefore teaching's medium—in the same way that sports plays are coaching's medium, and drafting is writing's medium. And students' work—the equivalent of the videotapes the coach made or the hard copy I print of my latest draft—is crucial to teachers' learning from practice.

Today, many American schools are in a state of crisis instilled by external demands for accountability. The consequences of the crisis are not yet clear. Will most students benefit or not? Much depends, I think, on whether teachers can reinvent accountability to fit what teaching really is. This involves resisting the transmission view of teaching, since efforts to accelerate transmission impair the relationships on which effective teaching depends. One sees the signs of such impairment in classrooms where test preparation crowds out teaching. To reinvent accountability to fit real teaching, teachers must study their students' performances. Such study closes the accountability loop—not only to elicit performances of understanding and to assess them against a set of demanding standards, but to use the experience of this assessment to adjust teaching. Sadly, however, there are few traditions of on-the-job study by teachers in American schooling. Ordinarily, for example, there are no study groups or professional seminars built into the American teacher's work week, no groups focused on curricular exploration or pedagogical conversation as in some other countries (Ma, 1999).

What is needed here are new school designs that make room for teacher learning on the job. Such designs will depend on policy changes at all levels of the system, and these will not be easy to obtain. Still, in introducing David Allen's (1998) edited collection of essays about "looking at student work," Howard Gardner speculates that the field of professional education for teachers may be ready for a kind of purification. The objective would be to achieve the methodological consensus around training that some other professions enjoy: medicine with its case conferences, business with its case studies, and law with its study of precedent-setting cases. Why shouldn't education have cases drawn from actual student work? he asks. And why shouldn't these constitute both the basic and advanced texts for teacher learning?

The appeal of this strategy for both Gardner and Allen is not just in its potential simplification of a now chaotic environment, but also in its symbolic focus on the core enterprise—the coaching of performances of understanding—and in the respite it offers from the reductive habit of substituting test scores or course grades for learning. Indeed, the whole title of Allen's edited volume is *Assessing Student Learning: From Grading to Understanding*. In several chapters, the volume also explores how we might better assess schools—from "grading" them on crude measures like average cross-sectional test scores to "understanding" them in terms of the quality of the work they encourage and expect.

As I say, the policy changes necessary to get there from here will not be easy to achieve. Meanwhile, we must not mistake structural change for cultural change. Providing teachers more time to meet together and plan together, for example, can have little impact on their learning if the teachers lack experience in talking with each other about their work, and lack models of how to look at their students' work in systematic ways. Similarly, without such cultural change, "school quality reviews," "walkthroughs," and other inspection-based accountability strategies are likely to be more compliance audits than learning opportunities for school faculties (Institute for Learning, 1997; Smith & Ruff, 1998; Wilson, 1996).

What can propel the necessary cultural change? In this chapter, I report on the work of several intermediary organizations that have created models of supporting teacher learning through exploring student work, and that are engaged in various kinds of activities designed to teach teachers how to use the models.

STORY: LEARNING TO "WORK THE DIAMOND"

Once upon a time, when the standards movement among the states was just gaining speed, a group of teachers in the largely poor northeast quadrant of Connecticut formed a study group. They wanted to learn how to "look at student work." They were not clear in the beginning about what kind of looking they had in mind, nor about why they thought this would be helpful in their work. But it had something to do with the accountability pressures beginning to build up.

Supported by a small Goals 2000 grant administered by a regional educational assistance center, the teachers worked with me and a British friend of mine, Simon Clements, formerly one of Her Majesty's Inspectors of Schools (HMI). I taught the Connecticut teachers certain elaborate methods of looking at student work (what I called there, and here, *protocols*). They included the Collaborative Assessment Conference from Harvard Project Zero, the Tuning Protocol from the Coalition of Essential Schools, the Minnesota Slice from the Bush Educators Program, and the Eileen Barton Protocol, named after a Chicago teacher who had taught it to both Simon and me. Simon taught the teachers still other protocols, including one he called the Yorkshire Setaside (Clements, 1998). Adapted from an HMI protocol Simon used when he was an inspector in Yorkshire, the Setaside convenes a small group of teachers after school for 45 minutes of time "set aside" to say what interests them in a particular child's drawing or a page of math, or anything else collected that day in a class or two. Each teacher has a moment to say what he or she particularly notices in the piece of student work. Everyone present has a moment to respond, and once the responses have all been given, an open discussion ensues.

Simon and I drove together to Connecticut on days when we worked with the teachers in this study group, including one day when we heard on the radio the news from Scotland about a gunman who had invaded an elementary school and murdered many children. Schoolhouse murders were not so common then as now. The news affected us deeply, and we talked a little about it with the Connecticut teachers. There is, of course, a vast difference between a threat to one's life and a threat to one's sense of professional power. Yet I think our conversation about these murders helped the teachers acknowledge to themselves and each other the sense of vulnerability they were feeling in the face of Connecticut policy changes. The acknowledgment helped them in turn to figure out what to do.

It was shortly afterward that the teachers turned the study group into a consulting group. They decided that "looking at students' work" involves a fundamental and beneficial shift of teaching attitude, and they wanted to help other teachers make the shift. In the manner of all consultants in those days (this was before the widespread use of Powerpoint), they used overhead transparencies to convey what they meant.

On one transparency they drew an isosceles triangle, with its narrow base at the top and its long equal sides pointing down. This triangle, they said, represents the state's new standards and assessments. Alone on the page, they said, this triangle feels to the teacher "like a dagger to the heart." Then they drew the same figure on the other transparency, but this time pointing up. This triangle represents teaching practice, they said, "like a tall mountain—impossible to move, hard to scale."

Next they overlaid the transparencies so that the "dagger's tip" penetrated the "mountain's top." (Try this yourself on a blank sheet of paper). The result was the construction of a new plane figure, a parallelogram the teachers called "the diamond." This is the plane of genuine accountability, they said, where it's hard to distinguish dagger from mountain, though both are close at hand (Caprioni et al., 1997).

The last time I talked with this group of teachers, they were planning to have T-shirts made up with the motto, "Work the diamond."

QUESTIONS RAISED BY THE STORY

Why did these Connecticut teachers take so much interest in looking at student work? In providing us with both the images of the dagger and the Scottish gunman, the story suggests the tension these teachers felt when they started this work, though they were not then articulate about it. In fact, one can read the story as the emergence of a teacher's voice, paralleling the emergence of a clearer public demand for accountability in schooling (McDonald, 1988, 1992). Pressured to be more productive and more accountable in their own work, these teachers instinctively retreated in order to "look" at their students' work. It was not, at first, that they wanted to evaluate the work by the light of the state's new standards or the implicit demands of its new statewide assessments. It was more that they wanted to evaluate the standards and assessments by the light of the work. The state says all children should know and be able to do such and such. But what do Justin or Maritza's experiences say to that? In looking for such answers, the teachers began to discover what many other teachers have discovered who have undertaken such study—that light shines both ways.

Simon and I offered the teachers an attractive alternative to two other possible responses that they found unattractive. They did not, on the one hand, want to damn the pressures from the state and retreat into the isolation of their own best intentions—though doubtlessly some of their colleagues were then doing just that. Nor, on the other hand, did they want to accept the assumption that "higher-ups" knew more about their students' learning than they did. They took a position in between these other possible positions, and it is one that has been little explored in the literature of school reform. "Work the diamond" is at once a splendidly concrete image and an ambiguous one. Is the work that of a jeweler or of a diamond miner? In either case, the image signifies the painstaking nature of the enterprise of using high and universal standards in the actual practice of teaching inevitably diverse students.

Why were the teachers able to "own" this third option so quickly, and to characterize it so aptly as in the logo and the motto? Why, within the space of a few months, were they able to change their conception of their role from workshop participant to consultant? First of all, I must fill an important gap in the story as told above. Encouraged by the Connecticut Department of Education, the agency that received the Goals 2000 grant in Connecticut actually planned a study group for principals, not teachers. When the agency called me, I thought that sounded like a good idea, but when I met the principals, it seemed clear that they really had little interest. As I recall, it was they who suggested inviting some teachers in their place. This is an important detail inasmuch as it acknowledges that reform in practice is often messier than reform as planned and funded. Indeed, the tendency to carry out reform as planned and funded (and/or evaluate it accordingly) is often responsible for the failure of reform to have a lasting impact (Schön & McDonald, 1998). But it is important also because it suggests that both the principals and the teachers who replaced them understood that this project was inherently about teacher learning. I believe that the teachers were especially drawn to it because the learning for once promised to relate quite closely to their actual practice, drawing on their students' own work.

The story suggests the role that a massacre of Scottish children may have played in catalyzing the teachers' responses to what they were feeling and learning. Sometimes extrapolating from extraordinary circumstances helps one recognize more ordinary tensions and to begin to deal with them. In this case, the ordinary tensions concerned the threat of a particular kind of victimization: being the target of behaviorist policymaking. By taking charge of their own learning, the teachers changed the culture of Connecticut policymaking as it affected them. But an important factor also was that Simon and I forced the issue. After a first session in which we provided some student work samples with which to explore several protocols for "looking," we told the teachers that we would not return to Connecticut to meet with them again unless they were willing to supply their own work samples. Later, we told them that there was no point to what we had taught them if they failed to build some new contexts for using it.

Indeed, Simon and I never thought of ourselves as workshop leaders—responsible to an agency for "delivering" some "in-service professional development" to teachers. We felt responsible instead to the teachers themselves—to aid them in their efforts to move in the direction they seemed intuitively headed. And we felt responsible also to the traditions into which we felt we were inducting them. In the process, we passed to them some tacit assumptions of these traditions—at least as we understand them. The first is that protocols for looking at student work collaboratively, while exacting in their demands, do not require elaborate training and expertise. What they do require, as Kathe Jervis (personal communication) has usefully put it, is a willingness to bend the rules. I would also say a willinness to suspend disbelief. Possessing these, any teacher can participate with little preparation, and any thoughtful participant can move in relatively short order to facilitator. The second assumption is that these protocols, while designed and promoted by particular organizations, belong to the community of teachers at large. And the third assumption is that members of this community can use the protocols as they see fit, adapt them to local circumstances, and teach them to others—again, in the spirit of a willingness to bend the rules.

It is important to note that the assumptions Simon and I passed on are not universally held across all the organizations active in this field. Sometimes, for example, particular adaptations of protocols are controversial among the original designers, and some organizations object when they hear that someone is facilitating a protocol they developed without what they regard as the proper training, experience, or authorization. However, the tug of the teacher underground seems stronger than any organization's or individual's power to maintain what they take to be principled standards of usage. I myself have sometimes marveled at how something I have had a hand in inventing shows up on my path strangely transformed. I believe, however, that the best course of action in such circumstances is to point out the roots of a protocol. This is not just to acknowledge its creators, but to acknowledge as well (and make available for critique) the theoretical assumptions attached to these roots. Indeed, that is one of the purposes of this chapter.

What are these methods—or protocols—that we taught them? Where do they come from? How do they work? Two of the three mentioned in the story, the Collaborative Assessment Conference and the Tuning Protocol, are well documented and described in David Allen's (1998) edited volume mentioned above, and in a companion volume (1999) by Tina Blythe, David Allen, and Barbara Powell, *Looking Together at Student Work*. The Tuning Protocol is also described in my 1996 book, *Redesigning School*. Each represents a distinct tradition in the history of teacher learning from student work, as I describe below.

Two other protocols mentioned in the story, the Yorkshire Setaside and the Eileen Barton Protocol, are described currently only in the underground of teacher networks, workshops, and handouts. Both are good examples of simple-to-use protocols meant to be accommodated easily into the ordinary rhythms of a teacher's week—for example, during a common planning period, or some setaside time after school. The Barton method raises three questions about a single piece of student work: What do you see here? What do you not see? What questions do you have? It is in the same tradition as the Collaborative Assessment Conference. But the Yorkshire Setaside represents still a third tradition, as I describe below. It shares this tradition with the final protocol mentioned in the story, the Minnesota Slice. This is one that I designed for the Bush Educators Program at the University of Minnesota, with input from both Simon Clements and David Green, another former HMI. It is descibed in Kathleen Cushman's November 1996 issue of *Horace*, the publication of the Coalition of Essential Schools, and also on a web site devoted to protocols for exploring student work (www.aisr.brown.edu/LSW). The web site was developed by a collaborative of researchers and staff developers, and is maintained by the Annenberg Institute at Brown University.

TRADITIONS OF DISCIPLINED CONVERSATION

Protocols for helping teachers learn from students' work tend to share certain overarching features. The most obvious is that they involve actual student work on the table, and not necessarily the most polished work. Another is that the protocols invite conversation about this work and about the teaching associated with it. This is startling inasmuch as teachers generally do not speak with each other about their students' work. The protocols presume that teachers can learn more about teaching well by talking intimately and honestly with other teachers about their practice and its effects.

Like most conversations, the conversations provoked by these protocols are relatively unbounded in terms of what any party may think to notice or to say. This spontaneity is part of their appeal. Unlike most conversations, however, these are highly structured in terms of who may speak when and in what fashion. Indeed, the term *protocol* suggests that these conversations are as scripted in format as a researcher's interview or a meeting between diplomats. Paradoxically, though, the discipline is also part of their appeal. As with research or diplomacy, the activity of talking productively with peers about the intentions behind and the actual effects of one's work demands assertiveness and frankness, but also delicacy and some buffer against quick judgments and harsh words. Participants in the protocols generally recognize quickly—though usually after an initial period of discomfort—that the discipline makes the process safe. Finally, all the protocols explicitly or implicitly involve standards. Even protocols like the Collaborative Assessment Conference that aim at first to suspend rather than encourage teachers' evaluative instincts ultimately do so in order to hone these instincts.

Protocols for Suspending Judgment

In a recent description of the Collaborative Assessment Conference, a protocol he and his Harvard Project Zero colleagues designed in 1988, Steve Seidel had this to say:

Like works of art, the things children make can be highly engaging. They can captivate, confuse, charm, and alarm the viewer/reader. But if we think we know everything about children, their work, this kid in particular, and so on, we won't watch with such care. The protocol is a trick, then, to focus the attention and encourage engagement. (Seidel, 1998, p. 31)

Seidel's analogy is hardly incidental. He is himself an artist as well as an educational researcher, and Project Zero was founded in order to study cognition and education in the arts (McDonald et al., 1999). One might say the same thing of all the protocols described in this chapter that he says of the Collaborative Assessment Conference—that it aims through formality to trick people into spontaneously doing what ought to come naturally but does not. This one, however, uses the aesthetic device of making the familiar strange: it invites speculation about what might otherwise seem quite ordinary. In the presence of a child's drawing, as in the presence of a museum piece or following a film, the Collaborative Assessment Conference presumes that the people who experience the work together can gain much by wondering aloud about it. This includes sharing what they noticed, raising questions, and speculating about significance without necessarily pinning it down. However, such deliberate wondering is unusual. "That was a great performance by so and so," we might say as we exit the theater; then we talk about other things. One result is an aesthetic offense—failure to allow an aesthetic object to do what it was made to do. Another result is a cascading loss of learning over time—in the same way that the absence in our lives of the books we should have read or the music we should have heard diminishes our understanding of all the books and music to follow.

The Collaborative Assessment Conference counters an impulse conditioned by the teacher's daily pressure to make hundreds of quick judgments—Who's got it? Who doesn't? Who's paying attention? Who isn't? The protocol forces participants to look closely at a piece of student work as a work rather than as an answer or an indicator of achievement. Participants describe in turn what they see in the work without making judgments. They raise questions about it. They speculate about what the student was working on. Meanwhile, the teacher who brought the work to the group's attention remains silent. Paradoxically, the artifice allows an intimate and authentic conversation to form and begin to flow. Once this happens, the protocol relaxes—the teacher joins in and answers questions, the other participants offer advice, and everybody reflects on what they have learned.

In its suspension of judgment, its emphasis on observation and description, and its use of guided, collegial conversation, the Collaborative Assessment Conference is like Descriptive Review. Associated with the work of Patricia Carini and her colleagues at the Prospect Archive and Center in Vermont, Descriptive Review is a set of processes for teachers' learning about children and their work (Carini, 1979, 1982; Himley with Carini, 2000; Kanevsky, 1993). The Prospect Center's efforts were arguably the first efforts within a longer tradition of child study to treat the work of children as text for exploration. In doing so, Carini and her colleagues explicitly invited teachers to regard their students' work not as transparent indicators of development or achievement, but as complex, culturally embedded constructions that must be "read" (Himley, 1991).

Helen Featherstone (1998) describes how a group of Philadelphia teachers, members of one of the Prospect Center's networks, have used Descriptive Review in weekly after-school gatherings since the late 1970s:

> The Descriptive Review of a child has six parts. First, the chairperson gives the child's name (a pseudonym) and age and the teacher's guiding question [for example, how to help the child as a developing reader]. Then the presenting teacher describes the child, using five broad headings: physical presence and gesture; disposition; connections with others, both children and adults; strong preferences and abiding interests; and modes of thinking and learning. Third, the chairperson restates the presenting teacher's themes as she hears them. Then the participants ask questions that they hope will clarify the descriptions and the context. Fifth, the chairperson summarizes new information. Finally, returning to the teacher's original question, group members make recommendations. (p. 70, citing Kanevsky, 1993)

As with the Collaborative Assessment Conference, the protocol for Descriptive Review is at once demanding and liberating. For example, one of the Philadelphia teachers told Featherstone that the group makes no attempt to reconcile conflicting recommendations, and discourages the presenting teacher from responding to any of them. The effect of the discipline of suspending judgment is that the teacher finds her capacity to make judgments enriched by other perspectives. Like the Collaborative Assessment Conference, Descriptive Review pushes teachers to delve deeply for answers to questions about their students, even as it acknowledges paradoxically the role of uncertainty in teaching. It does the latter by insisting on the complexity of children and their work, by forcing participants in the Review to adopt multiple frames for viewing the child and his or her work, by forcing continual reframing, and by avoiding summary judgment.

The tradition in which I place both the Collaborative Assessment Conference and Descriptive Review stretches back to the child study movement of the late 19th and early 20th centuries, and through later movements that have also situated themselves in opposition to the powerful influences of standardized testing in American schooling. These later movements include the influential North Dakota Study Group on Evaluation.

The child study movement was especially championed by the early psychologist G. Stanley Hall. It aimed to make teachers researchers in their own practice by closely studying their students' learning. "The teacher must know two things," claimed Hall: "the subject matter to be taught, and the nature and capacity of the minds in which it is to be rooted." In his typically grandiloquent fashion, Hall claimed that child study would help prevent "the mutilation which so powerful an engine as the modern school may inflict upon the tender souls and bodies of our children, and thus upon our entire national future"(quoted in Lagemann, 2000, p. 26). Hall was an opponent of the mental measurement movement, championed by such other early psychologists as Edward Thorndike and Lewis Terman. However, his personality, and what Lagemann (2000) calls his evangelicism in support of child study, alienated many of his contemporaries.

This alienation was perhaps a factor in the marginalization of child study within 20th-century U.S. schooling.[1] The more important factor, however, in ensuring that child study became the sideline to mental measurement's mainline was the American romance with efficiency (Callahan, 1962; Tyack, 1974). This ensured the success of such instruments for understanding students as Terman's Stanford-Binet intelligence test and his Stanford Achievement Test—precursor of today's generation of standardized achievement tests.

By 1972, when the North Dakota Study Group on Evaluation was founded under the leadership of Vito Perrone (1991, 2000), standardized testing was well established in American schooling, and with it a derivative culture of classroom testing emphasizing factual recall, short answers, objective scoring, and the separation of assessment from instruction (Shepard, 2000). For the last 30 years, Perrone and his colleagues in the North Dakota Study Group have published critiques of the testing culture in U.S. schooling and have promoted alternatives to it. Patricia Carini was an original member of the Group. Other influential members have included Lillian Weber (1997), Kathe Jervis (1996), Eleanor Duckworth (1996), Helen Featherstone (1998), and Deborah Meier (1995). Meier has been, with Theodore Sizer (1996), a leader of the Coalition of Essential Schools, and also of the anti-testing movement in Massachusetts (Lindsay, 2000).

Even as the testing culture triumphed by the end of the century in the enactment of an astounding series of state and federal policies promoting testing, such voices as these have ensured a counterculture that has affected many of the national organizations now promoting teachers' ways of learning from student work. Such organizations include the Coalition of Essential Schools; the National Center for Restructuring Education, Schools, and Teaching (NCREST); Project Zero; the Rural Challenge; the Rural School and Community Trust; the National School Reform Faculty; the National Writing Project; and the teacher networks of the Bread Loaf School of English.

Protocols for Tuning Judgment

Yet the phenomenon that concerns us in this chapter straddles the ideological divide between those who dislike standardized testing, and those who regard it as an important tool in ensuring high achievement and equity. Thus important protocol inventors, trainers, and promoters—in addition to the organizations listed above—include the Institute for Learning at the University of Pittsburgh, the Education Trust, and the Annenberg Institute. These organizations are prominent in what is often called the standards movement. In encouraging teacher learning through explorations of student work, these organizations have tended to make the role of standards explicit and emphatic. They are therefore important participants in a second tradition, one founded not on the value of suspending judgment but on the value of tuning it to higher standards.

Of course, protocols like the Collaborative Assessment Conference and the Descriptive Review implicitly involve the application of standards also, inasmuch as they invite a conversation about values and valued performances. Thus at one point in the Descriptive Review that Helen Featherstone (1998) observed, the presenting teacher, Lynne Strieb, says of her student Matthew: "His math is fine. He noticed the vertical pattern of numbers in the hundred chart. He's learning to tell time. He is interested in the 100th day project. He can tell that a dime is enough to get an eraser at the school store. He is not facile with numbers over 100 yet. He does fine with adding and subtracting" (p. 74). Strieb, a member of the North Dakota Study Group, may be said to be applying standards here, but ones that have arisen from her practice and her practiced observation of children. They are not the kind of standards that policymakers typically mean when they call for standards-based teaching. Indeed, Strieb's emphasis here on multiple descriptors and her emphasis in the overall review of Matthew's learning on multiple frames, as well as her withholding of summary judgment, are intended to complicate the conventional idea of standards. At least within the reflective space created by this and similar protocols, external standards are bracketed, and the child's uniqueness accentuated.

The emphasis goes the other way in a protocol designed by Ruth Mitchell for the Education Trust. The protocol is called Standards in Practice. It is part of a larger process described in Mitchell's (1996) monograph, *Front-End Alignment*, whose title signifies the underlying strategy of orienting teacher learning and teacher practice to a set of public standards. Mitchell explains:

> The first step in using the standards is getting them into the schools. Some communities have tried to do this by immediately designing assessments based on their new standards. However, we suggest moving more slowly and allowing everyone in a school—teachers, students, administrators, parents—to become familiar with the standards over at least a year. During this time, you should use the standards to look at the student work actually going on in the school, and ask two vital questions: Is this work good enough to meet the standards? If it isn't, what are we going to do about it? (Mitchell, 1996, p. 26)

This is where the protocol fits in. On numerous occasions over the course of a year, teams assemble to look at the standards side by side with student work. A team always includes teachers as well as other members of the community—for example, parents and school board members. The student work is a complete class set of work responding to a single assignment. The protocol requires first that all the members of the team complete the assignment as given to the students. This is a novel requirement among protocols, and can lead to great insight. Next the team generates a rough scoring guide based on a reading of the standards, and on its experience in completing the assignment. Then members of the team individually score each of the student papers in the class set, using the new scoring guide. When finished, they engage in a facilitated conversation focused on the following questions: What does this student work tell us about the student's learning? Was this assignment well designed to help students acquire knowledge and exercise skills? A recorder writes the group's answers to the questions. Finally, the team plans some action steps based on its analysis.

As with all the protocols discussed in this chapter, Standards in Practice involves a discipline concerning what may be said and when. Mitchell describes one facet of this discipline:

> Teachers typically will look for the work of students they recognize and will want to bring into the discussion personal information about those students. You don't want this to happen. Instead, you want teachers to look at the work only in the light of the standards, not to exclaim about the growth Jasmine has shown since last year or to point out that Antonio had missed three days before the assignment in question. (p. 30)

As the protocols discussed above require the supension of judgment so as to promote greater understanding of a student's unique characteristics, this one forces judgment so as to promote an honest accounting of gaps between expectations and actual achievement. An explicit premise of this second tradition is that such honest accounting is crucial to efforts to improve conditions of learning for all students. An implicit premise is that the portrayal of students as unique individuals has a dark side in American educational history—namely, the century-long effort to classify students based on their presumed abilities and academic destinies. It is such presumption that this tradition seeks to suspend.

As the first tradition discussed above arose in opposition to the testing culture of American schooling, this second tradition arose partly from a testing subculture. Mitchell, for example, traces the roots of Standards in Practice to group scoring practices in standardized testing introduced to teachers over the course of the last 25 years as part of state and district efforts to assess writing and other performance tasks. Indeed, for many teachers, group scoring provided their first serious encounters with work by students other than their own, and many have reported the experience as powerful professional development (King & Campbell-Allan, 1998).

However, this tradition of teacher learning from student work has other roots as well. A particularly important one involves the efforts by reform networks to put teachers and schools in closer touch with one another. One of the protocols mentioned in the story of the Connecticut teachers is the Tuning Protocol, and its name signifies the objective of these efforts. Some colleagues and I at the Coalition of Essential Schools developed the Tuning Protocol to provide some schools we were working with wider access to images of quality—images available in the teaching practice of other schools, and also in the work practice of adults in the community. We hoped that the schools might "tune" their practices to these images. Over time, the Tuning

Protocol spread to many schools and school networks associated with the Coalition, and also to two important policy contexts. One is California, and Joel Kammer (1998) tells the story of the California Protocol in David Allen's volume. The other is New York, where in the mid-1990s the State Department of Education introduced an adaptation of the Tuning Protocol called the New York Peer Review.

New York's Commissioner of Education, Richard Mills, had the idea of introducing what were then the state's new Learning Standards by illustrating them with exemplary lesson plans by New York teachers. He also proposed honoring the teachers whose work was chosen by inducting them into a new entity called the New York State Academy for Teaching and Learning. As his staff, joined by consulting staff from the Annenberg Institute, including me, began to plan the Academy, we realized that membership could be more than an honor. This insight developed as we talked about a peer review process to judge submitted lesson plans. Our first image of this process was that of a contest judged by peers who would review the work "blindly" and send their reviews to Albany. Then somebody said, "But what if the teacher were *there*?" What if the teacher did not send a lesson to Albany to be judged, but brought it to Albany in person, and what if the judges were others who had brought their own lesson plans to Albany? What if the contest became a conversation?

One of the first members of the Academy, Linda Dagle, a middle school teacher, recalled her experience of "induction":

> I brought a teaching idea I call "Reading the Newspaper
> Intelligently" to what I thought was a show-and-tell of successful
> teaching practices. I came armed with visual aids such as video-
> tapes of my seventh-grade students, writing they had done in
> response to newspaper photographs, my assessment of that
> writing, and the rubrics I used. But when I got to the three-day
> conference in Albany, full of other teachers bearing other
> packages, I found out this was not another "show-and-tell," but
> something I had never really done before. The next morning I
> presented my lesson to nine of my peers, some representing
> English at the middle level and others with diverse backgrounds.
> And the experience didn't end for me there. I then went off to be
> a peer reviewer for other people's lessons. In fact, everybody at
> the conference was both a presenter and a reviewer. And we were
> all felt like pioneers. (personal communication, October, 1992)

The protocol of the New York State Peer Review features a facilitator, a teacher-presenter, and up to eight reviewers, one of whom acts as recorder. The facilitator gives an overview of the process, sets the tone for the review, and describes the ground rules. The teacher-presenter sets the context for what is called the learning experience, including targeted learning standards and performance indicators as listed in the New York State Learning Standards guides. He or she may also direct the reviewer's attention to a focus question of particular interest—for example, "Do you think my assessment plan for this learning experience is as strong as it can be?" The peer reviewers listen silently for 10 minutes. Then, as the presenter stays silent, the reviewers respond in "warm" and "cool" terms with special reference to a set of criteria that highlight the standards the teacher has identified as learning targets. Warm comments are empathetic, appreciative. Cool comments are comparative, critical (McDonald, 1993). One aspect of the discipline in this protocol is that reviewers may not combine warm and cool in the same comment. Another is that they and the facilitator (who may participate in the review) must maintain an overall balance of warm and cool. Following their comments, the presenter responds to any of the comments he or she chooses to repond to, while the reviewers remain silent. Finally, everyone joins in general conversation. Following the departure of the reviewers from the table, the facilitator, presenter, and recorder meet to debrief. The aim of this part of the process is to ensure that the presenter is well oriented for the work of revising her learning experience. It is only after revisions are complete that he or she is inducted into the Academy.

Today, more than 1,300 New York teachers have participated in Statewide Peer Reviews, and thousands more in regional and district-level versions. Although the state still uses reviewed lesson plans to illustrate its Learning Standards on a web site devoted to the purpose (www.nysatl.nysed.gov), it has long since realized that Peer Review has a larger purpose than supplying illustrations. Indeed, from the enthusiastic comments of the first participants like Linda Dagle, the state realized that the process of Peer Review is at least as important as its products. These participants often say that the experience has been their best professional learning experience since student teaching. Doubtlessly, one factor affecting its reception is that the review here is indeed conducted by peers, and that all reviewers are presenters and vice versa. It may also be that teachers are hungry for the kind of professional development experience that closes what I called above the accountability loop—one that makes concrete links among standards, teaching plans, and actual student learning as represented in classroom work.

Protocols for Extending Judgment School-Wide

The third tradition of teachers learning from students' work is different from the other two in its objectives, methods, and sources. For example, it targets schools rather than individual teachers, and emphasizes inquiry over speculation and the application of specific standards to practice. While the first tradition has roots in the American child study movement and the second in the American standards movement, this third has particular roots in the English tradition of school inspection as adapted to the American context (Wilson, 1996, 1999; Jervis, 1997).[2] You will recall from the Connecticut story that Simon Clements, a former HMI (Her Majesty's Inspectors of Schools), taught a protocol to the teacher-consultants called the Yorkshire Setaside. Based on collecting some work during an ordinary day in school and then engaging the school's teachers in an after-school conversation, the Yorkshire Setaside is a good example of this third tradition.

In adapting to the American context, school inspection has, of course, mixed with native traditions, especially the residues of early 20th-century school surveying and teacher-led curriculum study (Lagemann, 2000), and the more established traditions of instructional supervision (Glickman, 2000) and school accreditation (Wilson, 1999). One finds the impact of the standards movement, too—for example, in the Walkthrough, a protocol developed originally by Anthony Alvarado and his colleagues in New York City's Community District 2 (Elmore & Burney, 1997), and modified and promoted by the Institute for Learning at the University of Pittsburgh (Institute for Learning, 1997).

Walkthroughs have three different modes, depending upon who participates in them: supervisory, collegial, and observational (when an outsider accompanies an insider). The protocol begins with a discussion of the eight Principles of Learning, a set of standards for schools developed by Lauren Resnick for the Institute for Learning (Rothman, 1996). These especially emphasize students' capacity to learn rigorous intellectual habits and content, learning as apprenticeship, and habits of "accountable talk." Following the discussion, the participants tour the school, entering its classrooms and other work spaces, looking for and examining student work, talking with students and teachers, and in all these activities searching for evidence of the Principles of Learning in practice. Following the Walkthrough, participants discuss their findings with each other, offering evidence from their notes to support the judgments they make. Then one of their number, typically the principal, writes a post-Walkthrough letter to the teachers summarizing the findings.

As with the Walkthrough, most of the protocols of this third tradition of teacher learning from student work focus on accountability.
They also promote judgment-making. However, they tend to take a
more complicated view of both these things than is true of the protocols in tradition two. Wilson's (1996) account of the English school
inspection is helpful in understanding the difference. What is desir-
able in this tradition is more than the skillful application of rubrics.
Judgment is viewed as the weighing of multiple sources of evidence,
steeped in the wisdom of teaching experience and moderated by peer
conversation.

Like both of the other traditions, the protocols of the third tradition cover a range of scale and complexity—from the intimate and
simple Yorkshire Setaside, to the regional and state-level school quality review systems inspired by the work in the United States of former
HMI David Green. Examples of the latter include the School Quality
Review Initiative of the Southern Maine Partnership, which Debra
Smith and David Ruff (1998) describe in David Allen's edited volume;
the SALT initiative (for School Accountability for Learning and Teaching) of the Rhode Island Department of Education (Hole, McEntee, &
the SALT Leadership Team, 1999); and the School Quality Review of
Boston's Pilot Schools (the city's quasi-charter schools), coordinated
by the Boston Center for Collaborative Education.

In the midrange of scale and complexity are the Walkthrough, and
also the Minnesota Slice, another protocol mentioned in the Connecticut story. It was created as a professional and school development tool
for the Bush Educators Program of the University of Minnesota,
founded and led by John Mauriel of the university's Carleton School
of Management.[3] Over the course of 25 years, the program enrolled a
majority of Minnesota's superintendents of schools, a good proportion
of its principals, and a share of its central office and teacher leaders.
Most recently, its program featured a succession of problem solving inquiries. These began with cases drawn from the actual practice of school
leaders at various levels, proceeded in phase two with on-the-spot inquiries in schools and districts, and culminated in a phase three, team-
led project in the Bush Fellows' own schools and districts.

The Slice was developed as part of a tool kit for phase two. Each
year, some Bush alumni volunteeered their districts or schools to be
the subject of a Bush cohort's inquiry, and posed a focus question. One
year the question was, What seems to be the purpose of education in
Owatonna, Minnesota? These inquiries served double duty from the
perspective of the Bush Program—contributing to the quality of Minnesota teaching and learning directly in the places where they were

conducted, and contributing indirectly by teaching the Bush Fellows how to pursue such questions in their own places. Thus Bush Fellows learned how to conduct focus group interviews and in-depth interviews; they learned how to design, conduct, and tabulate telephone surveys; they learned how to organize a large-scale community meeting on a particular focus of inquiry; they learned how to shadow students; and they learned how to conduct a Slice. Most importantly, they learned how to weigh all the resulting evidence, and how to make judgments based on the evidence and moderated by spirited conversation.

The Slice gets its name from the constraints on the student work sample it analyzes. The aim of a "slice" is to capture a very broad but manageable array of student work that is also ordinary in terms of the range of qualities it includes. One year, the Bush Program collected all the work done between the morning of January 10 and noon on January 11 (including homework) in a sample of elementary classrooms (two classrooms at each grade) in two socioeconomically different schools within the district of Owatonna. It also collected all the work done within the same time parameters by a sample of secondary students in the district. The secondary sample cut across curriculum "levels," and drew equally from students considered by their schools to be high-achieving, low-achieving, and in the middle. At the elementary levels, the teachers collected the work, while at the secondary levels, the students themselves were the principal collectors. The definition of student work at both the elementary and secondary levels was as follows:

> . . . artifacts that teachers might use to understand students' learning: the completed homework assignment or math worksheet, the drawing or composition, the attempted graph, the reading log or science journal entry, the report on an experiment, the notes taken while listening to a presentation, the contributions to a class discussion or learning group (captured on audio or video tape), the construction of a model (captured in a photo), the draft of a poem or story, the script of a skit or the skit itself (captured on video tape), and so on. (unpublished memo, Bush Educators Program, 1996)

The result in the end was a substantial but highly bounded sample of student work. Reading and responding to such a sample requires some kind of protocol. Other organizations that have collected slices— for example, the Southern Maine Partnership, as described in Chapter 7—have developed their own protocols (Smith & Ruff, 1998). But the Bush protocol goes as follows:

Bush Fellows (the outsiders) and teachers and administrators of the host distrist (the insiders) gather for an afternoon and evening of slice-based conversation. The evening starts early—just after school lets out—with a two-hour quiet exploration of the student work. The written work (with all personal and school identifiers removed) should be arranged according to grade level, and laid out on tables, with plenty of chairs for browsers. Browsing should be encouraged, inasmuch as it is usually impossible to attend closely to every bit of a slice in just two hours. But the browsers should also be encouraged to take notes on what they notice, bearing the focus question in mind [for example, What seems to be the purpose of education in Owatonna?]. These notes will prove very useful at the seminar. Photographs should be laid out on a table also, or posted on bulletin boards, and there should be a room for video viewing. The video should be played museum-style—in one or more continuous loops.

Following the quiet browsing, everybody has dinner together, chatting about whatever they choose. Diners should be seated to ensure a mix at each table of outsiders and insiders. Following dinner, a two-ringed seminar begins. The inner ring of ten chairs—the only ring empowered to talk during the seminar itself—is first occupied by a selection of Bush Fellows. For up to forty-five minutes, they discuss the slice in terms of the focus question. As in any text-based seminar, the facilitator asks them to cite evidence from the text to back the statements they make, asks them to respond to each other's observations, and tries to keep the conversation moving ever deeper. After a half-hour to forty-five minutes (the facilitator's call), those in the inner ring cede their places to "insiders"—that is, to teachers and others from the schools where the slice comes. They are asked to continue the conversation rather than to start all over. After another half-hour to forty-five minutes, the facilitator calls a halt to the seminar proper, and begins a general conversation open to everyone in the room. (unpublished Bush Program memo, 1996)

ARGUMENT: THE VALUE OF MIXING TRADITIONS

Of all the problems facing U.S. schooling today, three of the most critical involve teacher learning. The first concerns gaps in teachers' understanding of what their students can do. The second concerns teachers' lack of skillfulness in assessing and assisting their students' growth along a continuum tuned to high and authentic standards. And the third concerns teachers' reluctance or incapacity to work collaboratively and accountably across classrooms and grade levels to ensure that all the students in a given school meet these standards in the end. Each of the traditions described above of teacher learning from student work especially focuses on one of these three problems, and each tradition has proven its effectiveness in numerous settings.

My argument concerns the fact that while the three problems are obviously related, the three traditions are not. If a teacher is unpersuaded that his students can do intellectually challenging work, then it seems pointless to teach him how to use rubrics for assessing such work. Meanwhile, the efforts of individual teachers who believe in children's capacities and who use rubrics to assess the children's work can be easily swamped by the contrary efforts of their colleagues in the same school. In general, if we keep our eyes on the child—in Kathe Jervis's (1996) evocative phrase—we recognize the need for solving all three problems, and thus for using all three of the traditions explored in this chapter.

Tradition number one, represented by methods like the Collaborative Assessment Conference and Descriptive Review, has proven to be a powerful learning aid for teachers in understanding the real capacities of students, and in fighting a century's practice of classifying students on the basis of premature judgments of their incapacities. This is because the protocols of this tradition explore difference without the presumption of deficit, and involve what Peter Elbow (1986) calls playing the believing game—suspending doubt in an artificial way in order to find grounds for supporting development. James Comer has said that many if not most American schools operate on the assumption that children cannot develop intellectually and morally, and that the school's business is to adjust them to their natural fate (personal correspondence). Stevenson and Stigler (1992), among other scholars, have pointed out that such prejudice is uncharacteristic of many other nations' schools. It seems inconceivable that such lofty goals of achievement as those represented by most states' standards documents and by many state assessment systems can possibly be reached absent the effort to make such prejudice uncharacteristic here, too.

Meanwhile, tradition two is about learning to act on the presumption of capacity. What is the point of believing in children's capacity if one lacks a sense of how to work with it and to what ends? As Deborah Meier has said, the phrase "All children can learn" is either a banality or an incomplete sentence (personal correspondence). The real issue is, learn *what*? Can all children learn the hard stuff that many standards documents say they should? And if so, how? The protocols of tradition two take these questions on, and in the best possible circumstances—with actual student work on the table, actual standards, and practically oriented conversation among teachers themselves. Anyone who thinks for long about the problem of raising standards of achievement for all American students will realize that there is no way from here to there without such conversation.

But individual teacher learning is simply not enough. The school itself must become a learning organization (Senge, 1990). What is needed for this is a transformation of the school culture from one focused on processing to one focused on invention in the interest of accountability. Too many schools in the United States today operate as if they were impassive public facilities. As Hill, Foster, and Gendler (1990) explain, schools acting as public facilities tend to distance themselves from the users of the facility by a preoccupation with their own smooth running. The bus station sees itself accountable for providing its patrons a clean and safe place to wait for their bus; it takes no responsibility for their enjoyment of the trip (McDonald, 1996). That is, of course, as it ought to be with regard to bus stations, but schools must have a larger purpose. They must stand for something. Their teachers must act continually and collaboratively to make sure that their commitments play out in their actions. And they must assume collective responsibility for the quality of the outcomes of these actions. The protocols of tradition three are all about helping teachers learn how to do such things—about building up the capacity to articulate values, about seeing and understanding the effects of their teaching at a schoolwide level, about making good judgments with respect to those effects, and about taking corrective action as necessary. No other accountability devices now in use by states, districts, or networks approach these protocols in terms of their power to do these things. Certainly average test scores released to newspapers in the form of "school report cards" do not come close.

At various points above, I have alluded to disputes between partisans of one or another of the traditions I have described. Such disputes are, of course, a natural outcome of the passions that people must invest in their reform efforts in order to have any impact. They are also exacerbated by the political cachet of school reform today: politics typically accentuates difference. But sometimes it happens too that politics can reconcile difference when the need for coalition seems evident and a rationale for supporting it is available. This is the kind of politics I advocate in this case: an effort undertaken across reform efforts—whether those of states, networks, intermediary organizations, or districts and schools—to put aside ideological concerns in the interest of promoting different protocols for different needs. The rationale for such a coalition is the one that the Connecticut teachers provided us in the motto they chose for their consulting group: the need to "work the diamond." It is not incidental to their story that they wanted to learn and teach to others as many protocols as possible.

NOTES

Acknowledgment. I wish to acknowledge the helpful comments made on an earlier draft of this chapter by David Allen, Simon Clements, Kathe Jervis, and John Mauriel.

1. John Dewey also advocated a kind of child study, as exemplified in the work of the University of Chicago Lab School when he presided there. However, according to Lagemann (2000), when Dewey left Chicago for New York in 1904, abandoning direct work with teachers and students, he also left behind much of his potential for influencing how child study would develop. Meanwhile, child study endured at the margins—its champions there including Lucy Sprague Mitchell (1954) and her colleagues at Bank Street College.

2. Many champions of "looking at student work"as a vehicle of teacher learning would admit a fourth tradition besides the three I explore in this chapter. Best represented by the Primary Language Record and its derivative, the California Language Record (Barr, Ellis, Hester, & Thomas, 1988; Falk & Darling-Hammond, 1993; Falk, 1998), this tradition orients teachers' looking at their own student work in the context of their own teaching. It may also lead to conversation among teachers inasmuch as the protocols are practiced school-wide. Considerations of length prevented me from exploring this tradition here.

3. The Bush Program, begun in 1975, admitted its last cohort of school leaders in 1998, and closed with a celebration of its impact in June 2000.

REFERENCES

Allen, D. (Ed.). (1998). *Assessing student learning: From grading to understanding*. New York: Teachers College Press.

Barr, M., Ellis, S., Hester, H., & Thomas, A. (1988). *The Primary Language Record*. London: Inner London Education Authority/Centre for Language in Primary Education.

Blythe, T., Allen, D., & Powell, B. S. (1999). *Looking together at student work*. New York: Teachers College Press.

Bruner, J. (1990). *Acts of meaning*. Cambridge: Harvard University Press.

Callahan, R. (1962). *Education and the cult of efficiency*. Chicago: University of Chicago Press.

Caprioni, L., James-Stebbins, K., Maurice, M., Maynard, T., McGinley, M., Overcash, M., Ozmun, C., Patrylak, R., Page, D., & Woods, M. (1997). *Guide for looking at student work*. EastConn. Unpublished.

Carini, P. (1979). *The art of seeing and the visibility of the person*. Grand Forks: North Dakota Study Group on Evaluation.

Carini, P. (1982). *The school lives of seven children: A five-year study*. Grand Forks: University of North Dakota/North Dakota Study Group on Evaluation.

Clements, S. (1998). *A Yorkshire setaside: Models for in-service groups*. Unpublished paper.

\

Cushman, K. (1996, November). Looking collaboratively at student work: A toolkit. *Horace, 13*(2). Oakland, CA: Coalition of Essential Schools.

Duckworth, E. (1996). *"The having of wonderful ideas" and other essays on teaching and learning* (2nd ed.). New York: Teachers College Press.

Elbow, P. (1986). *Embracing contraries: Explorations in learning and teaching*. New York: Oxford University Press.

Elmore, R., & Burney, D. (1997). *Investing in teacher learning: Staff development and instructional impact in Community School District #2, New York City*. Cambridge, MA: Consortium for Policy Research in Education, Harvard Graduate School of Education; New York: National Commission on Teaching and America's Future, Teachers College, Columbia University.

Falk, B. (1998). Looking at students and their work: Supporting diverse learners with the Primary Language Record. In D. Allen (Ed.), *Assessing student learning* (pp. 40–65). New York: Teachers College Press.

Falk, B., & Darling-Hammond, L. (1993). *The Primary Language Record at P.S. 261: How assessment transforms teaching and learning*. New York: National Center for Restructuring Education, Schools, and Teaching (NCREST), Teachers College, Columbia University.

Featherstone, H. (1998). Studying children: The Philadelphia Teachers' Learning Cooperative. In D. Allen (Ed.), *Assessing student learning* (pp. 66–83). New York: Teachers College Press.

Gardner, H. (1999). *The disciplined mind*. New York: Simon and Schuster.

Glickman, C. D. (2000, April). *The power behind school success: Where goeth instuctional supervision?* Invited keynote address, Special Interest Group on Instructional Supervision, annual meeting of the American Educational Research Association, New Orleans.

Hill, P. T., Foster, G. E., & Gendler, T. (1990). *High schools with character*. Santa Monica, CA: Rand.

Himley, M. (1991). *Shared territory: Understanding children's writing as works*. New York: Oxford University Press.

Himley, M., with Carini, P. (2000). *From another angle: Children's strengths and school standards*. New York: Teachers College Press.

Hole, S., McEntee, G., and the SALT Leadership Team. (1999). *Examining student work: A self-study activity guide*. Providence, RI: Rhode Island Department of Elementary and Secondary Education.

Institute for Learning. (1997). *Walkthrough: Developing a learning community* (Version 7). Pittsburgh: University of Pittsburgh, Learning Research and Development Center.

Jervis, K. (1996). *Eyes on the child: Three portfolio stories*. New York: Teachers College Press.

Jervis, K. (1997). *Conducting a School Quality Review in a cross-cultural Setting (The New York State School for the Deaf)*. New York: NCREST, Teachers College, Columbia University.

Kammer, J. (1998). Three takes on accountability: The California protocol. In D. Allen (Ed.), *Assessing student learning: From grading to understanding* (pp. 105–122). New York: Teachers College Press.

Kanevsky, R. D. (1993). The descriptive review of a child: A way of knowing about teaching and learning. In M. Cochran-Smith & S. Lytle (Eds.), *Inside outside: Teacher research and knowledge* (pp. 150–162). New York: Teachers College Press.

King, S. P., & Campbell-Allan, L. (1998). Portfolios, students' work, and teachers' practice: An elementary school redefines assessment. In D. Allen (Ed.), *Assessing student learning: From grading to understanding* (pp. 147–163). New York: Teachers College Press.

Lagemann, E. (2000). *An elusive science: The troubling history of education research.* Chicago: University of Chicago Press.

Lindsay, D. (2000). CON-test. *Education Week*, April 5.

Ma, L. (1999). *Knowing and teaching elementary mathematics.* Mahwah, NJ: Erlbaum.

McDonald, J. P. (1988). Emergence of the teacher's voice: Implications for the new reform. *Teachers College Record*, (Summer), 471–486.

McDonald, J. P. (1992). *Teaching: Making sense of an uncertain craft.* New York: Teachers College Press.

McDonald, J. P. (1993). Three pictures of an exhibition: Warm, cool, and hard. *Phi Delta Kappan, 74*(6), 480–485.

McDonald, J. P. (1996). *Redesigning school.* San Francisco: Jossey-Bass.

McDonald, J. P., Hatch, T., Kirby, E., Ames, N., Haynes, N. M., & Joyner, E. T. (1999). *School reform behind the scenes.* New York: Teachers College Press.

Meier, D. (1995). *The power of their ideas.* Boston: Beacon.

Mitchell, L. S. (1954). *Know your children in school.* New York: Macmillan.

Mitchell, R. (1996). *Front-end alignment: Using standards to steer educational change.* Washington, DC: The Education Trust, American Association for Higher Education.

Perkins, D. (1992). *Smart schools.* New York: Free Press.

Perrone, V. (1991). *Expanding student assessment.* Alexandria, VA: Association for Supervision and Curriculum Development.

Perrone, V. (2000). *Lessons for new teachers.* Boston: McGraw-Hill.

Rothman, R. (1996). *Organizing so all children can learn: Applying the Principles of Learning.* Washington, DC: National Center on Education and the Economy.

Schön, D. A., & McDonald, J. P. (1998). *Doing what you mean to do in school reform.* Providence, RI: Annenberg Institute for School Reform, Brown University.

Seidel, S. (1998). Wondering to be done: The Collaborative Assessment Conference. In D. Allen (Ed.), *Assessing student learning: From grading to understanding* (pp. 21–39). New York: Teachers College Press.

Senge, P. M. (1990). *The fifth discipline: The art and practice of the learning organization.* New York: Doubleday.

Shepard, L. (2000, April). *The role of assessment in a learning culture.* Presidential address, annual meeting of the American Educational Research Association, New Orleans.

Sizer, T. R. (1996). *Horace's hope: What works for the American high school*. Boston: Houghton Mifflin.

Smith, D. R., & Ruff, D. J. (1998). Building a culture of inquiry: The School Quality Review Initiative. In D. Allen (Ed.), *Assessing student learning: From grading to understanding* (pp. 164–182). New York: Teachers College Press.

Stevenson, H. W., & Stigler, J. W. (1992). *The learning gap*. New York: Summit Books.

Tyack, D. (1974). *The one best system*. Cambridge, MA: Harvard University Press.

Weber, L., with Alberty, B. (Ed.). (1997). *Looking back and thinking forward*. New York: Teachers College Press.

Wilson, T. A. (1996). *Reaching for a better standard: English school inspection and the dilemma of accountability for American public schools*. New York: Teachers College Press.

Wilson, T. A. (1999). *Visiting accreditation: Strengthening the regional accreditation process: Report to the Commission on Public Secondary Schools, New England Association of Schools and Colleges*. Providence, RI: LAB at Brown, Brown University.

Wiske, M. S. (Ed.). (1998). *Teaching for understanding: Linking research with practice*. San Francisco: Jossey-Bass.

About the Contributors

Ann Lieberman is an emeritus professor from Teachers College, Columbia University. She is currently a Senior Scholar at the Carnegie Foundation for the Advancement of Teaching and a visiting professor at Stanford University.

She is co-director of the Carnegie Academy for the Scholarship of Teaching and Learning (CASTL) for K–12. She is also working on a book with Diane Wood about the National Writing Project.

Lynne Miller is a professor of Educational Leadership and director of the Southern Maine Partnership at the University of Southern Maine. Before entering academia, she worked as a high school English teacher, an alternative school director, and a building and central office administrator. Lynne has written widely in the areas of school renewal and teacher development. She is co-author (with Ann Lieberman) of *Teachers—Transforming Their World and Their Work* (Teachers College Press, 1999).

Derrick P. Alridge is an assistant professor in the Department of Social Foundations of Education at the University of Georgia. He writes and teaches in the field of African-American and American educational history and philosophy, with interests in Du Boisian educational thought, intellectual history, and historical educational policy analysis.

Jacqueline Ancess is the associate director of the National Center for Restructuring Education, Schools, and Teaching (NCREST) at Teachers College, Columbia University. Her research and publications focus on urban secondary school reform, assessment, and accountability. For over 20 years she worked in the New York City school system as a district administrator, founding director of a middle school, staff developer, and English teacher.

Marilyn Cochran-Smith is professor of Education and director of the Ph.D. program in Curriculum and Instruction at the Lynch School of Education at Boston College. She is also the editor of *The Journal of Teacher Education*. For years she has written about inquiry, diversity, and social justice in teacher education. She is co-author, with Susan L. Lytle of many articles on teacher inquiry as well as the book *Inside/*

Outside: Teacher Research and Knowledge (Teachers College Press, 1992). They are currently working on a new book, *Inquiry as Stance*, also to be published by Teachers College Press.

Anna Richert Ershler is the Sarlo Professor of Education at Mills College in Oakland, California, where she co-directs the Teachers for Tomorrow's Schools Credential and M.A. programs. Her research is on teacher learning and school reform. In this domain of study she is concerned with changing conceptions of teacher knowledge and learning, and conditions that support or inhibit knowledge construction by teachers. She links questions of reform with teacher learning that results in changed practice at both the classroom and school levels. She has written several papers and chapters exploring these topics, including the recent ASCD publication "Resurrecting Hope: Knowing the Facts, Imagining the Future" in *A Better Beginning: Supporting and Mentoring New Teachers* (Marge Sherer, Ed.) and "Teaching Teachers for the Challenge of Change" in *Teaching about Teaching: Purpose, Passion and Pedagogy in Teacher Education* (John Loughran and Tom Russell, Eds., 1997).

Beverly Falk is an associate professor at the City College School of Education, City University of New York. She has served in a variety of roles—teacher, administrator, researcher, and consultant—at the school, district, state, and national level. Her most recent book is *The Heart of the Matter: Using Standards and Assessments to Learn.*

Sarah Warshauer Freedman specializes in literacy studies, particularly the teaching and learning of writing. She is especially interested in issues of equity and in teacher education for urban multicultural settings. Her most recent books, *Exchanging Writing, Exchanging Cultures* and *Inside City Schools,* explore these issues from her disciplinary perspective. Her current work at the University of California, Berkeley, focuses on understanding how to teach untracked English classes.

Carl D. Glickman is University Professor of Social Foundations of Education and chair of the Program for School Improvement at the University of Georgia. His work focuses on public schools, education, and democracy through school renewal networks and collaborations. His most recent book is *Revolutionizing America's Schools.*

Maxine Greene is Professor Emeritus of Teachers College, Columbia University, where she has been a professor of philosophy and education since 1973. She is past president of the American Educational Research Association, the American Educational Studies Association, and the Philosophy of Education Society. Her best-known books include *Teacher as Stranger: Educational Philosophy in the Modern Age* and *The Dialectic of Freedom* (Teachers College Press, 1988)

Judith Warren Little is a professor at the Graduate School of Education, University of California, Berkeley. She focuses her research on teachers' work and careers, the contexts of teaching, and professional development policy and practice. For the past several years, she has been studying the conditions of teaching in the context of school reform, with an emphasis on high schools.

Susan L. Lytle is an associate professor of Education at the Graduate School of Education, University of Pennsylvania. She chairs the Language in Education Division and directs the Program in Reading/Writing/Literacy and The Philadelphia Writing Program. Her research focuses on inquiry, professional development, critical feminist pedagogy, and the literacies of teaching.

Joseph P. McDonald is a professor of Teaching and Learning in the School of Education at New York University. He is the author of several books about teaching and schooling, including *Teaching: Making Sense of an Uncertain Craft* (Teachers College Press, 1992), and he conducts research on school reform.

Milbrey W. McLaughlin is the David Jacks Professor of Education and Public Policy at Stanford University and co-director of the Center for Research on the Context of Teaching.

Laura Stokes taught writing and directed a site of the National Writing Project at the University of California at Davis for 11 years. She received her Ph.D. in educational policy from Stanford in 1999. She is currently senior researcher for Inverness Research Associates, an education evaluation and policy analysis group headquartered in Inverness, California.

Diane R. Wood is an Assistant Professor at Southern Maine University. Her most recent articles, one that describes how narrative practices can be used in the professional development of teachers, and another written with Ann Lieberman about professional development in the National Writing Project, appear in *Anthropology and Education Quarterly* and *The International Journal for Leadership in Education*, respectively. She has co-edited *Transforming Teacher Education: Lessons in Professional Development*, a book to appear this spring. Currently, she is working with Ann Lieberman on a book about the National Writing Project and school reform.

Joel Zarrow is a doctoral student in Administration and Policy Analysis at Stanford University's School of Education.

Index